A Rebel and Her Cause

To my grandmother
Zahida Suroor
a feisty woman far ahead of her times

A Rebel and Her Cause

the life and work of Rashid Jahan

RAKHSHANDA JALIL

women
UNLIMITED
an associate of
kali for women

IGNCA

A Rebel and Her Cause
was first published in India in 2014
by
Women Unlimited
(an associate of Kali for Women)
7/10, Sarvapriya Vihar
New Delhi – 110 016
www.womenunlimited.net

in association with
Indira Gandhi National Centre for the Arts
C.V. Mess, Janpath
New Delhi – 110 001

ISBN: 978-81-88965-86-1

Cover design: Neelima Rao

Typeset at Sanchauli Image Composers, New Delhi – 110 059
and printed at Raj Press, R-3 Inderpuri, New Delhi – 110 012

Acknowledgements

I wish to acknowledge the generous help of the Indira Gandhi National Centre for the Arts for making this book possible. The project of studying Rashid Jahan's life and legacy was part of the "Confluence of Traditions and Composite Cultures" programme of the Janapada Sampada Division. I must gratefully acknowledge the assistance offered by Prof. Molly Kaushal in facilitating this project and allowing me to complete it in a timely fashion, as well as by Dipali Khanna, Member Secretary, IGNCA, in seeing this project through in its present form.

Among those who helped in the writing of this book I must first mention those who actually knew Rashid Jahan and therefore helped me understand her. My mother, Mehjabeen, knew her and her husband, Mahmuduzzafar, as a child. She was able to recall in minute detail what Rashida was like and how much she influenced all those who came in close contact with her. Others who knew Rashid Jahan and helped me paint my portrait of her include: Birjees Kidwai, Bano and Naren Gupta, Sarwat Rahman, Munibur Rahman and Rashid Jahan's niece and nephew, Shahla Haider and Salman Haider. Shahid Najeeb, Mahmud's nephew who lives in distant Australia, sent me a tranche of family photographs; some of them have been used in this book; others, rare and remarkable as they are, could not be reproduced for technical reasons.

Others who have helped in different ways in locating material and providing insights into the working of the Communist Party during its early days, as well as on the links between the Progressive Writers' Association and the Indian Peoples' Theatre Association, include: the late Raza Imam, M. M. Mehdi (Mamujaan), Shamim Faizi, Ali Javed, Sharib Rudaulvi, Shamim Hanfi, Jitendra Raghuvanshi, A. K. Sharma (Panditji), Ranjan Kaul, Shakil Siddiqui, Noor Zaheer, Arjumand Ara, and the late Attia Abid. I am grateful in particular to Ali Javed for his constant support and solidarity in my literary ventures.

As in the past, writing and research would be a lonely exercise were it not for the companionship of Najmi, Aaliya and Insha. It is they who make me carry on; and it is to them I say: 'Tum mere paas raho...'

Preface

The Indira Gandhi National Centre for the Arts is a premier resource centre engaged in research, documentation, publication and dissemination of knowledge in the field of arts. It is visualised as a Centre encompassing the study and experience of all the arts, each form with its own integrity, yet possessing a dimension of mutual interdependence and inter-relatedness.

The present book, *A Rebel and Her Cause: The Life and Work of Rashid Jahan* has emerged out of research conducted by the author, Rakhshanda Jalil, and is part of the Centre's programme, "Confluence of Traditions and Composite Cultures". Dr. Rashid Jahan (1905- 1953) was a multifaceted personality: doctor, dedicated member of the Communist Party of India and one of the founders of the Progressive Writers' Movement. The aim of this particular research was to revisit Dr. Jahan's legacy and to examine it for both its humaneness and its individuality. The author has used a variety of sources to construct a biographical sketch of Dr. Jahan; her corpus of writings is incorporated in the book and her short stories and plays have been translated. The book also includes some rare photographs collected by the author from members of Dr. Jahan's family.

The "Confluence of Traditions and Composite Cultures"

programme maps the processes responsible for cultural symbioses and interactions in the realm of the arts, leading to the creative transcendence of diverse identities. One important aim of the programme is to disseminate knowledge about multiple streams present in the shaping of our Urdu literary heritage. One such project, *Echoes from the Heart: A Compilation and Translation to English of Writings in Urdu by Muslim Women (1920-1950)* has just concluded. Besides, the Centre has taken up a systematic study of performative traditions in Islam under the project "Aqeedat ke Rang: Expressions of Devotion in Islam".

The recent focus of the Centre has also been on Qasba Sanskriti. The Qasba is a site of religio-cultural synthesis, where pluralism refused to be a mere idea and instead defined everyday practices, thereby becoming the very way of life. As part of this programme, the Centre has produced three films entitled *Qasba Sanskriti: Amroha; Bilgaram;* and *Bareilly, My Bareilly.* The Centre also holds seminars, panel discussions, public lectures and film screenings as part of this programme.

Dipali Khanna
Member Secretary
Indira Gandhi National Centre for the Arts

Foreword

I cannot pretend to be objective about this book. Dr. Rashid Jahan was my aunt, my mother's eldest sister and a mainspring of our family life. Every now and then she would swoop down on us at home in Aligarh, or sometimes in Naini Tal, a dazzling figure who immediately took over, presiding over our daily routine of school and play. Under her watchful eye the growing tribe of her nieces and nephews imbibed many lessons of conduct and behaviour, striving to meet the standards she set for us. We were expected to take responsibility for ourselves, make our own beds, clean our own shoes, not leave these household chores to the servants, who always had to be treated with consideration. In an early assault on gender stereotypes, all of us, girls and boys alike, were required to learn how to knit and sew - knitting is now forgotten but I can still sew a button better than my wife. There was always activity and fresh excitement when she was there. The family circle would be in overdrive and a whole new group of friends, many from the Party, would be constantly in and out of the house, irresistibly drawn to her aura. Something was forever happening but in the midst of all the activity she always had time for the children. We adored her and did all we could to earn her attention and approval.

As we grew older, we became more aware of some of the

darker shadows. She was an active member of the Communist Party on account of which she was put in jail while her husband Mahmud went 'underground'. Even when not in jail, she was often tailed by the CID, and while outwitting them was a bit of a game, there were hardships to be borne. More sombre were her health problems. Her life had always been full of movement and activity, though from a young age she had problems with her thyroid for which surgical treatment became necessary. And then, later, she was afflicted with cancer that eventually would end her life. Yet these travails, as Rakhshanda Jalil recounts, scarcely slowed her down or took her away from her calling.

An intense commitment to social causes, especially those relating to women, was ingrained in Rashid Jahan from her earliest days. In this she owed much to the life and work of her parents, her father Shaikh Abdullah being a noted pioneer of girls' education, in partnership with his wife, Waheed Jahan. Their early struggles and steadfast commitment, the many prejudices they confronted, the practical problems they overcame, the enlightened cause they served, the dedicated persons attracted to them, and an ever growing community of educated, confident young women, all this was integral to Rashid Jahan's world. Ms. Jalil gives an insightful and sympathetic account of that world and of Shaikh Abdullah's signal achievements as a social reformer.

After her early studies in Aligarh and Lucknow, Rashid Jahan trained as a doctor at the Lady Hardinge Medical College in Delhi. After graduating and working in the provincial medical service for some years, she eventually established a practice in Lucknow and gained some renown in her field. Career mattered little to her, for her concern as a doctor was to bring succour to those in need, especially those immured in the zenana. By temperament and training she was very well suited to this task. I recall her clinic in Lucknow that Ms. Jalil describes, where dozens of people were always present in search of medical services not readily available elsewhere.

Medicine was only one part of Rashid Jahan's activity. The epitaph on her grave in Moscow describes her in three words: 'Communist. Doctor. Writer'. It is the third of these attributes that brought her greatest recognition and renown in her lifetime. From her student days she had been constantly engaged in writing short stories and also plays for stage and radio. The subjects she chose were related to ordinary people and everyday situations, which in itself was unusual at the time, and she wrote in plain, uncomplicated language without literary frills. Rakhshanda Jalil does not rate her literary work very highly, pointing out that what she wrote had to be fitted into the interstices of a very full life and was often left half done or sketchily completed. Yet her writing had an impact, for she wrote about real life and recognisable issues, especially women's concerns. Writers of sometimes greater renown took, and continue to take, inspiration from her work. In her lifetime what made her famous, even notorious, was the publication, *Angarey* in which she collaborated with three well-known writers of progressive inclination to produce a volume of short pieces on largely social themes. Given their views, what they wrote was seen as a radical attack on traditional society and attracted the loud denunciation of the conservatives, and as the only woman among the quartet Rashid Jahan drew more fire than the others. The British did *Angarey* the great favour of banning it and thereby making for it a permanent niche in the Urdu literature of the time. Even today the affair reverberates, and only a few years ago the Vice-Chancellor of Aligarh Muslim University banned a proposed observance of Rashid Jahan's centenary for fear that commemorating such a notorious figure could provoke an agitation! This faint-hearted decision can be regarded as an unintended tribute to Rashid Jahan after all these years.

Rashid Jahan is fortunate in her biographer. Rakhshanda Jalil has written about her with empathy and understanding, and seems drawn to the bold and remarkable woman she writes about. A lot of painstaking research has gone into the narrative, about Rashid Jahan herself and also about her family. In the process, Ms. Jalil has recreated an important moment in recent social history. The book is thus a many-sided account, and all the more valuable for its multiple dimensions. To add further value, there are a number of translations into English of some of Rashid Jahan's works. It is an admirable account of a gifted and committed individual who still has much to offer.

Salman Haidar
New Delhi

Contents

Introduction

Rashid Jahan was a woman of many parts: a doctor, a dedicated member of the Communist Party of India (CPI) and one of the founding members of the Progressive Writers' Association (PWA). She was also an active member of the PWA's sister cultural body, the Indian Peoples' Theatre Association (IPTA), a life-long campaigner for women's rights and a pioneering short story writer and dramatist in Urdu. Given her many-splendoured personality, it is unfortunate that her legacy today – a little over a half-century after her death – is celebrated by only one set of people, those who see her as an icon of the Progressive Writers' Movement, a movement that captured the public imagination as no other literary or cultural movement before or after. While the Movement and the Party shaped and moulded Rashid Jahan, giving form and substance to her desire to bring about lasting social change, it is important to revisit her legacy and examine it for both its humanity and its individuality.

Moving from the girls' school at Aligarh started by her parents, Shaikh Abdullah and his wife, Waheeda Begum, to the Isabella Thoburn College in Lucknow and then the Lady Hardinge Medical College in Delhi, Rashid Jahan's was a pioneering journey in search of education. Upon her graduation from Lady Hardinge in 1929, she embarked upon another journey, equally pioneering and inspiring for generations of young women who followed in her footsteps. As a doctor in the provincial medical services, she lived and travelled in the smaller towns and cities of the United Provinces (as it was then) till she was posted to Lucknow. Here she met a group of dynamic young people and co-authored an explosive book called *Angarey* in December 1932. Banned three months later in March 1933 by the colonial government on charges of being a 'filthy' and 'immoral' book that would hurt the religious sentiments of the Muslim community, *Angarey* has become something of an 'urban legend', for it is still more talked about than read. Rashid Jahan who, as a woman, had borne the brunt of the worst ire of those behind the *Angarey* furore and became (in)famous as 'Rashid Jahan *Angareywali*', is today regarded as the Scarlet Woman of Urdu Literature, one who wrote on provocative subjects and revelled in shocking people. Literary historians, too, have failed to give her the importance she deserves, for while she is placed as a marker in the evolution of literary radicalism in Urdu – just as *Angarey* is regarded as *sang-e-meel* (a milestone) – she is nevertheless relegated to the category of a minor writer, as one who was part of a larger literary grouping but not sufficiently talented or important, in purely literary terms, to deserve any serious study.

Such a simplistic reading of the life and career of a woman as remarkable as Rashid Jahan seems to me to be not merely unfair, but essentially flawed; for Rashid Jahan was more than a brave and brash woman who wrote on bold subjects with blithe disregard for the consequences. More even than a woman somewhat ahead of her times as the product of a radical and privileged background and education denied to most young, especially Muslim young, women. Most importantly, she was a woman deeply and passionately engaged with the great debates of her age: anti-fascism, anti-imperialism, feminism, nationalism, socialism, gender-justice, and more. As a member of the Communist Party of India – which she joined in 1933 at a time when the entry of women in active politics, especially in the Communist Party, was itself a novelty – she was actively engaged in the United Provinces wing of the Party; this engagement was reflected in her writings which covered a wide range of subjects including the position of women in a capitalist society; and why ordinary citizens should rise up in revolt against a corrupt and exploitative system. She not only served on the editorial board of the Party organ, *Chingari*, along with Party worthies such as K. M. Ashraf, Sohan Singh Josh, Firozuddin Mansur, Tikaram Sukhan and Harkishan Singh Surjeet, she also edited it along with comrades and fellow-writers Sajjad Zaheer and Mahmuduzzafar Khan, whom she married.

While much of her writing is about women or on women's issues such as the perils of a secluded and cloistered life, women's reproductive health, the need for birth control and the toll that early marriage and frequent pregnancies take on their well-being, and on the importance of education for women, she also wrote about other pressing social issues: colonisation, exploitation, democracy, nationalism, poverty, racial and religious prejudice. The sort of writing-for-women being done by male writers of her time was not for her; for while she used the speech and idiom of women speaking to women and displayed an uncanny ability to mimic the dialect of women – both the *begumati zubaan* of upper-class women from *sharif* households as well as the rough and ready slang of the lower classes – her message was radical. She was spot-on in her depiction of scenes from a woman's life and demonstrated remarkable empathy for women who lived less-than-empowered lives, no matter how far removed those lives were from her own, but she was clearly not writing for a female audience alone. This is evident in the fact that her work was published in mainstream literary journals or left-leaning magazines, and her plays were written for the radio or for theatrical performances under the banner of IPTA. She saw women as political actors at par with men and challenged commonly-assumed notions of superiority and masculinity in a patriarchal world. She was the first woman to raise the banner of revolt in Urdu literature, and appropriated a space in public and intellectual life, a space that no one – least of all women – even knew existed!

A generation of women writers – notably Ismat Chughtai, Attia Hosain, Razia Sajjad Zaheer and Sadiqa Begum Soharvi – acknowledged the influence of Rashid Jahan on their lives and writing. For her own part, Rashid Jahan was doubtless influenced by the European writers she read in her youth as well as by the new currents of socialist thought that her friends in the Party exposed her to from the early 1930s. She must also have been affected by ideas about a new sort of writing that was being propagated by the Young Turks she met in Lucknow, but it must also be said that she refused to write under ideological compulsion. Given the force of her personality and her individualism, and regardless of the fact that she was a card-carrying member of the Party, it is unlikely that she wrote in accordance with Party diktat. Her home, always a centre where the city's intellectuals gravitated, was no doubt a place for eclectic and intense discussions on a variety of subjects, but going by the testimony of those who knew her and by the portrayal of strong-willed, outspoken, independent-minded women in her writings, it seems she, more than any of the other Progressives, neither craved approval nor paid much attention to what her fellow Progressives thought of her. Rashid Jahan's work, both literary and social, spoke for itself, it needed neither champions nor defenders. The 'Angareywali' was, evidently, a woman of immense self-assurance.

Dogged by frequent bouts of ill health, Rashid Jahan moved between Lucknow and Dehradun where her in-laws lived, and it was in Dehradun that her evolution into a politically-aware, committed Party worker was completed. Running a busy medical practice and writing stories and plays continued alongside. Always in a hurry, always on the go, her many interests came together in a heedless rush in the last years of her life: conducting adult education classes, talking about reproductive health in sweepers' colonies, gathering women from Arya Samaj mandirs to join hands on women's health and education issues or participating in trade union rallies and protest marches, she was busy cramming the work of a lifetime into one short decade. Her friend and comrade, Hajra Begum, describes the gamut of her concerns: always for others, never for herself. When she was not busy raising funds for underground colleagues through her practice or bullying her many admirers to contribute to her many 'causes' (such as the release of imprisoned co-workers or securing safehouses for underground comrades), she would be writing, translating and editing political pieces for *Chingari*. From a short story writer she had evolved into a playwright, journalist and editor.

Her friend, the writer Ale Ahmad Suroor, in a moving epitaph for this unusual woman who touched many lives through the courage of her convictions, observed: 'Dr Rashid Jahan had a magic, and that magic was her *khuloos*, her sincerity.' It was this magic that drew the most talented and gifted people of her generation to her in the course of her brief but meteoric life and literary career: Sajjad Zaheer, Firaq Gorakhpuri, Josh Malihabadi, Hiren Mukherjee, Mian Iftikharuddin, among hordes of young men and women. A handful of those who are alive and were interviewed for this account spoke eloquently of how Rashid Jahan touched their lives in some way, of how different she was not just from most Muslim women of her age and class but how she defied conventional labels and revelled in breaking stereotypes. The picture that emerges from these various accounts – a picture that I have attempted to outline in the following pages – is of a headstrong and wilful, but also a brave and compassionate woman, one who was not content to merely record the need for change, but who was willing to *be* the change.

Rashid Jahan died at the age of forty-seven in 1952 in Moscow, where she was undergoing treatment for uterine cancer, and is buried in a cemetery there. Her epitaph reads: 'Communist Doctor and Writer'; it seems an apt summing up of her life. She had agreed to undertake the long and circuitous journey, knowing that there was little hope for her, simply so that her husband could travel to the USSR, an opportunity denied to Indian communists due to visa restrictions. Brief though her life was and slender her literary output, together they serve to illustrate the fact that Rashid Jahan single-handedly paved the way for other women writers. Equally importantly, she opened a window of immense possibilities for young Muslim women. Her life continues to inspire, and her legacy lives in the lives of all those who raise their voices whenever they encounter oppression and injustice. Her life and her literary output together serve to illustrate the truth in the poet Majrooh Sultanpuri's words:

Main akela hi chala tha jaanib-e-manzil magar
Log saath aate gaye aur caravan banta gaya.

I set off alone for the journey's end
But others kept joining me, a caravan was formed.

Rakhshanda Jalil
New Delhi

I. Life & Times

1

Rashida: Her Father's Daughter

Duain dein mere baad aane wale meri wahshat ko
Bahut kaante nikal aaye mere humrah manzil ke

Let those who come after me send benedictions for me
Many a thorn has been removed from their path due to me

– Saquib Lucknowi

Shaikh Abdullah and the school at Aligarh

It was during the Christmas holidays in the year 1888 that a young lad of fifteen and a student of Standard VII happened to attend an event organized by the Mohammadan Educational Conference in Lahore.[1] His name was Thakur Das; he was the son of Mehta Gurmukh Singh, grandson of Mehta Mast Ram, lambardar of a village in Poonch district, Kashmir. In later years, this boy would be known as Shaikh Abdullah (1874–1965) or, more fondly, by generations of women as Papa Miyan.

Thakur Das attended the Conference in the company of his beloved teacher and mentor, Maulana Nooruddin. This was the first time the Kashmiri Pandit boy had set eyes on the revered Sir Syed Ahmad Khan (1817–1898), distinguished founder of the MAO College whose fame had reached distant Lahore. There he sat on the dais, a short distance from Thakur

Das, flanked by Maulvi Nazir Ahmad (1831-1912), the orator, educationist and author of Urdu's first best-selling novel, *Mirat al-Urus*.[2] The impressionable boy narrates the chit-chat he heard on stage, the bonhomie and good cheer he witnessed between the two principal speakers and the effect these two powerful orators from Delhi had on their enraptured Lahori audience. For young Thakur Das, it had been a long journey in search of an education. After receiving his primary education at the village school, the boy had gone first to Jammu and, then onwards to Lahore to complete his schooling.

Possibly under the influence of his mentor, Maulvi Nooruddin, Thakur Das embraced Islam in 1891 while still at Lahore and took the name Shaikh Muhammad Abdullah. Initially, he became a Qadiyani as Maulvi Nooruddin was an Ahmadiya[3]; it was many years later, in Aligarh, that he began to profess the Sunni Muslim faith. In the same year as his conversion, on May 14, 1891, he reached Aligarh to begin his education at the MAO College and it was here that he truly flowered and found a real family in place of the one he had left behind in Poonch.

Aligarh accepted him with open arms. It gave him the freedom to be exactly who or what he wished to be. Free of the ties and trappings of caste, culture and class, Shaikh Abdullah was like virgin clay, ready to be moulded. Yet, like clay, he had certain innate distinctive qualities. His peers and teachers were quick to spot these traits: earnestness, optimism, determination, and an infectious never-say-die spirit. He joined the Anjuman al-Farz or Duty Society, set up by Sahibzada Aftab Ahmad, an Old Boy, to foster a sense of voluntary service among students and further Syed Ahmad's vision of a class of people devoted to selfless service for the *qaum*. Set up in 1889, during Syed Ahmad's lifetime, the Duty Society was a small, select group of elected members and consisted primarily of earnest young men who wished to propagate the 'idea' of the college at Aligarh and collect funds for the education of those who could not afford it. Acutely aware that only the sons of the rich and landed classes could study within the hallowed portals of the MAO College, self-consciously designed by its founder to be the 'Cambridge of the East', members of the Duty Society sacrificed their holidays and much of their leisure time and took upon themselves the onerous task of collecting funds by going from house to house and town to town, like mendicants begging for alms. Not just that, members of the 'Duty' as it soon came to be called, set up tea stalls, served tea, even washed soiled cups and saucers with philanthropic zeal; by 1895, they had collected a grand sum of Rs 5000.[4]

For young Shaikh Abdullah, his stint at the Duty Society provided a valuable early lesson in resourcefulness and public-spiritedness. It was important to have an idea, he knew; what was equally important, he learnt in the company of men like Aftab Ahmad Khan, was how to go about putting it into practice with single-minded determination. Strategising, organising, mobilising people and funds – all these would come in handy when it came to putting his own dreams into practice with the establishment of the Women's College. At the same time, he was influenced by Syed Ahmad's model of *nai taleem* or a 'new education' which, though not necessarily in English, taught modern subjects such as mathematics, geography, economics through the vernacular and, yes, even in Urdu – hitherto considered inappropriate when it came to school curricula. The Scientific Society set up by Syed Ahmad in 1863 and the journal *Tahzeeb-ul Akhlaq* in 1871 provided the young man with ample fodder to chew on. In fact, while still a student, Shaikh Abdullah became quite close to Syed Ahmad and had the opportunity to run small errands for him, such as take notes, reply to letters, and clean up copy for publication. Also, at the encouragement of Syed Ahmad, Shaikh Abdullah began to write short journalistic pieces; in the years to come, this experience would be useful when he set up his own journal for women, *Khatun.*

The All-India Muhammadan Educational Conference, set up by Syed Ahmad in 1886, met for its eighth annual meeting in December 1893 in Strachey Hall, Aligarh. Shaikh Abdullah attended, but not as a star-struck provincial lad looking from afar at the galaxy of stars in the Muslim firmament, as at the Lahore Conference of 1888. Now, as an active member of the Duty Society, the Muhammadan Educational Conference and as a recognized name in Aligarh's student circles. he had a more active role. He heard Syed Ahmad Khan, by now a lion in winter, make one last impassioned plea to the assembled Muslim intelligentsia drawn from all over the country and from different backgrounds: to make Aligarh the centre or *markaz* of all Muslim educational enterprises. Not everyone agreed. Some differed on locating it in Aligarh; why not the Punjab, for instance, argued the adherents of the Anjuman Himayat-i Islam. Others objected to western-style boarding-school education such as the one being proposed at Aligarh. Still others found the Aligarh School not sufficiently kosher in terms of its religious foundations. In this cacophony of voices, the concerns centred around the education of Muslim men. No one, in this Tower of Babel, was speaking for women.[5]

In much the same way that the traditionalists and Muslim clerics were bitterly opposed to the western-style education for boys being propagated by Syed Ahmad, the venerable Syed himself was vehemently opposed to the education of women on purely moral grounds.[6] In response to an appeal by the women of Punjab, he defended his position thus:

> O my sisters, believe me, there is no community in the world where the lot of women has been improved before the condition of men. And there is no community in the world where the condition of men has been improved and that of women has

not... It is my belief that attempts to improve the education of boys lie at the root of improving the educational status of girls.[7]

However, in the matter of education for Muslim women, Shaikh Abdullah was convinced that Syed Ahmad was paying mere lip service when it came to making public responses; in his heart the venerable old educationist was adamant: education would bring waywardness and cause women to abandon parda and compete with men.[8] Shaikh Abdullah believed that Syed Ahmad's opposition to the education of women did not stem from religious convictions; its roots lay in tradition: *qadamat parasti* and *parda parasti*, as he put it, preferring antiquity and the segregation of the sexes that parda ensured.[9] Both were anathema to young Shaikh Abdullah who had freed himself so thoroughly from the bonds of family, caste and creed and had embraced Islam with such vigour because of its essentially egalitarian underpinnings.

Already, the writings of a new breed of Urdu writers, men like Maulvi Zakaullah (1832-1910), Nazir Ahmed (1836-1912), Altaf Husain Hali (1837-1914), and others were creating a stir in the stagnant waters of Urdu literature where the creative writer and the social reformer were coming together in a new, radical way. Though their frame of reference remained a quintessentially colonial one, they nevertheless urged their Muslim brothers to actively participate in the changes that were unfolding around them. What is more, in a departure from tradition, they were speaking of and to Muslim women; thus implying, for the first time, that there was a female readership too. Through his enormously popular novels Nazir Ahmad was expounding his views on women's education and talking, for the first time, of going beyond *deeni taalim* or home tutoring in religious matters to *duniyaavi taalim* or a more worldly education. This entailed that a carefully monitored but structured school syllabus be devised for a secluded, sheltered atmosphere similar to a *sharif* household.[10]

Despite Syed Ahmad Khan's reservations regarding the empowerment of Muslim women by providing them a secular education at par with men, the crusade for women's education soon acquired a momentum of its own. While Calcutta, Dacca and Bhopal responded to the need for girls to go to schools and colleges, Delhi, Lucknow and a large swathe of Upper India still dragged its feet. At such a time, Hali's impassioned plea struck a chord in middle-class families; his *Majalis un-Nisa* (Conversations among Women, 1904-05) demonstrated how educated women make better wives and mothers who, in turn, can propel the engine of reform within Muslim society. Hali's heroine, Zubaida Khatun, is taught the Qur'an, Arabic, Persian and Urdu as well as mathematics, geography and history by her father. The *Majalis* was given a cash prize of Rs. 400 by the imperial government, thus putting the stamp of colonial approval on the need for women's education. Despite the presence of these reformist trends, women's education along the lines conceived of – and put into practice by – Shaikh Abdullah a few years later was still a cry in the wilderness. What men such as Nazir Ahmad, Hali and others – who formed a bridge of sorts between Syed Ahmad and a younger generation of Muslim reformers such as Shaikh Abdullah and Karamat Husain – were willing to conceive was reformist but not radical, enlightened but not extremist, modern but not revisionist. While the education of women was encouraged (for the larger good of the family), patriarchal values were maintained; the unspoken question being: 'If families are to be reared upon women's earnings, why should there be men?'[11]

A measure of literacy among women is evident by the sudden profusion of writings for them. Syed Mumtaz Ali (1860-1935) founded the first women's Urdu newspaper, *Tahzib un-Niswan* in 1898, in partnership with his wife, Muhammadi Begum (d. 1908).[12] Others joined in – from different cities such as Bhopal, Hyderabad, Aligarh, Lahore and Lucknow.

Shaikh Abdullah launched the monthly educational journal, *Khatun*, from Aligarh in 1904; it was followed by Rashidul Khairi's literary magazine, *Ismat* in 1908. These emerging women's newspapers and magazines not only fostered enlightened housekeeping and debates on women's rights but also ushered in a new kind of writing never seen before in the world of Urdu journalism.[13] Still, there was nothing in them that seriously threatened the status quo and so, while they occasionally caused ripples of dissent and disagreement, they did not cause the sort of outrage and uproar unleashed by someone like Rashid Jahan with her explosive contribution to *Angarey* in 1932.

While these reformist currents ebbed and flowed in the consciousness of the Muslim elite, the Muhammadan Educational Conference could not remain indifferent to the need – articulated in different ways, at different fora – for providing some sort of formal education to Muslim girls. In 1896, it passed a resolution to establish a Women's Education Section headed by two long-time advocates of formal education for women: Karamat Hussain, a Professor of law at Aligarh and Syed Mumtaz Ali. Over the next few years, while the Muhammadan Educational Conference met with unfailing regularity, little work was done for the cause of women's education save impassioned speeches on its urgent necessity. And so it continued, with the Women's Education Section having no more than a notional existence. Reform-minded poets and polemicists wrote in white heat. Much ink was spilt on the cause of women by enlightened men. Hali wrote:

Ai maaon, behnon, betiyon duniya ki zeenat tumse hai
Mulkon ki basti ho tumhin, qaumon ki izzat tumse hai

O sisters, mothers, daughters, you are the ornaments of the world
You are the life of nations, the dignity of civilisations rests with you

While many agreed that something had to be done, the

questions of what, where and how bedeviled these champions of the cause.

The year 1902 proved to be a momentous one for Shaikh Abdullah who had all along nurtured the dream of opening a school for girls in his beloved Aligarh, the city that had given him so much, the city he knew should give their rightful share to Muslim girls as it had to Muslim boys. Two events form a vital link in the chain of events that led to setting up the school for girls and, for the larger purpose of this account, allowed a woman like Dr Rashid Jahan to chart her destiny.

On February 1, Shaikh Abdullah and Begum Wahid Jahan, the youngest daughter of Mirza Ibrahim Beg, a leading light of Delhi's cultural elite were married. What is more, Mirza Ibrahim Beg, though a minor official in the city municipality believed – under the influence of intellectuals who had brought about the Delhi Renaissance, men such as Deputy Nazir Ahmad, Zakaullah and Hali – in educating girls. His own daughters had received informal education in their home in the Farrashkhana area and his only son, Bashir Mirza, had been a friend and contemporary of Shaikh Abdullah at Aligarh. Wahid Jahan, known for posterity as Ala Bi, just as her husband was called Papa Miyan by legions of Old Girls, had studied Urdu and Persian as well as received rudimentary instruction at home in English and arithmetic from an Englishwoman. Ala Bi's influence on Shaikh Abdullah, his life and work, would prove to be enormous.

In December 1902 the Muhammadan Educational Conference held its annual meeting when the city of Delhi geared up to celebrate the crowning of King Edward. This was a landmark event in the history of women's education in India. Its inaugural session was presided over by the Aga Khan, and Her Royal Highness the Begum of Bhopal also attended. On this occasion, Shaikh Abdullah, who had by now completed his law degree from the MAO College and established a legal practice in the city, gathered some friends and convinced them that since no one else seemed to want the secretary's post (vacant after Karamat Husain moved to Allahabad, first to teach law at Muir College and then to practice it), he should be made secretary of the Women's Education Section. Once appointed, Shaikh Abdullah embraced the cause with passionate intensity. In his own words:

From the day I was appointed secretary, from that day itself my mind was consumed with the idea of making this Section functional. I began to think of nothing except how, through this organization, I could draw Muslims towards educating their girls. I told the late Begum Abdullah (his wife) to speak to her friends and make enquiries as to what could be done... She organized a small function at her home and invited a lot of ladies from the neighbourhood... [14]

Shaikh Abdullah writes how the year 1903 passed by in a flash; for all the good talk no one, till that point, was even willing to think of an ordinary school ('normal school', as he puts it) for girls. At best, the community felt a school should be set up to train teachers who would, in turn, educate Muslim girls from sharif families *within* the confines of their homes. But in his heart he knew such a scheme was not practicable; schools that provided elementary education to girls were the real need of the hour. Those who argued that even Muslim countries or theocratic states had not attempted to establish separate madrasas for women could not conceive that any sharif family in India would ever think of sending their daughters to school. What was worse, detractors of such new-fangled ideas declared that Muslim girls from such families would end up meeting non-Muslim girls or those from non-sharif families. As the debates went on, the nub of the argument for and against educating Muslim girls appeared to be parda. *'Sub se zyada rona parda ka tha aur iss bahas mein auratein bhi hissa le rahin theen.'* ('The greatest arguments were about parda and women too were taking part in this debate.')[15] Separate but equal schooling for women seemed to offer a viable option, that is, secular education along the same lines as men but one that made due provision for parda.

A year passed, and in December 1903, at the next session of the Muhammadan Educational Conference in Bombay, yet another milestone was crossed. Women attended; they saw and heard the proceedings from behind the screens (*chilman ke peeche se*). Shaikh Abdullah once again seized the opportunity of meeting and interacting with delegates, this time with the express agenda of soliciting their views on starting a 'normal school' for girls. He succeeded in getting a resolution passed for starting such a school but the assembly agreed that it could not be opened in Aligarh because of the large number of boys present there! Shaikh Abdullah objected; in whichever city they might agree to open a girls' school, surely there would be boys there too. The women of two influential Bombay families, the Fyzees and Tyabjis, related to each other by marriage, pledged their support to the cause.

Shortly after his return to Aligarh, freshly enthused and energised to do something concrete, Shaikh Abdullah launched the journal, *Khatun*, with the specific intention of using it as a platform to speak about women's education. Shaikh Abdullah himself, Ala Bi and her sisters wrote on a range of subjects: personal hygiene, domestic science, household tips; Hali wrote his famous poem *Chup ki Daad* (In Praise of the Silent, 1905) especially for the journal. The same year, Shaikh Abdullah also secured a resolution from the recalcitrant Muhammadan Educational Conference to locate the proposed girls' school in Aligarh. However, an assured annual grant from the Begum of Bhopal – an enlightened ruler who had done much to patronise women's education in her own state – clinched matters. Slowly but surely, the caravan with Shaikh Abdullah as its guiding light or *rooh-e-rawan*, moved on. In 1905, a group of liberal-minded young men from the MAO College travelled to Bombay to gather subscriptions. The dynamic sisters, Zohra and Atiya Faizee, helped collect Rs 400 from well-to-do Muslim families. By 1905, when the Muhammadan Educational Conference met again, this time in Aligarh, the Women's Education Section with Shaikh Abdullah at its helm, held an exhibition of art and craft done by women: paintings, calligraphy and needlework to showcase the hidden talent of unseen women.[16]

In 1906, Shaikh Abdullah led a deputation to meet Sir James LaTouche, the Lt-Governor of the United Provinces. With him were Raja Naushad Ali Khan, a taluqedar of Awadh; Muhammad Nasim, a lawyer from Lucknow; and Ghulam-us Saqlain, an enlightened Old Boy and friend from Shaikh Abdullah's boarding-house days. Since a government grant could only be given to an existing school, not the 'idea' of a proposed school, the deputation returned empty-handed. However, the Lt-Governor promised a grant-in-aid *should* such a school ever see the light of day, and *should* it receive a favourable report from the inspector of schools. The promise, though tenuous, was enough to spur Shaikh Abdullah to turn his dreams into a reality. The same year, in October 1906, he hired a house in the Balai Quila (or 'Ooper Kot' as it was and still is called by locals) neighborhood and without further ado opened the Aligarh Zenana Madarsa with seventeen students on roll. Ala Bi's family helped find a suitable *ustani* (a lady teacher) from Delhi; Ustani Akhtari agreed to come to Aligarh only if her entire family too could stay with her. Shaikh Abdullah agreed. Ustani Akhtari taught the girls, her husband was put in charge of security, a scholarship was fixed for her daughter and the ustani's mother was hired for a small fee for washing the *takhtis* (wooden boards on which the pupils wrote). Three *dolis* (small covered palanquins) were hired, along with bearers. Classes were held in strictest parda under the personal supervision of Ala Bi and her sister, Sikandar Jahan.

Ala Bi was everywhere: minding her home and growing family, juggling finances, taking classes and teaching as many subjects as she could. Since she had studied elementary Persian with her father and also possessed a fine hand, she taught these two subjects with special fervor. With classes under way, Shaikh Abdullah shot off a letter to the Lt-Governor, an inspectress was duly sent who gave a favourable report and the Aligarh Zenana Madarsa received a lumpsum grant of Rs 17,000 with an additional monthly amount of Rs 250.[17] Now there was no looking back. The school at Aligarh would grow and grow, provide shade and shelter, nurture talent and allow dreams to become reality for countless young women, including Shaikh Abdullah's own daughters. Here was a space that valued women. In that small hired kothi in the congested quarter of the old city (shehr as it was and continues to be called by those who live in the 'University' areas), Shaikh Abdullah created a space – enclosed by high walls and guarded by watchful eyes – that, in the years to come, opened up a world of immense possibilities.

Women's education and the making of a doctor

The Abdullahs had six daughters and two sons, of whom five daughters and one son survived beyond infancy. Rashid Jahan, their second daughter, was born on August 25, 1905. She was followed by two more daughters, Khatun Jahan and Mumtaz Jahan, and a son, Mohsin Abdullah, and another named Saeed who died at the young age of thirty. Saeed was followed by Khurshid Jahan, the prettiest and most vivacious of the siblings who later became known as the popular film actor, Renuka Devi, in the Hindi film industry, followed by the youngest, Birjees Jahan who is today the only surviving child of the Abdullahs. A close-knit and fun-loving family, there was never a dull moment for the Abdullah children with books and reading interspersed with picnics, card games, visits to their grandparents' home in Delhi as well as to the homes of the local worthies in Aligarh and boisterous games in the sprawling Abdullah Lodge. At the same time, they had a strict puritan upbringing. As Khurshid writes:

> Papa did not smoke, intake of alcohol was considered one of the seven mortal sins. To tell a lie was to burn in the fires of hell. We were a happy, healthy and wholesome family unit. Our rights as individuals were respected and we respected the rights of others, particularly the servants and the women dependents of Abdullah Lodge.'[18]

Known as Rashida by friends and family, Rashid Jahan's life and that of the girls' school started by her parents a year after her birth are intertwined. As Rashida grew, so did the school. Hoping to encourage others by their own example, it was to this school that the Abdullahs sent all their children, beginning with young Rashida, barely a year older than the school itself. Travelling each morning in a covered palanquin, Rashida went to the school to receive a rounded education that included both a study of the Qur'an and modern science. At home, her father, Papa Miyan would read her stories from Shakespeare, while her mother introduced her to the world of women's journals such as *Khatun*[19], *Ismat* and *Tehzeeb-e-Niswan*. In school, her teachers, particularly the headmistress, a young Bengali Christian from Calcutta named Miss Hazra, introduced her to revolutionary new ideas such as swadeshi, Home Rule and the ills that sprang from the partition of Bengal, as well as the writings of Tagore and Bankim Chandra.[20] Early exposure to issues of national importance led her, in later years, to her finding common cause with a host of major struggles of her times – communism, feminism, nationalism, secularism.[21] Talking about her years growing up in the midst of a family as eclectic and liberal as hers, Rashid Jahan once observed, 'We slept on the mattress of women's education and covered ourselves with the quilt of women's education from our earliest consciousness.'[22]

The Abdullahs' home attracted many visitors who left their mark in different ways, moulding the mind of a young woman who saw nothing contrary about *being* a woman and *being empowered*. Some of these visitors were the Begum of Bhopal, a woman who, despite her strict adherence to parda, nonetheless took an active part in the social and political discourses that concerned the Muslims of India; the elegant Atiya and Zohra Fyzee who brought a whiff of the cosmopolitanism of Bombay to provincial Aligarh; Bi Amma, the mother of Mohamed and Shaukat Ali (the famous Ali Brothers), who so impressed a young Rashid Jahan that she decided to henceforth wear only khadi[23]; and Aabru Begum, the sister of the erudite Maulana Abul Kalam Azad. Of these, possibly someone as well-read and well-travelled as Atiya Fyzee would doubtless have left a lasting impression on a young girl such as Rashida. Daughter of Hasan Ali Effendi and Shareefun Nisa Tayabali, Atiya (1877-1967) was born in Constantinople with the proverbial silver spoon in her mouth. However, unlike other well-born women of her age and station, she chose to engage with the great intellectual debates of her time, and used her wealth and status to broaden her horizon in a manner that had never been attempted before by any other Muslim woman in this part of the world.[24]

The school whose birth and evolution were directly related to the life and career of Rashid Jahan, moved from rented premises in the old city to its present location on Marris Road in 1909. Soon, the sharif families of Aligarh – impressed by the dedication of the Abdullahs and mindful of the stringent observance of the parda as also the diligent teaching of the Holy Qur'an – began sending their daughters to this new school, the first of its kind in Upper India. The Tyabjis and Fyzees of Bombay, early patrons of Shaikh Abdullah's innovative scheme of a 'normal' school for Muslim girls, continued to gather generous donations from the wealthy Muslim merchants of Bombay Presidency. As word spread of the good work being done and the personal supervision of Ala Bi, a well-born lady from a sharif family of Delhi, the Old Boy network of MAO College sprang into service. These Old Boys, many of whom were by now well-settled, well-to-do professionals and esteemed members of the Muslim middle class, living in cities across the length and breadth of Muslim India, donated generously to the cause. So did the rajas, taluqedars and minor royalty – both Muslim and non-Muslim. Unlike the MAO College – and this must be stressed – the school for girls was avowedly non-denominational. While Shaikh Abdullah was no doubt moved by the plight of Muslim girls who had remained in abject ignorance and illiteracy while the boys had moved on, his intention was never to keep non-Muslims away. If anything, he appointed several Christian, Hindu and Sikh teachers and, as the school moved from elementary to middle to higher education, ensured it remained free from communal bias.

While funds were no longer a problem, the school was not without its share of critics and troublemakers. A disgruntled section of malcontents who objected to the very idea of a school for Muslim girls always existed. Moved partly by envy for Shaikh Abdullah and partly by misplaced religious zeal, they expressed their outrage in ingenious and entirely dishonourable ways. Shaikh Abdullah's autobiography mentions many such instances: how street urchins were 'encouraged' to accost the *dolis* carrying pupils to and from school, raise the curtain and shout obscenities at the little girls cowering inside; or, how seemingly respectable folk spread false stories about goings-on at the school; or, how the more scurrilous-minded came up with accounts of the school teaching singing and dancing to produce 'nautch girls'! Shaikh Abdullah handled

each of these situations with forceful dignity, a quality that
Rashid Jahan inherited in ample measure and would display in
later years when she herself came under fire from hypocrites
and bigots over the *Angarey*[25] furore.

Undaunted by the underhand tactics of his detractors,
Shaikh Abdullah was however faced with a real problem. Girls
tended to drop out midway through their schooling as soon as
they reached puberty. The fear of a stain on family honour
propelled even liberal-minded families to pull out adolescent
girls. The only way out of this impasse, the Abdullahs decided,
was to convert their day school into a boarding house, one
where parda could be more rigorously implemented than in
the most scrupulous of sharif households. Behind the high
walls of a boarding school, not only would the girls be spared
the daily trauma of a commute from their homes, fraught as it
was with all manner of perils, but a boarding school would
allow the Abdullahs to cast their net wider. Girls from far-
flung parts of the country could attend, in much the same way
as boys from all over India gravitated to the MAO College.
Already, there was a group among the staff and students of
MAO College who were lobbying to convert their College into
a strictly residential campus. There was much to be said for
students living under close supervision of teachers, enjoying
the full benefits of an education that included games, sports
and extra-curricular activities and the shared joys and sorrows
of communal living.

With the help of a handsome grant from the Begum of Bhopal
and an assurance from the government of an enhanced grant-
in-aid, Shaikh Abdullah bought a plot of land that he had long
admired on his daily walks. This was the heavily forested Nanak
Rai ka Bagh which contained not only a mango orchard but
several other tall and dense trees. However, being a mere mile
and a half away from the boys' College, the Shaikh's intention
of building a boarding school for girls set off alarm bells across

the hallowed portals of Syed Ahmad's all-male establishment. W. A. J. Archibald, Principal of the MAO College, expressed his displeasure at having a girls' school at such close proximity. He was joined by a chorus of protests from a cross-section of Muslim elites, both from Aligarh and outside, including some such as Dr Ziauddin and Viqar-ul Mulk who had initially supported the idea of women's education. No one thought to question the merits of the scheme envisaged by Shaikh Abdullah: the provision of mainstream education in a safe, secure and as home-like atmosphere as was possible to create at moderate expense.

Undaunted, Shaikh Abdullah went ahead with his plans for constructing a house that included classrooms, dormitories, dining halls as well as living quarters for teachers – all ensconced behind high walls. In 1911, Lady Porter, wife of the Acting Lt-Governor of the United Provinces, came to lay the foundation stone of the Muslim Girls' School and Hostel. The construction, completed in 1913, was marked by an elaborate ceremony attended by a galaxy of rich, powerful and influential women from distant parts of the country. Virtually the who's who of elite Muslim women descended in droves, coming in ladies' coupes till the railhead at Aligarh and thence in screened carriages to the shamiana erected for the festivities. The Begum of Bhopal inaugurated the new buildings; she was joined by the Fyzee sisters, Abru Begum, as well as Begum Shafi and Begum Shah Nawaz from Lahore and scores of well-heeled women from Delhi, Hyderabad and Lucknow. Dazzled by this display of influential patrons and well-placed supporters, the rabble-rousers of Aligarh were temporarily silenced.

Ala Bi spent much of her waking time with the girls at the boarding school, caring for them as a mother would. In the early years, her insistence on parda was so strict that even Shaikh Abdullah addressed the girls from behind a screen or from a chair at the gate of the Waheedia Hostel (the spot known for posterity as 'the window') where only his wife and daughters could 'come out' to meet him. It took the feisty Ismat Chughtai to make a public admonishment that it was shameful that girls should observe parda from their fathers; only then did Papa Miyan begin to speak face to face with the girls. However, the fallout of this rigorous implementation of the parda (which the Abdullahs accepted as a practical necessity) was that more and more sharif families took to sending their girls to study in the care of the husband and wife duo. With nine students in 1914, the majority being family or wards of friends, the school grew in strength; by 1926 it had become an intermediate college and by 1937, it was offering graduate courses with over 250 students in various classes. Two of the Abdullah sisters – Khatun Jahan and Mumtaz Jahan – obtained post-graduate degrees from England and Lucknow, respectively, and returned to serve as principals of the College. A great many former students took to teaching as a profession. Every girl who emerged from behind the high walls of the Aligarh Women's College, irrespective of whether or not she earned a living, regardless also of whether she put her education to any gainful use or not, nevertheless felt empowered. In her empowerment lay an affirmation of Shaikh Abdullah's deep-seated belief that education was the cornerstone of overall progress and development. The innumerable articles and editorials in *Khatun* as well as his first-person testimony in his autobiography bear ample evidence: 'It is important to tie children to the rope of education from their infancy, and the way an educated mother can go about doing this very important job, a father never can.'[26]

Lady Hardinge College and the years until *Angarey*

At the age of sixteen Rashid Jahan left the sheltered world of Aligarh and the safe confines of the girls' school to study at the Isabella Thoburn (IT) College in Lucknow.[27] Here, new intellectual vistas opened up. Though a science student, she read Dickens, Keats, Shelley and Thomas Hardy, as well as Tolstoy, Pushkin and the Russian masters as well as Maupassant and Balzac.[28] While still in college, she wrote her very first story called 'When the Tom-Tom Beats' in English; it was translated by Ale Ahmad Suroor, who would later become a close friend, into Urdu under the title 'Salma', and became quite popular.[29]

These two years between Aligarh and Delhi were carefree years filled with books, sports and the many extracurricular activities encouraged by the teachers at IT College. While still at an all-girls school like the one she had left behind at Aligarh, IT College was, in many ways, an altogether different world. For one thing, the emphasis on English was new to someone like Rashida[30] who, though she knew English, nevertheless came from an Urdu-speaking milieu. For another, the exposure to girls from different backgrounds was far greater and the emphasis on parda was negligible. Though housed in secluded quarters in the fabled Char Bagh campus, the girls were by no means cloistered. Inside the college, they swam, played tennis, badminton and basketball, debated and acted in plays, recited poetry, and were introduced to the latest cultural and literary trends. Outside the College, they were permitted to go to the movies and indulge in "Ganjing", a form of recreation unique to Lucknow comprising as it did a leisurely stroll along the colonnaded market of Hazrat Ganj.

Set up primarily for native Christian girls, IT (as it was generally known) drew girls from all the 'good' families – Muslim, Hindu, Sikh, Parsi and Christian. However, unlike the Christian girls – the majority of whom were on freeships or whose education was subsidised either by the Church or well-meaning members of the domiciled community – the non-Christian students paid full fees and were, naturally, from privileged if not aristocratic families. Liberal Indian parents of a certain class displayed more similarities than differences; their daughters, thus, tended to form a sorority of sorts, making close friendships across distinctions of religion, caste or culture. The benefits of a liberal English-style education mingled harmoniously – (in the case of Rashid Jahan and successive women writers such as Attia Hosain (1913-1998) and Qurratulain Hyder (1928-2007) who followed her at IT and came from similarly privileged backgrounds) with a family background steeped in the values of sharif culture. One can well imagine Rashid Jahan here from 1921-1923. The charmed world that the young women occupied in Char Bagh is showcased in the writings of both Qurratulain Hyder and Attia Hosain. Ismat Chughtai, who followed her beloved Rashida Apa from the school at Aligarh in 1933, has written colourful accounts of IT as well as drawn on several characters that she met during her days at the College in novels such as *Terhi Lakir* (The Crooked Line); she has also devoted a whole chapter to describing life among its porticoed halls, libraries and sports fields in her autobiography. Ismat describes how she could move about freely both inside the college and outside, go out to the bazars, meet people, even boys! She writes how the rule of freedom within reasonable limits implemented by her fair-minded American teachers went a long way towards making her what she was. Her views on the enforced parda and seclusion practised in most Muslim homes appear in different ways in much of her writing: 'The fear of the other sex that is planted in a girls' mind in her childhood has very deep and complex ramifications.'[31]

Rashida had discarded parda by the time she reached Lucknow; her mother, Ala Bi, had agreed that she would be singled out and her education might suffer if she continued with it. Free from its restrictive anonymity, Rashida blossomed. Always bold and fearless, she had been a natural leader since her childhood. Given her family background and the array of distinguished visitors who routinely visited Abdullah Lodge, she was attuned to the great national discourses of her time: the swadeshi, home rule, civil disobedience, khilafat movements were discussed in her parents' home by those most intimately connected with these great socio-political stirrings that were quickening the national consciousness. Her eclectic reading – thanks to teachers at Aligarh and Lucknow as well as the liberal humanism practiced by her parents – had opened her mind to the intellectual debates of the 1920s. Early exposure to nationalist leaders such as Maulana Mohamed and Shaukat Ali, their mother Bi Amman as well as Maulana Azad, members of the Fyzee and Tyabji clan introduced her to new ideas and new ways of seeing the world. While by no means dogmatic, the American missionaries who ran IT College were, essentially, preparing their pupils to live and cope in a colonised, deeply polarised world. Rashida could, from her early teens, see the cordon sanitaire that segregated the two worlds: the privileged/ under-privileged, educated/uneducated, rich/poor, coloniser/ colonised.

During holidays, she would return to Abdullah Lodge at Aligarh. But in Papa Miyan and Ala Bi's home, holidays were not meant to be an extended period of leisure; Rashida was expected to pitch in and lend a hand at whatever work needed to be done. It could be taking classes one day or informally teaching the servants and their children to read and write on others. Since Ala Bi had taught all her girls immaculate sewing and dress-making, Rashida would knit and sew, often making clothes for the extended family of helpers at the school or stitching woollen clothes for winter.[32] These chores would be interspersed with fun-filled family outings; Ala Bi would plan picnics to the waterworks at Narora or to a pond to pick water chestnuts and Papa Miyan would gather his flock for recitations from the choicest Urdu poets, or *King Lear*!

After completing her Inter-Science from Lucknow, Rashid Jahan moved to Delhi to study medicine at the Lady Hardinge Medical College in 1924. Noting how medicine and technology were central to polemical debates about modernity and colonialism and how colonial medical institutions (such as the Lady Hardinge Medical College meant exclusively to train women doctors) were themselves the result of politicisation of colonised women's bodies, Priyamvada Gopal writes:

As part of a relatively early cadre of women Indian professionals and, certainly, of Muslim women doctors, she [Rashid Jahan] found herself thinking about the relationship between the modern breed of "new women" to which she belonged and the constituency in whose name she had been created.[33]

It must be understood that schools such as the one at Aligarh provided women, especially Muslim women, the opportunity to partake of several of these colonial experiments in higher learning, especially in taking up professional studies, be it in teaching, medicine, nursing or other vocational courses. However, only a handful of them, like Rashid Jahan, were able to make the journey first, from the secluded spaces of the zenana to the relative confinement of a girls school (though it had due provision for parda) and then on to the freedom of a professional college. A trajectory such as Rashid Jahan's was a pioneering one, like a first flight into the great unknown.

Rashid Jahan's link with Aligarh did not break even after she left for higher studies; not only was it her parental home but, more importantly, the school started by her parents remained an integral part of her life. She would return, periodically, to mesmerise generations of young girls studying under the Abdullahs' watchful care as well as dazzle scores of young men from the nearby Aligarh Muslim University (as the MAO College came to be called from 1920) who had never seen so bold and brash a young woman before. With her cropped hair, her penchant for wearing either plain cotton saris or long kurtas over tight pajamas and no jewellery or make-up, her air of extreme self-assurance and her free and frank interaction with members of the opposite sex, she was quite unlike any other young woman from a sharif household. Studying in Lucknow and Delhi, she travelled alone by train. Her arrival, usually unannounced, created a ripple in the still waters of the girls' school; her sisters and a gaggle of young admirers would crowd around her, agog with anticipation of the stories she brought from the big world outside. Once, Khurshid recalls, how she showed up at night with a young girl; a 'secret conference' followed with her parents and Rashida left as suddenly as she had arrived leaving the girl in her parents' care. Years later, Khurshid discovered that the girl had been a victim of sexual abuse and she marvelled at her sister's courage and compassion in spiriting the girl away from her exploiters and bringing her to the safe haven at Abdullah Lodge.

Perhaps the most comprehensive account of the 'effect' of Rashid Jahan on young, susceptible minds is to be found in Ismat Chughtai's autobiography, *Kaaghzi Hai Pairahan* (The Raiment is Paper Thin). Chughtai (1911-91), the enfant terrible of Urdu literature, openly admits to being not merely influenced by this 'daughter of reform'[34] but also to copying her. In an interview, she said of Rashida:

> She actually spoiled me. That was what my family used to say. She spoiled me because she was very bold and used to speak all sorts of things openly and loudly, and I just wanted to copy her. She influenced me a lot; her open-mindedness and free-thinking. She said that whatever you feel, you should not be ashamed of it, nor should you be ashamed of expressing it, for the heart is more sacred than the lips. She said that if you feel a thing in your mind and heart and cannot express it, then thinking it is worse and speaking it better, because you can get it out into the open with words.[35]

Khurshid Jahan, thirteen years younger, writes of visiting Delhi where Rashida was studying and being taken for a Jackie Coogan film. 'I was completely awe-struck when I heard my sister enter into an argument with the Anglo-Indian manager of the cinema, demanding students' concessions for us. To my bewildered ears, she spoke flawless English.' Khurshid shares other memories of those years, such as Rashida taking her and her youngest sister Birjees (Biji) 'slumming to the bazar across the railway line', a part of town that was strictly out of bounds for members of sharif families, let alone girls raised in parda. Shortly after crossing the railway line that divides the city in two the girls, riding in a horse-drawn carriage, were accosted by a distraught woman; the woman's daughter had delivered a baby and was bleeding. Khurshid gave the woman some money and wanted to continue on their way but Rashida got off the carriage and went with the woman:

> She was gone all day and returned home quite late, hungry and exhausted but very happy to have arranged for the sick girl to be admitted to Lady Dufferin Hospital. She had promised to pay for all the food, milk and medicine. The next morning Apabi coaxed, cajoled and bullied us into contributing whatever we could, so that she could keep her promise to the girl. Biji and I grumbled a bit, but we couldn't refuse our large-hearted sister.[36]

For all the fame and name that Khurshid enjoyed in later years as a successful actor and, of all the Abdullah children, being the most visible and prominent sibling, she cannot help admitting to a twinge of something, perhaps envy, for the special place occupied by her dearly beloved Apabi:

> Apabi was our father's favourite child and *rose to the status of a son of the family* after she qualified as a doctor.[37]{ *italics mine*}

Rashida joined the Provincial Medical Service of the United Provinces after graduating from the Lady Hardinge College in 1929 and after a first stint as a medical officer in Bulandshahar, was posted to Lucknow in 1931. This second stint in Lucknow, longer than the first, would prove to be a turning point in her life and set her on a trajectory that would transform her from Dr Rashid Jahan to Comrade Rashid Jahan and thence to Rashid Jahan 'Angareywali'.

End Notes

[1] Shaikh Muhammad Abdullah, *Mushahidaat wa Taasurraat* (Aligarh: Female Education Association, 1969), p. 2-3. All translations from Urdu, unless otherwise specified, are mine.

[2] A cautionary tale of two sisters, was hailed as the first runaway bestseller in Urdu, given an award by the colonial government and made a part of the Urdu syllabus in many schools. Its opening lines were: "No one more thoroughly deserves to be called 'stupid' than a human being who does not sometimes ponder over the affairs of the world we live in. And although there are fit subjects for meditation in this world of a thousand different kinds, the most fundamental and important of all is human life itself."

[3] The district Qadiyan in Western Punjab is the home of Mirza Ghulam Ahmad, whom the Ahmadiyas hold to be the promised Messiah. The Ahmadiyyas consider themselves Muslims; most other Muslims consider them 'deviationists'. Often, the words 'Qadiyani' and 'Ahmadiya' are used indistinguishably.

[4] Mentioned by David Lelyveld, *Aligarh's First Generation* (Princeton: Princeton University Press, 1978), p. 289.

[5] This section draws from Shaikh Abdullah's autobiography.

[6] Sheikh Muhammad Abdullah, op. cit., p.200

[7] Ibid.

[8] Ibid., p. 206

[9] Ibid, p. 207. Shaikh Abdullah cites the instance of the plague which led to rioting in Kanpur when the Government insisted on removing the affected people away from their homes. Syed Ahmad, siding with the rioters, felt that removing women from parda and relocating them outside their homes, even to safeguard them from plague, was not acceptable.

[10] Gail Minault, *Secluded Scholars: Women's Education and Muslim Social Reform in Colonial India* (New Delhi: Oxford University Press, 1998), p. 35.

[11] Nazir Ahmad, *The Bride's Mirror: A Tale from Delhi a Hundred Years Ago,* English translation of *Mirat al-Urus,* Translated by G. E. Ward, with an 'Afterword' by Frances W. Pritchett (New Delhi: Permanent Black, 2001), p. 155.

[12] Gail Minault, 'Muslim Social History from Urdu Women's Magazines', in *Gender, Language and Learning,* op. cit., p.88.

[13] Rashidul Khairi (1870-1936) wrote on virtually every ill that beset Muslim society – widow remarriage, marriages of convenience in wealthy families, abuse and ill-treatment meted out by step-parents, rampant practice of polygamy, ill-treatment of servants (especially maids), among the many glaring malpractices in *sharif* Muslim households.

[14] Shaikh Muhammad Abdullah, *Mushahidaat wa Taasurraat*, op. cit., p. 211

[15] Ibid., p. 211

[16] The Abdullahs' fourth daughter, Khurshid Jahan, has given a detailed account of these early years in a chapter entitled 'The Struggle for Female Education' in her autobiography *A Woman of Substance: The Memoirs of Begum Khurshid Jahan*, Lubna Kazim (ed.) (New Delhi: Zubaan, 2005). Khurshid Mirza (1918-89) migrated to Pakistan with her police officer husband, Ali Akbar Mirza, and became a popular Radio and TV artiste; she was awarded the Pride of Performance award by the Government of Pakistan in 1985.

[17] Shaikh Muhammad Abdullah, op. cit., p. 233.

[18] Khurshid Jahan , op. cit., p. 73.

[19] The journal dealt with religious and social issues but in the light of modernism and liberalism instead of obscurantism. All through its existence, it gave especial importance to gender issues and to female education.

[20] Mentioned in the Brochure brought out in 2005 on the occasion of the centenary celebrations organised by the Female Education Association, Aligarh.

[21] Atia Abid, *Rashid Jahan: Selected Short Stories and Plays* (Aligarh, AMU Press, 2005), Introduction.

[22] Hamida Saiduzzafar, 'Rashida Apa', *Shola-e-Jawwala* (Lucknow: Indian Publisher, 1974), p. 1. Hamida Saiduzzafar (1921-1988) was the sister of Mahmuduzzafar, Rashida's husband. Hamida and Rashida became close friends. Hamida not merely published *Shola-e-Jawwala* after Rashida's death as a tribute to her dear sister-in-law but in her own autobiography, published posthumously by her friends, has devoted an entire chapter to Rashida whom she held in great esteem – as a sister-in-law, a friend, and a doctor. Hamida was a highly-trained ophthalmologist, a dedicated teacher and a practising doctor at Aligarh at the Mohan Lal Hospital (now known as the Gandhi Eye Hospital and affiliated to the Aligarh Muslim University), and also a keen photographer and avid bird-watcher. I had the great good fortune of knowing Dr Hamida Sauduzzafar as a child; I treasure the quotation from *Alice in Wonderland* she wrote in my autograph book. Incidentally, she operated me for my squint and befriended me during the lengthy post-operation exercises at the Gandhi Eye Hospital.

[23] According to Hamida Saiduzzafar, Rashid Jahan wore white khadi from the age of 14 onwards; in this she had the complete support and approval of her parents.

[24] A highly readable account of Atiya Fyzee's travels can be found in a travelogue-cum-memoir, first published in a journal and then as a book, called *Zamana-e-Tahsil*, in 1922. It has been translated into English by Siobhan Lambert-

Hurley and Sunil Sharma as *Attia's Journeys: A Muslim Woman from Colonial Bombay to Edwardian England* (New Delhi: Oxford University Press, 2010).

[25] The explosive book published in December 1932 with contributions by Sajjad Zaheer, Ahmed Ali, Mahmuduzzafar and Rashid Jahan.

[26] Shaikh Muhammad Abdullah, op. cit., p.481.

[27] Set up by an American missionary in 1870 to provide quality education to native Christian girls, it was a pioneering effort in women's education in India.

[28] Reminiscences of Hajra Begum entitled 'Kuch Rashid Jahan ke Bare Mein' published in special issue of Khatun, November 2005.

[29] Marjorie A Dimmitt (ed.), *When the Tom Tom Beats & Other Stories* (Lucknow: Methodist Publishing House, 1932), pp 92-104. The story was about arranged marriages; it first appeared in the IT College magazine called *Char Bagh Chronicle* sometime in 1923 or 1924.

[30] Rashid Jahan was called Rashida by family and friends.

[31] Ismat Chughtai, *A Life in Words: A Memoir*, Translated by M. Asaduddin (New Delhi: Penguin Books, 2012), p. 275.

[32] Khurshid Jahan, op. cit., p.75. Khurshid goes on to mention that Rashida (or Apabi as Khurshid called her) was always doing something for others. 'While she was in the Medical College, she learnt to knit and, from then on, our house was full of cheap wool and homemade needles. Everyone was taught to knit baby garments that she took away for the poor children at the hospital. Apabi would stitch and knit garments for her friends' and sisters' children since she adored babies.' (p. 91)

[33] Priyamvada Gopal, '*Sex Space and Modernity in the Work of Rashid Jahan* 'Angarewali', in Crystal Bartlovich and Neil Lazarus, (eds.) *Marxism, Modernity and Postcolonial Studies* (Cambridge: Cambridge University Press, 2002), p. 151.

[34] An expression coined by Gail Minault for the girls who emerged from the school set up by the Abdullahs.

[35] Interview, *Mahfil*, 8, 2-3 (Summer-Fall 1972), pp. 169-188.

[36] Lubna Kazim (ed.), *A Woman of Substance*, op. cit., pp. 93-94.

[37] Ibid., p. 93.

2

Rashid Jahan 'Angareywali'

Uth, ke ab bazm-e-jahan ka aur hi andaz hai
Mashriq-o-maghrib mein tere daur ka aaghaz hai

Arise, for the ways of the world are changing
Your age is about to dawn in the east and the west

– Muhammad Iqbal

The *Angarey* quartet: three angry young men and a woman

It was in Lucknow that Rashid Jahan blossomed and was drawn into a circle of intellectually-charged and politically-driven young people; and it was in Lucknow that she met a host of educated young men, some studying in the vibrant Lucknow University, others living or working in the city of nawabs, such as the *Angarey* group, namely Sajjad Zaheer, Ahmad Ali, and Sahibzada Mahmuduzzafar, whom she would marry in 1934.[1] While medicine remained central to her concerns, reading, writing, meeting people, discussing socio-political issues too became an important part of her life. Since she had been writing from her student days and had had enough opportunity to meet men and women from the world of literature and politics in Aligarh, it was but natural that in Lucknow too, she would meet, and impress, the city's Young Turks.

After the fall and decline of Delhi following the Great Revolt of 1857, Lucknow emerged as the cultural capital of Upper India.[2] With its glorious mix of educational institutions, law courts, clubs, cinemas, coffeehouses not to mention the lingering whiff of Awadhi decadence mingling with the liberalism of a vibrant new class of educated Indians drawn from across the length and breadth of colonial India. It was a veritable smorgasbord of people, places and ideas. Its very air was a heady cocktail of the past and the present, and a future that lay coiled waiting to unfurl among its many aesthetically-designed buildings, parks and pavilions.

Since there appears to be very little material on Rashid Jahan's time at the Lady Hardinge Medical College, we get only a glimpse of her life during her five years of medical studies in some of her short stories, such as *Mera Ek Safar* (One of My Journeys). We can only guess that she would have led an active life there, possibly acted in plays or written skits, participated in whatever extra-curricular activities the college had to offer, and emerged as a well-trained, competent doctor.[3] By the time she reached Lucknow to work at the Lady Dufferin Hospital, she was twenty-six years old. By all accounts she was free-spirited and beautiful, in a completely natural sort of way.[4] Dressed in the simplest of cotton clothes, her hair usually an unruly mop of curls, her manner did not betray the slightest trace of either vanity or self-consciousness; the sheer force of her personality was her greatest asset. Not only were her looks and appearance strikingly unusual for a woman from a *sharif khandan*, but her entire approach to life was unique, almost bohemian in its complete disregard for what were considered the 'proprieties'.

After a short-lived flirtation with the Congress,[5] possibly under the influence of new friends – many of whom were either pro-Left, had socialist sympathies or as in the case of Zaheer and Mahmud were already members of the Communist

Party of India – she came to see Marxism as crucial to understanding, and ultimately changing, many things that struck her as unfair, such as colonialism, imperialism, capitalism, industrialization, socio-economic developments and other forms of uneven, lopsided development. Though she joined the CPI in 1933 and remained an active member till her death, the pre-*Angarey* years found her increasingly drawn towards a socialist worldview. Her own experiences as a doctor no doubt reinforced her belief that in an essentially unfair world, women were more unfortunate than most. This appears to me to be the only logical way of interpreting why and how she chose to write the story and the play that she did for *Angarey*, her twin contributions to the incendiary book that placed her at the centre of a storm, brought her notoriety as Rashid Jahan Angareywali and – it must be admitted – earned her a place in Urdu literature not commensurate with the body of her work.

Commenting on her sister's growing nationalism, Khurshid Mirza wrote:

I had noticed in 1932 ... that my sister's patriotic zeal had taken a firmer hold upon her. She had impressed upon me from early childhood that wearing frocks was aping the English rulers who would never consider us their equals, no matter how much we tried to be like them. She taught me to say: 'I am a non-cooperative.' This was a few years before the non-cooperation movement was launched in India.[6]

Dr. Hamida Saiduzzafar who, after Rashida's marriage to Mahmud became not only a sister-in-law but also a dear friend, shows us another way of 'seeing' Rashid Jahan. Her detailed observations deserve to be quoted in length, for they provide a valuable insight into this unusual young woman:

Rashida always had a rebellious spirit. Quite early in life, she was aware of the social injustice and inequality in society. As a practical person, the diagnosis was not enough for her; she wanted a treatment, a cure. Of all the people of her class and her generation, Rashida had the least difficulty in identifying herself with, or relating to, the 'common people'. One reason for this was her family background, of course, where servants were treated as members of the family, and where class differences had been reduced to a minimum...

Another reason was that she came into contact with all sorts of people in her medical studies, and she made it a point to treat her patients not only medically but also psychologically which, of course, is half the battle.[7]

Hamida's comments about her 'mercurial' friend whom she describes as 'tactless' but also 'great fun and a great conversationalist', full of life and energy, but always unconventional, are useful because they give us a clue as to what might have led her to write the sort of stories she did, first for *Angarey* and then later:

Considering that Rashid Jahan was the first woman in Urdu who addressed herself squarely, consistently and forcefully to the myriad problems of the middle and lower-middle class woman in Indian society, she can rightly be called Urdu literature's first 'angry young woman'.[8]

In the light of these observations from two younger women who knew her well, it is clear why this angry young woman might have joined hands with three angry young men, and produced an angry book with little thought or regard for the uproar it might generate.[9] *Angarey* was simply the outcome of four young people giving vent to a deeply-felt sense of inequity. That it would one day be hailed as a beacon of progressive thought and be regarded as the precursor of the Progressive Writers' Movement was possibly beyond their ken at that point.

Let us briefly examine the book and the careers of the four young writers. *Angarey*, published in December 1933, comprised ten segments, namely five short stories by Sajjad Zaheer: *Neend*

Nahin Aati (Sleeplessness), *Jannat ki Bashaarat* (The Glad Tidings of Heaven), *Garmiyon ki Ek Raat* (A Summer's Night), *Dulari,* and *Phir Yeh Hungama* (Again this Commotion); two by Ahmed Ali: *Baadal Nahin Aate* (The Clouds Don't Come) and *Mahavaton ki Ek Raat* (A Night of Winter Rain); a story and play each by Rashid Jahan: *Dilli ki Sair* (A Tour of Delhi) and *Parde ke Peechche* (From Behind the Veil); and one short story called *Jawanmardi* (Virility) by Mahmuduzzafar.[10]

Zaheer's five stories constitute the bulk of *Angarey.* Written in the stream-of-consciousness technique made popular by writers such as Virginia Woolf and Marcel Proust, *Neend Nahi Aati* is a rambling story about heaven and hell, poverty, hunger and the place of religion in society. It uses two iconic images to make its impact: the notion of hell and the archetypal image of an Awadhi courtesan; by the end of the story, both images are turned upside down in a mock denouement. *Jannat ki Basharat* is a provocative story about a pious maulvi who falls asleep on the most blessed of all nights, when he ought to be up praying, dreams he is in heaven, only to find he has slept through the night. To be fair to Zaheer, though, he seems to be mocking religiosity more than religion, and attacking *maulviyat* rather than *Islamiyat. Garmiyon ki Ek Raat* is a biting critique of social and economic inequalities that cannot be bridged by religion. Through his depiction of an encounter between a clerk and his peon on a summer evening, Zaheer seems to imply that the poor will remain as poor as ever despite progress and development in the cities; in the existing social order, they can do nothing but watch the petit bourgeoisie move up the social and economic ladder. *Dulari* is not only the finest story by Zaheer but also the sharpest in *Angarey;* in its denunciation of the lot of *laundis* or slave girls sold for domestic labour in sharif households, it holds up a blinding mirror to genteel society. The Urdu critic, Khalilur Rehman Azmi, considered *Dulari* the first serious study of the position of women in a patriarchal society, a subject that would be repeatedly taken up by other Urdu writers who followed in Zaheer's footsteps.[11] *Phir Yeh Hungama*, the weakest link in *Angarey*, is a pastiche of several mini-stories and a jumble of thoughts full of sound and fury, signifying little.

Ahmed Ali's *Badal Nahi Aate* also uses the stream-of-consciousness technique and employs a range of images to weave a compelling story of the sexual exploitation of women by their husbands; however, the sense of defeat and helplessness gives way to anger and the first stirrings of awareness: 'Why can't we do anything? If we had our own money why would we have to tolerate such humiliation?' In his second story, *Mahavaton ki Ek Raat*, we once again hear a woman's voice, but this time in the form of an interior monologue to ask a litany of existential questions: 'Why doesn't God listen? Does He even exist or not? What is He? Whatever He might be, He is very cruel and very unjust. Why are some rich? And some poor?'

Mahmud's *Jawanmardi* is an eloquent portrait of an early but loveless marriage between two radically different people – the husband has been educated abroad but remains a quintessentially Indian man with a feudal mindset. Knowing very well that he has a sick wife, he nevertheless impregnates her to stop tongues from wagging and to demonstrate his 'manliness'. The wife dies in childbirth but he draws consolation from having proved his virility. While it is difficult to invest the story with any real literary merit, it is nevertheless a self-deprecatory admission, from a male, of the evils that men do and a useful intervention on a gendered perspective, one that would be picked up later by Ismat Chughtai, Khadija Mastur and others to make sharper, more psychologically penetrating observations.

Rashid Jahan's *Dilli ki Sair* is a short story – a mere three pages, about the complacency of men and the complete lack of *sair-o-tafri* (leisure travel) in the lives of women. A burqa-clad suburban housewife from Faridabad is taken by her husband on a trip to Delhi. He meets a friend at the station, leaves her sitting atop a pile of luggage and goes off. By the time he returns several hours later, she has had her fill of the sights and sounds – the crowds of passengers and porters, the rush and clamour of trains coming and going, the lascivious looks of strangers and the babel of strange tongues. She is scared, tired and hungry; all she wants is to go home. Yet, on her return, she tells and retells the story of her day-trip, regaling her women friends with her journey: 'After all, how often does one get treated to such juicy, delicious talk in a place like Faridabad. No wonder women come from far away to listen to Malka Begum's tale.' Despite its brevity, *Dilli ki Sair* is a penetrating reflection on life behind the parda and the blindness of male privilege towards the experience of women who lead cloistered lives. Worse still, in using the device of a woman telling the story of her aborted trip to a group of women friends and neighbours, there is a sense of shared bonhomie and cheerful acceptance: men *are* like that; women know it and can do nothing about it.

Parde ke Peeche is an extended dialogue between two women from sharif families living in a typical Muslim household. Drawing from her own experiences as a 'lady doctor' to reveal intimate and exact details of the lives of married women, as well as her experiences in her grandparents' home in Delhi, Rashid Jahan presents a harrowing picture of affluent women who are little more than sexual slaves of their husbands. When the lady doctor who comes to examine the younger woman, Muhammadi Begum, comments on the co-relation between frequent pregnancies and the patient's poor health, Muhammadi replies: 'Oh miss, you are all right. You earn your living; you eat well and sleep soundly. It's not like that with us. These fellows (referring to men like her husband) don't care whether they go to heaven or to hell when they die. They know what they want here. They don't care whether their wives, poor wretches, live or die. Men want their satisfaction.'[12]

Married at eighteen, Muhammadi Begum has borne children in all the years since, except twice, once when her husband was abroad and the second time when they had fought. She suffers from pyorrhoea and has had several teeth pulled out, because her husband returned from abroad and told her that her breath stank. Her children are pale, thin, emaciated, querulous, under-nourished, ill-kempt and rowdy. It is evident that Muhammadi is a bad manager of her household and many of her troubles are a result of her not being good at keeping her house or her children in order. She is ill and therefore not up to it may be one reason, but perhaps she is also disorganized, and Rashid Jahan gives her plight a sexist twist. She links Muhammadi's troubles with her husband. Being a feminist, Rashid Jahan is not content with merely delineating social injustice; she gives it a gendered perspective. We hear more about men being worse than animals when it comes to assuaging their sexual appetite, in a manner reminiscent of Ahmed Ali's *Badal Nahin Aate* and Mahmuduzzafar's *Jawanmardi*.

To keep her husband from straying, poor Muhammadi Begum even has herself 'fixed up':

> My womb and all my lower parts had fallen. I got it put right so that he could get the same pleasure as he'd got from a newly-married wife. But when a woman has a baby every year how can she stay in shape. It slipped down again. And then he went on at me and threatened me until he got me butchered again. And even then he wasn't satisfied.

Rashid Jahan's youngest sister, Khurshid Jahan, writes: 'The story is poignant in its depiction of men's complete lack of concern for women's feelings.... [*Parde ke Peeche*] underscores men's utter disregard for the women in their lives and describes accurately the goings-on in the middle-class Muslim household of the 1930s.'[13] The play portrays the woman as a victim of domesticity, marriage and sexuality and becomes, as Gopal says, a 'subversive litany of the wrongs that men do and women endure'.[14] Why subversive? The answer lies in the next section when we examine why *Angarey* was considered incendiary.

The storm over *Angarey*

Printed by Nizami Press in December 1932, *Angarey's* publication costs were borne by Zaheer who was then living in Lucknow having completed his studies in England. Writing about it years later in *Roshnai*, he was almost dismissive about the book that caused such a furore and left such a lasting impression on Urdu literature:

> Most of the stories in this collection lacked depth and serenity, and contained a good deal of anger and agitation against obsolete and retrogressive values. In some places, where the focus was on sexuality, the influence of D. H. Lawrence and James Joyce was apparent. The reactionaries had used these weaknesses to make *Angarey* and its writers the subject of harsh propaganda. As usual, resolutions were passed in mosques. Maulvi Abdul Majid Daryabadi challenged us to battle. We received death threats. And finally the U.P. government confiscated the publication.[15]

Ahmed Ali differed; in fact, he stoutly defended *Angarey*, often spoke about it and was acerbic in his criticism of those who decried it or its significance in the larger context of the Progressive Writers' Movement. Calling *Angarey* 'that brave, adolescent book', he viewed the birth of the Progressive Writers' Movement in 'enthusiastic discussions preceding and followed by [its] publication'. Of those who condemned the book and called for its ban, he declared: 'People read the book behind closed doors with relish, but denounced us in the open. We were lampooned and satirized, censured editorially and in pamphlets, and were even threatened with death. The book was eventually banned by the Government of the United Provinces, and the orthodox and God-fearing heaved a sigh of relief.'[16]

Of the *Angarey* quartet, Ahmed Ali (1910-1994) was the most gifted in purely literary terms; *Mahavaton ki Ek Raat* had already appeared in *Humayun*, the literary journal from Lahore, in 1932. Of the four he was the only one who went on to have a long and distinguished career as a writer. He also knew Rashida as he was a friend of her brother, Mohsin, and a frequent visitor to their home in Aligarh.[17] After completing his M.A. in English from Lucknow University in 1931 where he also taught for a year (1931-32), during the *Angarey* episode he was teaching at the Agra College. A prodigiously prolific writer, and at different points in his career a teacher, translator, poet, critic, diplomat and commentator on the Holy Qur'an, he is best known to the English reader for his epochal novel, *Twilight in Delhi*; he is also the most enigmatic of the four. His varied career showed glimpses of a person who was both a part of the establishment, yet against it. And it was Ahmed Ali who spoke of *Angarey* in later years and held it to be the 'real' Manifesto of the Progressives Writers' Association.

Son of Sir Wazir Hasan,[18] the Chief Justice of Oudh, Sajjad Zaheer (1905-73), was then living in Lucknow after having completed one B.A. from Lucknow University and another from Oxford where he had been greatly influenced by communist ideas and had also made friends with a wide circle of writers and intellectuals such as V. K. Krishna Menon, Mulk Raj Anand, Shapurji Saklatvala, Viren Chattopadhyay, Saumendranath Tagore, N. M. Jaisoorya, Raja Mahendra Pratap. Writing in his *Yaadein* (Reminiscences), he speaks passionately of the tumult that grew inside him during his student days in England:

We were gradually drifting towards socialism. Our minds searched for a philosophy which would help us to understand and solve the difficult social problems. We were not satisfied with the idea that humanity had always been miserable and would always remain so. ... After the end of our university education, this was the beginning of a new and unlimited field of education.[19]

Mahmuduzzafar (1908-1954) had lived in England for the greater part of his life since he had been packed off to school by his father, Dr. Saiduzzafar, a professor of anatomy at the Lucknow Medical College and a scion of the Rampur royal family. He had studied first at Sherbourne School in Dorset at the age of twelve, and then at Balliol College, Oxford. Yet, when he returned to India, in 1931, he became an active nationalist, choosing to wear khadi and refusing to sit for the civil services examinations as was expected of someone of his class and privilege. Betrothed to his cousin, Zohra,[20] since childhood, he was swept off his feet by Rashid Jahan.[21]

Born in upper and upper-middle class Urdu-speaking homes, being English-educated, all four were bilingual;[22] also, while privileged on account of birth and education, they were nonetheless acutely aware of the social and economic disparities that cleft Indian society into unequal halves. Given their western-style education, their knowledge of English and western literature, given also their fairly well-known penchant for radical and avant garde movements (literary and otherwise), they were seen by their detractors as 'west-inflicted'. That is, their profligacy in writing a shockingly immoral book (as *Angarey* was deemed to be) was viewed as 'the result of cultural and intellectual contact with Europe'.[23] They were accused of being 'intoxicated by English education, brainwashed into attacking Islam and its tenets'.[24] In fact, a satirical play by a certain Mullah Shahadami – entitled *Aag Khaaein* (Let Us Eat Fire) published in the *Khasaf Nama* dated February 10, 1933 – played on their westernised outlook being the cause of their scandalous breach of good conduct.

Mullah Shahadami's play featured the four contributors to *Angarey* with the syllables of each contributor's name slightly altered and given an Anglo-Saxon intonation. For instance, Zaheer became Mistar Sejad and was described as 'a fashionable saheb'; Mahmuduzzafar appeared as Mistar Memad, 'a romantically-inclined gentleman'; Ahmed Ali was identifiable as Mistar Emad, an 'up-to-date professor'; and there was no doubt whatsoever about the identity of Miss Razida 'a lady doctor'. A crude line-drawing appeared with the play showing the men wearing western clothes, and two of them – Segad and Emad – also wearing hats. Mistar Segad is clutching Miss Razida and all four are looking fearful. All around them are what appear to be flames and the simple, almost crude, line-drawing is entitled *Ek Awaaz* (A Voice). The author relied upon much black humour to depict these creatures as foolish, ridiculously westernised heathens who shall 'eat fire' for their blasphemous views when they are consigned to hell.[25]

Remembering those heady days, we have Ahmed Ali writing about what drew them together and caused them to produce *Angarey*:

> ... we shared a love of art and literature, and inspired by the youthful discovery of the strange new world of European culture, were filled with a zeal to change the social order and right the wrongs done to man by man. Astheticism of a creative kind was not common in the India of those days and the meeting of akin souls was not without its fullness and gratification. That age mellows down the heart's instincts and colours everything with the falsifying light of expediency and experience had never entered or discoloured our thoughts. We dreamed of winning for Urdu and the regional languages the same respect, and for the Indian people the same dignity, which other civilized languages and societies enjoyed. Time has proved that neither were our dreams futile, nor has our achievement been insignificant.[26]

A brief notice in the *Hindustan Times*, dated February 21,

1933 entitled 'Urdu Pamphlet denounced: Shias Gravely Upset' carried a portent of the trouble that was brewing; it mentioned a resolution passed by the Central Standing Committee of the All-India Conference, Lucknow, condemning the 'heartrending and filthy pamphlet' which 'has wounded the feelings of the entire Muslim community... and which is extremely objectionable from the point of view of both religion and morality.'[27] From then onwards, the tone and tempo of the protest accelerated. A barrage of articles began to appear in the Urdu press denouncing the book and its contents, heaping abuse and invective on its authors. As pressure began to mount on the U.P. government to proscribe the book, fatwas began to be issued in mosques against it and its authors, and festive book burnings took place outside bookshops purported to be selling it. Recalling the hostility of those days, Ahmed Ali wrote:

> ... bourgeois families hurried to dissociate themselves from us and denied acquaintance with us, especially with Rashid Jahan and myself... We were lampooned and satirised... our lives were threatened, people even lay in wait with daggers to kill us.[28]

The torrent of abuse culminated with the Government of the United Provinces banning *Angarey* on March 15, 1933 under Section 295A of the Indian Penal Code. The proprietor of Nizami Press, Malik Ali Javed, had caved in much earlier after his press was raided under orders of the city magistrate. He had confessed to his mistake in bringing out the book and apologised in a written statement as early as February 27, 1933 for insulting the feelings of the Muslim community. He readily agreed to surrender unsold copies of the book to the government. All but five copies were destroyed by the police in the raid. Of the five, three were placed in the custody of the Keeper of Records in Delhi (in what is now the National Archives of India) and the remaining two were sent to London.

Under the provision of the Press Regulation Act, 1890 (Government of India), the British Museum obtained a copy on June 21, 1933.[29]

That *Angarey* continued to live on in the Urdu-reading public's imagination and to exercise a hold over popular perception – becoming something of an 'urban legend' since more people had heard of it than had actually seen or read it – has more to do with the purported scandalous nature of its contents than any outstanding literary abilities of its contributors. Almost eighty years after the publication of this book (routinely dismissed as a 'pamphlet' by contemporary chroniclers), the very mention of *Angarey* evokes awe or derision disproportionate to what it actually deserves. This might have to do with the mythology that has built up around *Angarey* over the years, the reaction it evoked and the hair-trigger impulse behind the tradition of book-banning in India.[30]

Regrettably the anomaly in seeing *Angarey* for what it was has not diminished with time. Those who defend or decry the book and its four contributors still fail to correctly interpret the impulse behind its publication in the first instance. Those who clamoured for its banning as well as those who capitulated were hardly interested in what drove this foursome. One group merely saw it as an affront to their religious identity; the other was concerned solely with buying peace; no one was interested in appreciating the intent behind the provocation. Unfortunately, the literary historian, while acknowledging *Angarey* as a *sang-e-meel*, a milestone, in modern Urdu literature makes no more than a passing reference to *Angarey*.

The overtly sexual references and the attacks on religion still draw both the defenders' and the decriers' attention away from what was, I would like to believe, the real purpose of the book: to introduce another sort of writing, one born of a keen awareness among the four young writers, exposed to new literary trends and sensibilities, to the possibility of a radically new kind of writing. With the benefit of hindsight, it seems easy to see *Angaray* for what it truly was: no more and no less than a self-conscious attempt to shock people out of their inertia, to show how hypocrisy and sexual oppression had so crept into everyday life, that it was accepted with blithe disregard for all norms of civilized society. This 'new' writing was not unduly concerned with literary finesse; it placed message over manner and revelled in its ability to shock. If allowed to grow unchecked, it *could* become subversive which would suit neither the religious nor the political powers-that-be. It suited the colonial administration, however, to thwart, suppress and malign such writing by allowing a religious colour to mask its real intent. Unlike the later work produced by the progressives, *Angarey* is unrelieved by optimism; its ten contributing segments make no attempt to provide solutions, let alone advocate change.

Angarey, then, is a document of disquiet; it makes no attempt at social reform. Each of the ten pieces deals with lives that, when not shabby and poor, are certainly marked by decay and disintegration and in the case of women (whose cause was championed with such vigour not only by the lone woman in the quartet but each of the four contributors) marginalisation and exclusion. This attempt at becoming the 'other', speaking in the voice of a completely alien, unrelated other, can be considered *Angarey's* single most important contribution in strictly literary terms. It opened the doors for many writers to speak in voices other than their own and yet sound convincing and real. Premchand had done this before the *Angarey* writers, but his characters, while no doubt poor and deprived, lacked this altogether new, earthy vitality. Women like Gangi in Premchand's *Thakur ka Kuan* (The Thakur's Well) spoke bitterly against the caste-ridden, unjust, unequal society but no one had spoken of women's bodies, reproductive health, marital rape, domestic abuse and such issues that were considered beyond the purview of civilized society. Also, the complete absence of sentimentality in the *Angarey* pieces made for a radical break from tradition.

Weathering the storm

Being a woman and having written so bravely and boldly about sexual matters in a largely puritanical, patriarchal milieu, Rashid Jahan naturally came in for the worst ire of those who most vehemently opposed *Angarey* and all it stood for. Obviously, different people viewed her in different ways: 'In progressive families she became a symbol of the emancipated woman; in conservative homes an example of all the worst that can occur if a woman is educated, not kept in purdah, and allowed to pursue a career.'[31]

Lampooned as Rashid Jahan 'Angarewali' by the baser elements in the vernacular press, she became the public face of *Angarey*. As Priyamvada Gopal notes: 'Rashid Jahan – as a woman and a doctor – writing about gender, medicine and the politics of space, became an icon of the literary radicalism of *Angarey* itself; decried by some and celebrated by others.'[32]

Aligarh was not just an important centre of protest in the *Angarey* furore, it was also Rashid Jahan's home. Writing about those days that brought such an upheaval in their sheltered life at the girls' college, Khurshid recalls:

> When *Angarey* came out, I was involved in preparing for the annual examinations and had no idea of the public reaction. There were defamatory articles written against the writers in the Muslim press every day. One day, as I was climbing the steps of the verandah after a strenuous game of badminton, a girl called out loudly to another one as I was passing by: "Do you know, a vulgar book called *Angarey* has come out. Rashida Apa has also written in it and the Muslims have threatened to chop off her nose." My lovely sister's face minus her nose swam before my eyes, everything blacked out for a minute, and I sank on the steps in a dead faint.[33]

Later, when Khurshid learnt that it was 'only a threat and
not a fait accompli' she requested a day scholar to get her the
book. 'I read *Angarey* with a group of students and sighed with
relief. There was nothing vulgar in Apabi's stories, and so I did
not bother to finish the book.' Her family received innumerable
threats from those who, like Khurshid, had not bothered to
read the entire book, but were willing to commit murder over
it. Again, we have Khurshid's testimony:

> My parents had faced public threats all their lives. First when Shaikh
> Abdullah changed his religion from a Kashmiri Brahmin to a
> Muslim. Then, later, when he advocated education for Muslim
> women in India and alienated even Syed Ahmad Khan, whom he
> respected greatly. Then, providing hostel accommodation to young
> Muslim women became a bitter controversy, although it facilitated
> education for women who came from all parts of India. So, when
> it came to the agitation over *Angarey*, my parents were angry but
> unfazed by the threats.
>
> A blackmailer by the name of Ahrari[34] decided to exploit the
> situation and targetted Shaikh Abdullah as the father of one of
> the writers of *Angarey*. All through the year 1933, he kept writing
> scurrilous articles in a local newspaper saying that the morals of
> the girls in Shaikh Sahib's school were questionable and that the
> daughters of Shaikh Abdullah were setting a bad example by writing
> "filthy" stories. He pleaded that the Trusteeship of the Muslim
> Girls' College be taken away from him. We later learnt he was a
> dismissed employee of the university. This man sent his emissaries
> to Papa [Shaikh Abdullah] demanding a bribe of Rs 2000 to
> contradict his own accusations. Of course, Papa was not going to
> give in to coercion, and refused to pay.[35]

Instead, he took the blackmailer to court by filing a defamation
case against him in 1934. 'Ahrari lost his case and was awarded
sixteen months of hard labour in jail and a fine of about Rs
5,000,' records Khurshid.

We get another recollection about the *Angarey* episode from
Ismat Chughtai when she reminiscences about her Aligarh days

and how she first heard of *Angarey*. She begins by marvelling how these 'smouldering crackling' embers could have been published in Urdu 'the language over which Muslims have a feudal hold', and then goes on to substantiate Khurshid Jahan's account of the uproar fuelled by Ahrarvi who launched an attack on the Girls' College and brought out a paper to propel his tirade against the Abdullah family. 'According to him the Girls' College was a whorehouse and it should be closed down immediately. He also published obscene caricatures of Rashida Apa and other writers.' Intrigued by all the fuss, Ismat writes: 'I had not read the book, but Ahrarvi made me want to read it.' Someone smuggled in a copy and the girls 'lit lanterns, hung quilts over window-panes' and read the book overnight.[36] However, Ismat writes, 'We were faced with a dilemma. We looked hard for obscenity and filth, and couldn't find it.' But such are the pressures of respectability upon *sharifzadis*, she rues, that 'no one had the guts to say that *Angarey* was not obscene. A respectable girl saying that *Angarey* was not obscene would have been considered shameless.'[37] With this astute observation, thrown in carelessly among a host of inanities, Ismat has put her finger on the nub of the controversy surrounding the book. Perhaps, inadvertently, she also gives us a clue to the blanket condemnation of *Angarey* both in the press and in private: a certain herd mentality among the *shurfa* that sees the slightest deviation as a direct affront to public morality.

However, Ismat, a rebel even at that young age, chose to speak up. She wrote a long and impassioned letter challenging Ahrarvi: 'As it is Muslim girls are backward and deprived; on top of that bigots like Mullah Ahrarvi have become our enemies. By all means close down the college, but only our dead bodies will go out from here.' The article, published in the *Aligarh Gazette*, appealed to 'our six thousand brothers, our senior professors and teachers' to not 'sit back quietly'. In her

autobiography, Ismat noted with not unjustified glee that the
boys of the university gave Mullah Ahrarvi such a beating
that he disappeared soon afterwards. The girls celebrated their
victory by holding a mushaira to which the boys too were
invited. Later, a procession of Mullah Ahrarvi was taken out
and his effigy was burnt. 'For months we were intoxicated with
this victory,' notes a jubilant Ismat.[38] And, best of all, her
beloved Rashida Apa, who was fast becoming some sort of
idol, praised her hugely.

As for Rashid Jahan herself, she continued ploughing her
own furrow, unconcerned with the fuss and fury that surrounded
her literary attempts. If anything, she lent her name to a rejoinder
that appeared in *The Leader*, a newspaper from Allahabad.
Entitled 'In Defence of Angare: Shall We Submit to Gagging?'
it was published on April 5, 1933 and bore the signatures of
all four contributors.[39] Utterly lacking in any expression of
apology, the letter affirmed the writers' freedom of speech
and expression; what is more it explained why they 'have chosen
the field of Islam': 'not because they bear any special malice,
but because, being born into that particular society, they felt
themselves better qualified to speak for that alone. They were
more sure of their ground there.'

The Marxist worldview that had initially brought together
the *Angarey* quartet acquired a sharper hue and, in the aftermath
of the book-banning episode, drew Rashid Jahan towards
organised communism. In the absence of any direct testimony
from either Rashid Jahan or Mahmud, we have only the
conflicting versions presented by Ahmed Ali and Sajjad Zaheer.
Ahmed Ali was at pains to establish the pro-nationalist, anti-
imperialist sentiment of the *Angarey* quartet:

> Whereas we were ardent nationalists and anti-British, Marxism
> was not a ruling passion, though a Progressive outlook was inherent
> in the revolt; and as the group expanded, leftist leanings, vague in

some and pronounced in others, did become apparent, for there seemed no other way out of the social and political morass.[40]

At the same time, he was keen to stress the non-political nature of the *Angarey* outburst: 'The intention of the sponsors then, i.e. in 1932-33, was a literary one, with no forecast of any affiliation with any political ideology ...'[41] Also, believing that *Angarey* 'grew into the Progressive Movement, and the formation of the Progressive Writers' Association was announced in the *Leader*...' Ahmed Ali invested *Angarey* with more importance than others, going so far as to say: The most earth-shattering utterances of the Movement are to be found in *Angare*, which, in spite of it adolescence and immaturity, exposed discredited doctrines and dogmas which no one had dared attack, and set into motion a whole chain of actions and reactions.[42]

Zaheer, on the other hand, differed. His *Roshnai* opens with the line: 'In 1935, some Indian students set up the first circle of the Progressive Writers Movement, in London.' He then goes on to describe how a group of young men – Dr. Jyoti Ghosh, Dr. Mulk Raj Anand, Promode Sengupta, M.D. Taseer and he himself drafted a Manifesto, sent copies to prominent Indian intellectuals, including Premchand, and returned to India to organise the first meeting of the All-India Progressive Writers' Association in Lucknow on April 11, 1936. From the 'defence' published in the *Leader* till the Lucknow Conference of 1936, we see no evidence of 'progressive' activity. During the lull, with Zaheer away in England, his *Angarey* colleagues lay low and waited to regroup. We will see, in the next chapter, the trajectory Rashid Jahan marked out for herself as she married Mahmud and joined the CPI.

Increasingly, as Rashid Jahan was drawn towards organised communism and party-based politics, a certain section of writers – including most prominently, Ahmed Ali, who had been fellow travellers all along – began to make a distinction between the political and non-political faction among the progressives. Ahmed Ali grew apart from his *Angarey* colleagues as he believed

> ... progress or progressivism could not be narrowed down or confined to Communist channels, and that it applied equally to the middle classes and literature produced by them, of which all of us, the founders of the Movement, were members, so that we had taken it upon ourselves to show the way of progress by example and precept; and that good literature had nothing to do with class war or classes as such ...

We shall also see how class consciousness began to overlay everything for Rashid Jahan; her concern for ordinary people now became a dominant motif in her life and work. The dichotomy of the home and the world that reveals itself in the two *Angarey* pieces is replaced with broader, all-embracing concerns that move from the domestic and private space occupied by women in cloistered societies to span the open vistas of the national and public. Also, with tumultuous events taking place in India and abroad, we will see a perceptible change in her vision and understanding of writer's role in society.

End Notes

[1] Rashid Jahan was working for the Provincial Medical Service (PMS) and posted in Bahraich when she got married. She drew upon her experiences in Aligarh, Delhi (where she studied medicine), Bulandshahr (where she did her first stint as a doctor), Kanpur (where she had her second posting), Lucknow (where she studied at IT College and later worked), Amritsar (where her husband worked) and Dehradun (where her in-laws lived). Obviously, she travelled a great deal and her journeys by train feature in many of her writings. Rashid Jahan left the PMS in 1934 and thereafter had a private practice, first in Amritsar and later in Lucknow. Her practice thrived as she was a good doctor and very much in demand.

[2] The impact of the British annexation of Awadh on the culture of Lucknow has been comprehensively examined by: Rosie Llewellyn-Jones, *A Fatal Friendship: The Nawabs, the British and the City of Lucknow* (New Delhi: Oxford University Press, 1985); Veena Talwar Oldenburg, *The Making of Lucknow: 1856-1877* (New Jersey: Princeton University Press, 1984); Violette Graf (ed.), *Lucknow: Memories of a City* (New Delhi: Oxford University Press, 1997); and Michael H. Fisher, *A Clash of Cultures: Awadh, the British and the Mughals* (New Delhi: Manohar, 1987).

[3] Hajra Begum mentions Rashid Jahan participating in the cultural life of the medical college; 'Her vivacious temperament would not allow her to remain quiet here, too. She prepared a play in English, called 'Lala Rukh', which was very successful.' Quoted in 'Kuch Rashid Jahan ke Bare Mein', *Khatun*, op. cit., p. 9. I tried to locate this play or unearth some evidence of Rashid Jahan's activities at the Lady Hardinge Medical College through the Alumni Association but could not find any old records.

[4] My mother, Mehjabeen, is the daughter of Ale Ahmad Suroor. She remembers Rashid Jahan very well from the time her parents, Rashid Jahan and Mahmud were close friends in Lucknow. She has described Rashid Jahan's appearance and mannerisms to me in vivid detail – her clothes, her smile that lit up her face, her slightly prominent teeth that made her smile so attractive, her short hair that was such a novelty for a Muslim woman, and above all her great personal charm which was effective on everyone regardless of age, gender or class. My mother's account has been corroborated by others who knew her such as Dr Naren Gupta and Dr Sarwat Rahman whose testimonies appear elsewhere in this narrative. My interest in Rashid Jahan predates this study, as I had always heard many stories about her not only in my own home but in the Urdu-speaking milieu where she was talked of with great affection, even awe.

[5] Hajra Begum mentions, in passing, Rashid Jahan being influenced by Gandhi and being briefly drawn towards the idea of an armed revolt. Ibid., p. 10.

[6] Lubna Kazim (ed.), *A Woman of Substance, op.cit.,* pp. 99-101.

[7] Ibid., p. 95.

[8] Ibid., p. 104.

[9] For a detailed study of *Angarey* and the progressive writers' movement see my book, *Liking Progress, Loving Modernity,* forthcoming from Oxford University Press.

[10] Mahmuduzzafar was apparently 'pressed into service' at short notice by Zaheer and asked to pitch in since he wanted something to flesh out the slender book. Universally referred to as Mahmud, he was a friend and comrade from Zaheer's stay in England. *Jawanmardi* was possibly originally written in English and then translated by Zaheer, for it was several years later that Mahmud learnt to read and write in Urdu. In an interview to Shabana Mahmud in Karachi in February 1987, Ahmed Ali said that Rashid Jahan's two pieces and Mahmud's story were 'written within a few days to raise the number to ten'. See Shabana Mahmud, op. cit., p. 452.

[11] Khalilur Rehman Azmi, *Urdu Mein Taraqqui Pasand Adabi Tehrik* (Aligarh: Educational Book House, 2002), p. 180-181.

[12] Translations of 'Behind the Veil' are from Ralph Russell, *Hidden in the Lute: An Anthology of Two Centuries of Urdu Literature* (New Delhi: Viking, 1995), pp. 34-46.

[13] Lubna Kazim (ed.), *A Woman of Substance,* p. 101

[14] Priyamvada Gopal, op. cit., p. 40.

[15] Sajjad Zaheer, *The Light: A History of the Movement for Progressive Literature in the Indo-Pak Subcontinent,* translated by Amina Azfar (Karachi: Oxford University Press, 2006), p. 6.

[16] Ahmed Ali, 'The Progressive Writers' Movement and Creative Writers in Urdu', in Carlo Coppola (ed.), *Marxist Influences and South Asian Literature,* South Asia Series, Occasional Paper No. 23, Vol. I, (East Lansing: Michigan State University, 1974), p. 35.

[17] Lubna Kazim (ed.), *A Woman of Substance,* op. cit., p. 81.

[18] Sir Wazir Hasan had gone on deputation to England with Mohamed Ali in 1913 to put forth the wrongs done to the Indian Muslims but according to Sajjad Zaheer his father was more a 'cultural Muslim' who subscribed to a liberal democratic ideology than a religious one. In an interview for the NMML's Oral History Project, Sajjad Zaheer said his father was a product of the wave generated by Syed Ahmad Khan; unfortunately, men like Sir Wazir Hasan, he said, found themselves left out of the mainstream of the nationalist movement

even though the latter joined the Congress after his retirement as a judge.

[19] Sudhi Pradhan (ed.), *Marxist Cultural Movement in India (1936-1947)*, Vol. 1 (Calcutta: National Book Agency, 1979), p. 36. Apart from penning the history of the PWM in *Roshnai*, Sajjad Zaheer wrote in dribs and drabs about his own life. A great deal has been written on him in Urdu but much of it is hagiographical and repetitive. Zaheer's daughter Noor Zaheer in her book, *Mere Hisse ki Roshnai* (Shahadra: Medha Books, 2005), brings to light many lesser-known facets of her father's personality and life.

[20] This information was revealed in an interview with Dr. Sarwat Rahman, Mahmuduzzafar's neighbour in Dehradun. Zohra, also belonging to the royal family of Rampur, like Mahmud, later became famous as the dancer-actress Zohra Segal. Her autobiography, *Close-Up: Memoirs of a Life on Stage and Screen* (New Delhi: Women Unlimited, 2010), does not mention an engagement to Mahmud; though she does talk very fondly of Mahmud's father whom she called 'Memphis'.

[21] Sajjad Zaheer, like many others, was drawn towards Rashid Jahan; however, he went away precipitously after the furore over *Angarey* and she got married to Mahmud in 1934. In Zaheer's writings in *Roshnai*, there is nothing but affection and respect for her and Mahmud.

[22] Aijaz Ahmad has noted how the bilingualism and 'polyglot ease in communication' was 'typical' of the intelligentsia of late-colonial India. For a detailed explanation, see *In Theory: Classes, Nations, Literatures* (London: Verso, 1992), p. 76.

[23] Priyamvada Gopal, *Literary Radicalism in India*, op. cit., p. 16.

[24] Ibid.

[25] I am grateful to Ahmed Ali's son, Urooj Ahmed Ali, who gave me a copy of this drawing from his father's collection.

[26] Ahmed Ali, 'The Progressive Writers' Movement and Creative Writers in Urdu', op cit.

[27] Khalid Alvi, *Angarey ka Tareekhi Pasmanzar aur Tarraqui Pasand Tehrik* (Delhi: Educational Publishing House, 1995), p. 104. I have used Alvi's version of *Angarey* for the purpose of this account, though I also have a copy of the 'original' version given to me by Prof Asghar Wajahat. Alvi has compiled an extensive collection of clippings from the Urdu press on the *Angarey* debate; for further details on reactions in the Urdu press, see my forthcoming book.

[28] Quoted by Carlo Coppola in 'The Angare Group: the enfants terribles of Urdu literature' in *Annual of Urdu Studies*, Vol. 1, 1981, p. 61.

[29] For details of the book in its present location in the India Office Collection see Shabana Mahmud, 'The Founding of the Progressive Writers' Association', *Journal of Modern Asian Studies*, Vol. 30, No. 2, May 1966, p. 450.

[30] For a detailed study of banned literature in colonial India, see N. Gerald Barrier, *Banned: Controversial Literature and Political Control in British India, 1907-1947* (Delhi: Manohar, 1978).

[31] Carlo Coppola and S. Zubair, 'Rashid Jahan: Urdu Literature's First "Angry Young Woman"', *Journal of South Asian Literature*, 22:1, 1987, p. 170.

[32] Priyamvada Gopal, op cit., p. 42.

[33] *A Woman of Substance*, op. cit., p. 102.

[34] Khurshid Jahan has the name slightly wrong. It was not Ahrari but Shahid Ahrarvi.

[35] *A Woman of Substance*, op. cit., p. 103.

[36] Interestingly enough, Kaifi Azmi, another founder member of the PWM, describes encountering *Angarey* for the first time in much the same way: behind closed doors in an atmosphere of prurience and secrecy. In his version of the first encounter, the place is not a room in a girls' hostel but a small room in the Shia seminary, the Sultan ul Madaris, where his maulvi sahib lay in bed and two or three other boys sat huddled around him, reading the book. The secrecy around it and the desire to read it despite the directives (both religious and lay) not to, added to the intrigue and drama behind *Angarey*.

[37] *Ismat: Her Life, Her Times*, Sukrita Paul Kumar and Sadique (eds.) (New Delhi: Katha, 2000), p. 77.

[38] *A Life in Words: A Memoir*, Translated by M. Asaduddin (New Delhi: Penguin, 2012), p. 154.

[39] I have a copy of the original typed version which I found amongst Ahmed Ali's collection in Karachi. I am grateful to his son, Urooj Ahmed Ali, for giving it to me. The presence of that document amongst Ahmed Ali's papers lends credence to Urooj's assertion that the 'defence' was drafted by Ahmed Ali and that he was at the forefront of the movement that led to the formation of the PWA, as well as to Ahmed Ali's assertion that the 'defence' was actually the earliest manifestation of the Manifesto that was later drafted (and altered) by Sajjad Zaheer, Mulk Raj Anand and others in London in 1935.

[40] Ahmed Ali, , op. cit., p. 36.

[41] Ibid. p. 35.

[42] Ibid., p. 40.

3

Comrade Rashid Jahan

Tere maathe pe yeh aanchal bohut hii khub hai lekin
Tu iss aanchal se ek parcham bana leti to achcha tha

– Asrarul Haq Majaz

This veil on your forehead is pretty indeed
Better still had you turned it into a banner

Charting new directions

Always a stormy petrel, Rashid Jahan had become first 'Doctor' Rashid Jahan, in itself a novelty for the daughter of a respectable Muslim family, and after the publication of *Angarey* and the furore it caused, she was being called Rashid Jahan 'Angarewali'. Possibly as a fallout of the fuss and fury over *Angarey* or as a process of natural evolution, she now became 'Comrade Rashid Jahan'. Path-breaking and unconventional as she was, and militantly independent-minded too, it would be facile to suggest that she joined the party under the influence of committed friends like Zaheer or Mahmud, both Communists by the time she met them. She joined the Communist Party of India as a full-time member in 1933 and became an active member in the U.P. wing.

On October 14, 1934, while still working for the Provincial

Medical Services (PMS) and posted in Bahraich, she married Mahmuduzzafar.[1] Thereafter, began a period of short stays in different cities, doing whatever work was expected of her by the Party and combining it with her own abiding interests: writing and medicine. When Mahmud took up the only full-time employment he was to engage in his entire life – that of vice-principal of the MAO College in Amritsar where, in addition to his administrative duties, he also taught English – she resigned from the PMS and went to live and work in Amritsar from 1934-36. With Mahmud busy with his teaching and administrative tasks, Rashid Jahan found herself once again at the centre of a charged circle. The notoriety that came in the wake of the *Angarey* episode and made them (in)famous in the Urdu-speaking world possibly added to the aura of this unusually well-known Communist couple.[2] The Punjab of the 1930s, alive to the call of communism, already had one of the most active communist units in the country (after the ones in the Bombay and Calcutta presidencies). Sohan Singh Josh, who was arrested and tried in the Meerut Conspiracy Case, was active in the Punjab; he would join hands with Zaheer and Mahmud to launch a newspaper called *Chingari* in 1936. Rashid Jahan wrote for *Chingari* and edited it when Mahmud and Josh were underground. The seeds of communism, sown by members of the Ghaddar party, had found rich soil in the land of the five rivers. Trained in Moscow by the COMINTERN, many Ghadrites brought back an organised, cadre-based system of functioning; they attached special importance to increasing memberships in workers' bodies and kisan sabhas. By the mid-1930s, Rashid Jahan and Mahmud would have found plenty of like-minded people. Mahmud may, (and this is conjecture on my part), have accepted the assignment to teach in Amritsar with the 'blessings' of the Party.

Even before the Jallianwala Bagh incident of April 1919 had seized the national imagination, Amritsar was known for

its vibrant cultural and political life. One of the largest cities
in the Punjab and the spiritual centre of Sikhism, it was the
home of Saadat Hasan Manto and Abdul Bari Alig, a city
throbbing with literature inspired from the Russian Revolution.[3]
The entry of a couple as charismatic, intellectually alive, and
attuned to the socio-economic concerns of their times as Rashid
Jahan and Mahmud would, no doubt, have created a stir. Their
cosmopolitanism and the whiff of controversy that surrounded
them would, doubtless, have added to their aura as an
unconventional, even bohemian pair.

Faiz Ahmad Faiz, then a young lecturer in English at the
MAO College from 1935-1942, records meeting Rashid Jahan
and Mahmud:

> ... it was in that city (Amritsar) that I became politically conscious.
> Largely due to the friends I had made there – Mahmood-uz-
> Zafar (sic), Dr. Rashid Jahan and, later, Dr. Taseer.[4] I had entered
> a new world. I began to work in the trade union movement,
> became involved in a league for civil liberties and joined the
> Progressive Writers' Movement. Never before had I felt so much
> at peace with myself and my environment.'[5]

Faiz also recollects his introduction to communism and his
first reading of the Communist Manifesto, about which he later
said: 'I read the Manifesto once, and the way ahead was
illuminated.'[6] In fact, one can trace the perceptible movement
away from *shabab* (romanticism) to *inquilab* (revolution) in Faiz's
poetic ouvre as he was introduced to socialism in the company
of Rashid Jahan, Mahmud, Zaheer, Taseer and others. In a
poem such as *Mujhse Pahli si Muhabbat Mere Mahboob Na Mang*[7]
(Don't Ask Me for that Old Love, My Love), for instance,
Faiz acknowledges the heart-tugging beauty of the beloved
but he can also see the other sorrows of the world which claim
his attention. He juxtaposes the beloved's beauty against the
miseries and ugliness of the world, a world which has hunger,
disease and deprivation, a world that can never let him love

her as he once did, for a love that is divorced from social reality is too individualistic, too meaningless:

Aur bhi dukh hain zamane mein muhabbat ke siwa
Rahatein aur bhi hain wasl ki rahat ke siwa

There are other sorrows too apart from love
And other pleasures too apart from that of union[8]

Rashid Jahan's only surviving sibling, Birjees Kidwai, remembers visiting her sister and brother-in-law while she was still a student at the girls' college in Aligarh.[9] Like Sajjad Zaheer, she was taken in by the sounds and sights of Punjab, so different from her sheltered world in Aligarh. She recalls the commune-like atmosphere in her sister's home and the company of several young men, such as Faiz, who joined them on large, rambunctious picnics in the countryside. However, the Amritsar days were not days of hedonism; for the first time, Rashid Jahan came in close contact with workers.[10]Hajra Begum writes:

> While she had adopted Communism at an ideological level by the time she arrived in Amritsar, hitherto her experience of the poor working class was confined to her medical practice and training. She knew the *mazdoor* as a patient, not as friend and comrade who could work alongside her, shoulder-to-shoulder. She had studied the principles of socialism in theory; so far she had not had the opportunity of putting them into practice. Her personal life was separate from her political life. Perhaps that is why when you read her early stories in the collection entitled, *Aurat* you sense something is missing. Her characters are alive, their troubles and sorrows are real, but when you finish reading the story you sense an incompleteness. Either she holds out no solution for the suffering men and women, or the solution appears artificial, even unreal.[11]

In 1935, while Mahmud and Rashid Jahan were still at Amritsar, Sajjad Zaheer returned from England. In London, while ostensibly studying for the Bar-at-Law, Zaheer and a group of young men had drafted a *Manifesto* of the All-India Progressive Writers' Association, a copy of which Zaheer had mailed to several prominent Indian intellectuals and writers, including Premchand. Taken in by the *Manifesto's* rousing call to throw off the shackles of convention and forge a new sort of literature, one that would be attuned to the radical changes taking place in society, Premchand published its Hindi translation in the October 1935 issue of his influential literary journal, *Hans*.[12] Soon after reaching India in November 1935, Zaheer made his way to Allahabad where his father, Sir Wazir Hasan worked in the Allahabad High Court. Within days of his arrival, he re-established contact with his *Angarey* comrade, Ahmad Ali, who in turn introduced him to his colleagues at the University and opened the door to the intellectual life of this vibrant city located at the confluence of two mighty rivers.

An opportunity presented itself for the *Angarey* quartet to meet: an Urdu-Hindi Writers' Conference in Allahabad in December 1935 organised by Tara Chand[13] under the aegis of the Hindustani Academy. Recalling that time, Zaheer writes:

> Dr. Rasheed Jahan (sic) arrived from Amritsar. We were already in correspondence with her about the Progressive Movement, and we wanted her to be present in our discussions with other writers, so that on her return to Punjab she could facilitate our contacts with the writers there.[14]

The *Angarey* group set about meeting – and convincing – a galaxy of writers about the need for a new literary grouping: Premchand, who instantly offered his unstinting support to an all-India body of writers devoted to socially-engaged writing; Maulvi Abdul Haq, the Baba-e-Urdu who had been running a humongous dictionary project from Hyderabad, proved to be just as cooperative in appending his signature to the *Manifesto* Zaheer showed him[15]; Josh Malihabadi, the poet who sang sweetly and robustly of revolution, willingly gave his consent to the idea of an all-India association of progressive writers;

Firaq Gorakhpuri, the legendary poet and teacher at Allahabad University, joined in; Munshi Daya Narayan Nigam, the editor of *Zamana* from Kanpur, similarly gave it his blessings. Soon, letters were pouring in: Sibte Hasan reported from Hyderabad that he had managed to get signatures from many prominent writers including the influential Qazi Abdul Ghaffar, the editor of *Payam;* Hiren Mukherjee wrote to say he was getting a group of writers together in Calcutta; soon branches of the PWA began to sprout in Bombay, Ahmedabad, Calcutta, Hyderabad, Aligarh.

Returning from the Urdu-Hindi Conference in Allahabad, Rashid Jahan suggested that Zaheer come to Amritsar with her and travel through the Punjab to create interest in the PWA. He agreed; in January 1936, Zaheer travelled to Amritsar and stayed with Rashid Jahan and Mahmud, in whose home he first met Faiz. Together, all four travelled to Lahore where Faiz introduced the progressives from U.P. to the intellectuals of Punjab. Zaheer's *Roshnai* carries a wonderful account of these days spent with Rashid Jahan and Mahmud, talking of progressivism, meeting some of the greatest Urdu writers of their time, discovering the delights of Punjab such as drinking *lassi* and the sight of men wearing voluminous *shalwars!* Mahmud's minute attention to detail in planning the trip, Rashida's disorderliness as well as her wilfulness and short temper, Faiz's shyness and Zaheer's own passion in advocating the cause of the PWA shine through. In describing a meeting between Sufi Ghulam Mustafa Tabassum, the gentle, soft-spoken, much-loved poet of Punjab, and the fiery Rashid Jahan, known to fly off the handle at the slightest provocation, Zaheer writes with wry perspicacity:

> There was sharpness in Rasheeda's disposition, she spoke what she believed was the truth, no matter how harsh it sounded to anybody. On the other hand, Sufi sahib was so polite that if there was the slightest likelihood of hurting somebody's feelings he would

not utter a word, keeping his views entirely to himself. Despite the disparity, the two of them got along like a house on fire.[16]

Amidst the bonhomie and good cheer of meeting writers and poets, of the mercurial Rashida teasing the quiet Faiz and Mahmud ensuring they met as many people as possible, the *Manifesto* was greeted with universal, and enthusiastic, approval. The Punjab trip crystallised the idea of holding a conference of All-India Progressive Writers' Association (AIPWA). It was held at the Rifah-e-Aam Hall in Lucknow on April 11, 1936, on the sidelines of the 49th Session of the All-India Congress. The *Angarey* quartet met, possibly to work in unison for the last time, for subsequent years would see differences emerging between Ahmed Ali and Zaheer. While Zaheer and Ali were responsible for organizational details such as who to invite and to set the agenda for the various sessions, Mahmud went around sticking posters announcing the conference in different parts of the city, and Rashid Jahan, who was well known in Lucknow as a lady doctor, sold three-rupee tickets for the reception committee. With a meticulousness that was characteristic of him, Mahmud also typed out resolutions and programmes for each session and took care of other administrative chores. On the big day, Rashid Jahan and Hajra Begum were incharge of selling tickets at the door of the Hall and ushering people to their seats. Years later, Hajra Begum recalled a sexist bias, claiming she and Rashid Jahan would end up doing:

> ... all the work which nobody else liked to do like putting on stamps, writing addresses and so on and we ran around, in fact so much so that when Munshi Premchand came, he asked Sajjad Zaheer: 'What is this, Banne, you are using these two girls?[17]

While Rashida didn't read a paper, Mahmud did; entitled 'Intellectuals in Cultural Reaction', his article made a rousing call to define progressivism in literature. Though not a creative writer of any stature or experience, Mahmud was astute enough to observe that:

> ... literary activities cannot be hemmed in and hedged around by dry and lifeless definitions. Literature, as all the arts, continually grows, expands, turns this way and that – and to be vital, it must have freedom to do so. When it is suppressed, it becomes sterile, lifeless, false.[18]

Mahmud was also unequivocal in his condemnation of 'non-progressive' tendencies:

> All tendencies towards sympathy with reaction, with Imperialism, with feudal superstitions, with fascism, Imperialist aggressions and war – we shall condemn as non-progressive and therefore to be mercilessly attacked and rooted out. All tendencies towards irrationalism, mysticism, introversion, sex-perversion or obsession, over-concern with the fate of the individual as against society as a whole, dreams of the irrevocable golden age or the never to be realised future – we shall regard as dangerous because they are the indirect allies of reaction, in that they detract from positive resistance, activity and struggle. All tendencies towards shocking for the sake of shocking, of blindly hurting people's cherished sentiments, tendencies towards literary terrorism or anarchy we shall regard as especially objectionable, in that they will tend to isolate the progressive intellectuals from the people and thus play into the hands of reaction.[19]

Speaker after speaker at this first seminal meeting of the AIPWA stressed the need for a new sort of writing and a radically new way of looking at the world. Premchand drew the road map for the country's intelligentsia in an Inaugural Address entitled *Sahitya ka Uddeshya* (The Aim of Literature):

> We will have to raise the standard of our literature, so that it can serve the society more usefully... our literature will discuss and assess every aspect of life and we will no longer be satisfied with eating the leftovers of other languages and literatures. We will ourselves increase the capital of our literature.[20]

We will return to the PWA and the extent of its influence on Rashid Jahan in the next chapter.

Rashid Jahan in U.P. politics

For Mahmud and Rashid Jahan, the Amritsar spell (1934-1937) was followed by a brief stint at Allahabad where Mahmud worked as personal secretary to Jawaharlal Nehru. With Mahmud installed in Anand Bhawan, there came into existence an intellectual group of known 'leftists' within the Congress who were regarded by other Congressmen as Nehru's protégés in the All-India Congress Committee's Secretariat located at Allahabad.[21] This group comprised Dr. Z. A. Ahmed[22] and his wife Hajra Begum[23], Dr. K. M. Ashraf[24] and Sajjad Zaheer. Nehru's open patronage of the communists can be traced to the Lucknow session of the Congress in April 1936; but in later years Nehru would speak with dry bitterness of those who embed themselves in the Congress and then undermine its basic creed.[25] Zaheer, too, recalled how proud Nehru was of the Muslim members in the core group of the AICC – Mahmud, Dr. Ashraf, Dr Z. A. Ahmad and Zaheer himself:

Pandit Jawaharlal Nehru was very proud of our group and he introduced us to Gandhiji and to Sardar Patel saying, "People say that Muslims are not coming in the Congress. Here is this brilliant group of young Muslims which went to England and took degrees there and has come back and joined the Congress." Anyhow... this was the time when Panditji started his Mass Contact Movement and from the Communist side, we too were trying to develop the Congress as a sort of united national front of all the anti-imperialist elements in this country. We wanted that more and more workers and peasants should join the Congress and that it should go more to the left rather than be dominated by the middle or the more rightist elements. So we particularly campaigned, for example, for mass membership of the Congress.[26]

However, according to Zaheer, the right-wing within the Congress resented the presence of the left and kept a watchful eye on the young comrades, reporting their activities to Gandhi and Patel. Hajra Begum, in her interview at the NMML, corroborated this and added that Acharya Kripalani was the link between the goings-on at the AICC and Gandhi. The admission of non-writers in a literary grouping such as PWA is also corroborated by Hajra Begum who was the 'contact' on behalf of the Party for a year-and-a-half, and approached well-known sympathisers in Allahabad University such as Firaq, Satish Chandra Deb and Ejaz Hussain. We also get a glimpse of the communist 'infiltration' into the Congress and the Congress Socialist Party in the same interview; not a writer herself, Hajra Begum nevertheless served as Secretary of the Allahabad PWA, as part of the Party's directive to work with the city's intellectuals: So, in the guise of the PWA, I would go to them, and in that way approach them also for whatever help the Party needed and that was one of my tasks, which was not openly known – openly I was doing work for the PWA.[27]

Meanwhile, the All-India Students' Federation, set up in 1936, had grown – with branches in almost all the important educational centres in the U.P. and the three Presidencies. The task of these 'intellectual' communists within the Congress was to keep an eye on its functioning, and familiarise students with extremist doctrines through the medium of study circles and training classes which they conducted according to the recognised principles of communist practice. The imperial government, for its part, was not unaware of this Trojan Horse in the Congress' camp. A Director, Intelligence Bureau (DIB) report[28] reveals a reference to Mahmuduzzafar Khan who worked as Jawaharlal Nehru's personal secretary[29] and visited London in the autumn of 1936 where he discussed the possibility of collaborating with the firm of Victor Gollancz and furthering the scope of activities of the Left Book Club.[30] The purpose of such a venture was to evade the restrictions under the Sea Customs Act and to publish Indian editions of left books from manuscripts which would be sent over from England. Gollancz himself had a 'lively interest in the dissemination of communist literature in India' and was determined to popularise the Left Book Club in India. A Left Book Club Discussion Group already existed in London for Indian students, under the charge of Promode Ranjan Sen Gupta (one of the original signatories to the *Manifesto*).

Another reference to Mahmud is found in a DIB Report dated November 27, 1937. Described as an 'intellectual' communist, he is said to have expressed his opinion (upon returning from Europe) that the CPI was growing in confidence, and was in a strong position as regards the Congress since many of its adherents, such as Dr. Ashraf, Z. A. Ahmed and Zaheer, were working in the Congress 'inner circle'. According to the report, this 'clique of intellectuals', most of whom were personal friends of the Meerut Conspiracy Case[31] accused and were at one time members of the Secret Indian Students' Communist Group in London, exert influence on the affairs of the Congress Central Committee, which is 'hard to distinguish from active membership'. B. F. Bradley, a British communist and the bête noir of the intelligence agencies, is described as the group's 'chief technical advisor' and 'confidant abroad' who had endorsed the 'open tactics' adopted by Indian communists and advised 'full speed ahead' along the triple line comprising workers, peasants and student groups.

The 'honeymoon' with the Congress was not destined to last; Nehru discovered the covert intentions of the bright young sparks who were increasingly beginning to cause no end of embarrassment to him and the Congress with their open support of kisan and workers' rallies, and recommended their expulsion from the Congress.[32] Mahmud and Rashid Jahan returned to Lucknow. Mahmud was appointed General Secretary of the CPI in UP and Rashid Jahan began private practice which, given her name and fame not to mention her impeccable training at the Lady Hardinge Medical College, as well as the nearly decade-long experience with the PMS, was lucrative. However, she gave all her earnings as a successful and much-sought-after gynaecologist to the Party; the Party, in turn, gave the husband and wife duo Rs. 50 each for their living expenses. Mahmud had very little to do with Urdu literature after *Angarey*. He wrote one play, *Amir ka Mahal,* which was possibly his last piece of writing in Urdu.[33] His major published work is the travelogue *Quest for Life*[34] (1954), in which he describes his travels in Russia, where he had gone with Rashid Jahan, who was at the time terminally ill with cancer. As he got increasingly drawn into the UP wing of the CPI, he spent many years either in or out of jail (August 1940 till June 1942, spent in the infamous Deoli prison in the company of some of the most prominent communists and revolutionaries who were jailed by the colonial government) or 'underground', after the Indian government came down on communist workers for instigating civic unrest (1948-1951).[35] On all such occasions, Rashid Jahan worked harder than before, throwing herself with ever-increasing zeal into a cluster of inter-twining activities. She was jailed for participating in the U.P. Railway Workers' strike, along with Hajra Begum, and was lodged in the Central Jail in Lucknow from March–May 1949. Hajra Begum read the jail manual and wrote to the authorities demanding to know on what grounds they had been arrested. The letter sanctioning their arrest was signed by Sarojini Naidu in her capacity as Governor of UP, but was dated the day she passed away. The two were set free three months later.

Plagued by frequent ill health, Rashid Jahan moved between Lucknow and Dehradun[36] where her in-laws lived. It was in Dehradun that her evolution into a politically-aware committed Party worker – begun in Amritsar – was completed. Treating the sick and writing short, stringent stories continued side by side, seamlessly bringing together her many interests. When she was not conducting adult education classes sitting on the floor of sweepers' colonies or gathering women from Arya Samaj mandirs to join hands on women's health and education issues, or participating in trade union rallies and protest marches, she was either busy running her practice to raise funds for underground colleagues or bullying friends and admirers to contribute to her many 'causes', such as the release of imprisoned co-workers or securing safe-houses for underground comrades.[37] Or, she would be writing, translating and editing political pieces for *Chingari*. From a short story writer, she had become a playwright, journalist and editor.

On September 10, 1934, the first issue of *Chingari* (Spark) had appeared from Saharanpur. This was the cyclostyled English organ of the UP Committee of the CPI, edited by Sohan Singh Josh. Its subsequent Urdu version, edited by Sajjad Zaheer and later by Mahmud, was meant to supplement the organ of the Central Committee of the CPI and to deal with problems specific to the UP. Culled from material that had appeared in the short-lived *Communist* from Bombay and *Inprecor*, *Chingari* made the first serious contribution to the introduction of pure communism into agrarian India, outside the Punjab. *Chingari* also revealed the nominal existence of the UP Committee of the CPI which, under the charge of Sajjad Zaheer, would increasingly play a bigger role with the establishment of the PWA. From 1938, the task of editing *Chingari* increasingly fell upon Mahmud, and in his absence on Rashid Jahan.[38] Also, by the late Forties, the government had begun to round up the comrades and imprison them at the Deoli Prison Camp near Tonk in Rajasthan. Mahmud, too, was imprisoned here along with the virtual who's who of the CPI.[39]

Naim Khan, who was summoned from Saharanpur to Dehradun to assist Rashid Jahan in Party work, recalls his first meeting with her and the attention and love she showered upon him virtually from that first meeting. A young man of nineteen or twenty, he confessed to coming completely under her thrall and how she changed the direction of his life with her forthrightness, attention to detail and the personal interest she took in the people around her: I could never have imagined that an educated lady from a big family would show such affection for an unknown, new Party worker like myself. From that day I began to call Dr. Rashid Jahan Rashida Apa. And this relationship remained intact till her dying day.[40]

From 1950 till her death Rashid Jahan refrained from taking active part in overtly political events due to her steadily failing health. She was diagnosed with cancer in 1950 itself, and was operated upon at the Tata Memorial Hospital in Bombay, but the disease never quite went away. In the last two years of her life, as her political activities declined, she moved to the relative peace and quiet of Dehradun. She returned for another operation to Bombay in March 1952 but by then it was too late; the cancer had spread. The Bombay doctors urged Mahmud to take her to Moscow, as the Soviet Union had made great strides in the medical field and it was possible that some miracle could occur. Rashid Jahan was well aware of the hopelessness of her situation but, despite her extreme weakness, agreed to undertake the long journey simply so that Mahmud could see his beloved Russia.[41]

Rashid Jahan and Mahmud

Interviews with the few persons still alive who knew Rashid Jahan, reveal an intense, driven and passionate woman. Dr. Sarvat Rahman[42] narrates her first impression of Rashid Jahan as a new bride at the reception given by her father-in-law; she wore a white sari, and she danced. There is nothing particularly bizarre about either, in fact it is not even very shocking now but in 1934 it was most unusual. The point Dr. Rahman was making was this: Rashid Jahan needn't have worn white (she could just as well have worn pale pink or pale blue if she didn't want to wear bridal red), and she needn't have danced. However, she *chose* to do both. Perhaps she liked, or wanted to, shock people, Dr Rahman concludes.

Still others have spoken of her aura, how she could fill a room with the sheer force of her personality. Naren Gupta recalls that she was beautiful in a completely natural way. As in her stories, there was an element of utter comfort while talking about the female body in her conversations too.[43] In the next chapter, when we examine her plays and stories, we shall see the same ease in speaking out on issues that were considered beyond the pale – not just of literature but of civilized conversation in sharif household; issues such as reproductive health, birth control, the prevalence of sexually-transmitted diseases among genteel folk, etc. Priyamvada Gopal – the only scholar in the West to have studied Rashid Jahan in some detail – notes how with her very first work in *Angarey*, she claimed for herself the authority 'to speak not only about women's bodies and sex, but about modernity, science, progress, ethics and epistemology'.[44]

We have seen, earlier, how Faiz declared that he was drawn into the activities of the PWA primarily because of Rashid Jahan; others too have testified to the great personal charisma that drew people to her like moths to a flame. Her house (be it in Amritsar, Lucknow or Dehradun) became a meeting place for a motley group of people – Party workers, poets, writers, patients, young girls seeking counsel, young men in search of political advice. This has been borne out by several people in the course of interviews: Naren and Bano Gupta, Aulad Ahmad Siddiqui and Munibur Rahman. Naren Gupta recalled the time they had spent in Lucknow as young doctors, both members of the CPI, both devoted to the Party and the people. They had hired a small place in Hazrat Gunj where they ran a free clinic for the poor. Dr. Bano Gupta, far junior to Rashid Jahan and also a doctor, had the opportunity to interact with Rashid

Jahan on numerous occasions because of Naren. She remembers Rashid Jahan as a warm, vivacious person who liked to have young people around her. Bano said she would stay over at Rashid Jahan's house, even wear her clothes on several occasions.

Rashid Jahan's generosity (mentioned by Hamida Saiduzzafar and Khurshid Mirza in their books) is borne out by Shaukat Azmi in *Kaifi & I* where she remembers an incident when Kaifi praised a kurta that Rashid Jahan was wearing; the kurta was her husband Mahmud's but it looked very fetching on her. Promptly, the next day, Rashid Jahan had it sent over. Kaifi wore it with pride and affection. Jitendra Raghuvanshi (National General Secretary of IPTA), recalls a similar incident. His father, Rajendra, has written about Rashid Jahan asking him in her typically forthright way, why his artistes wore such old and worn-out clothes in his plays for the Lucknow IPTA. Raghuvanshi replied that those were the only costumes he had. Rashid Jahan took him home, opened her cupboard and took out several handsome and obviously expensive sets of clothes, hers and Mahmud's, and gave them to him. These costumes, made of brocade and real zari, heavily embellished with gota, sequins, mirrors, as well as Mahmud's bridal shervani, were worn by several Lucknow theatre performers and used in IPTA plays for years to come.[45]

Her generosity and lack of sentimental attachment to material things can also be seen in the light of Marxian dialectics as yet another example of Rashid Jahan having 'declassed' herself. Incidentally, in a rare example of practicing what one preaches, Mahmud distributed his ancestral land and property near Rampur among the peasants who tilled the land; and the home he shared with Rashid Jahan, especially in Lucknow, has often been described as a commune. Naim Khan was 'in-charge' of it and at any given time, several people from Rashida's extended circle of friends, admirers and Party colleagues could be found living there. She had employed a low-caste boy to work in the kitchen and to those who objected, she retorted that he was cleaner than many high-caste people! Her sister, Birjees Kidwai, too, remembers going to Lucknow with her infant daughter and the commune-like atmosphere in Rashid Jahan's house.[46] People from all walks of life and of all political dispensations flocked around her. The house on 7 Bisheshwar Nath Road was a great meeting place for writers, intellectuals, poets and fellow comrades. Rashid Jahan's vivacity and quick-wittedness were the perfect foil for her husband's sobriety and courtesy. Together, they presented a picture of dedication to a cause that they considered larger than themselves.

Brimming with affection for Mahmud and Rashid Jahan, Sajjad Zaheer's *Roshnai* paints a vivid portrait of the couple: diametrically opposite in personality, temperament and background yet united in a common love for each other. She was untidy and unmethodical, whereas her husband was orderly and organized; she was like quicksilver, whereas he was patient and sober; she revelled in being chaotic, whereas he was precise and meticulous. Yet, the two were firm friends who appreciated the good and selfless qualities of the other. Zaheer wrote:

> The union of Rashid Jahan and Mahmud was really a meeting of opposites. Rashida hated orderliness. It used to astonish her friends and acquaintances that she was such a good doctor, and they could not understand why she was so popular with her patients. Losing and misplacing her belongings was a daily occurrence with her, while Mahmud never forgot anything. He remembered not only his own but also his friends' responsibilities and plans for work... he would always smoothen out the confusion spread by Rashid Jahan. Yet the golden chain of love that tied them together was a sight worth seeing. Both seemed to have substituted the care of humanity for their own selves. A serene domestic life was not in their stars. For Mahmud, the future held imprisonment, hard labour and anxiety related to his work for the homeland. For Rashida it held long periods of solitude, financial problems and physical

stress. But... whenever one went to their house one felt that it was suffused with happiness – the kind of happiness that springs like a clear pool of water from the meeting and harmony of two hearts and minds. It was a happiness that enlivened sad spirits, and brought lushness and music into their life.[47]

Dr. Sarvat Rahman captures the aura of a young Mahmud who had come back home in 1931 after spending fourteen long years studying in England:

The accomplished young man, product of an aristocratic and almost purely occidental education, came back with revolutionary ideas of social change. How much his idealism, his artistic gifts, his youthful good looks and distinguished Oxford accent must have appealed to his numerous girl cousins and other ladies of his generation![48]

Mahmud, who had studied economics and history at Balliol College, was also a keen painter. In fact, his travelogue *A Quest for Life* carried some fine drawings, causing his sister, Dr. Hamida Saiduzzafar, to lament in her *Autobiography* how Mahmud could have been a fine painter had he chosen art as his calling: 'He had a great talent for sketching ... Sad to say, Mahmud neglected this gift of his, and later in life devoted his time and energy to politics rather than drawing, painting and sculpture where his real talent lay.'[49] She remembers her much older brother being full of nationalist ideas on his return to India in 1931. Despite a thoroughly English education, Mahmud 'wore a Gandhi cap, wanted to wear khadi clothes, and tried hard to speak Urdu (or Hindi) rather than English'. He also gave his sister, then barely ten years old, Gorky's *Twenty-Six Men and a Girl* much to the chagrin of her snooty governess (who was 'of French descent' and disapproved of Mahmud's 'progressive' ways). Sarvat Rahman remembers Mahmud coming to their home to learn to read and write Urdu from her mother. Zaheer too noted Mahmud's great desire to learn Urdu, how whenever the rest of them 'quoted Persian or Urdu poetry, or discussed a subtle literary point of our own language, an expression of sadness would suffuse his face'; Zaheer continues:

> Mahmud was always troubled by the fact that he was not proficient in his mother tongue. He used to write poetry in English and sometimes even wrote short stories and literary essays, but he was well aware that no matter how hard we try, we can never produce a major creative work in a language that is not our own.

Mahmud was not just literary; his English upbringing and his study of philosophy, logic, and economics had endowed him with the ability to work untiringly and systematically.[50]

Elsewhere, in Hamida's *Autobiography*, one of her contemporaries, Dr. Ranjana Sidhanta Ash, remembers Mahmud as:

> ... the most polished and charming communist who would come round on his cycle to the [Lucknow] university intelligentsia selling "progressive literature". *I hope that genre of writing still finds its way to schoo-girls from the middle classes growing up in a world that rigidly silences Marxism.*[51] {Italics mine}

Dr. Ash remembers Mahmud as being 'not merely the bearer of Marx and Lenin, Gorky and the Gollancz Left Book Club orange volume' but also as the husband of Dr. Rashid Jahan and how the two 'charming and charismatic people', a 'wondrous couple', were her 'idols'.[52]

While Mahmud's career as an activist and Party worker is of interest to us not only because of Rashid Jahan but also because the Party, whose cause he served so selflessly, has given scant attention to forgotten foot soldiers like him, Rashid Jahan's mercurial, charismatic persona, and her brief but volatile literary career, deserve to be studied with some seriousness for the degree and extent to which she paved the way for future generations of women writers in Urdu. After *Angarey*, she published *Aurat aur Deegar Afsane wa Drame* (Woman and Other Stories and Plays); a collection of short stories came out after her untimely death at the age of forty-seven in 1952 and was called *Shola-e-Jawwala* (Sparks of a Volcano)[53]. Writing about her sister, Khurshid Jahan says forthrightly enough:

> Dr Rashid Jahan was better known as a progressive writer than as a medical practitioner. The writer's group that she was a part of, comprising Mahmuduz Zafar, Sajjad Zaheer, and Prof. Ahmad Ali, wrote against social conventions and the false interpretation of religion that had become the monopoly of a particular class of Muslim scholars. These precocious young intellectuals brought about a cultural as well as an artistic revolution in Muslim society because of their ability to see things clearly. They wrote stories without mincing their words and meanings, choosing sensitive topics that were not discussed. ... Their unique and bold style of writing and vocabulary gave a new impetus and vitality to Urdu literature. Rashid Jahan's writing was appreciated in literary circles for being energetic and lively, and for the introduction of colloquial speech into the narrative that made it immediately accessible to the reader, breaking with the conservative and formal mode of earlier writing. Later, Ismat [Chughtai] perfected this style in her literary works.[54]

Writing her obituary, her friend and admirer, Ale Ahamd Suroor, described her as 'brave', 'intelligent', 'fearless', 'a dedicated doctor', 'a peerless political worker', 'a respected writer', as someone who 'did not know how to be impressed by anyone. If she loved someone, she loved them wholeheartedly; if she disliked them, she did the same.'[55] When the end came and it was time to walk into the endless night, she displayed the same courage she had all her life. When Mahmud asked her: 'Shall we go?' she answered: 'I will go wherever you take me.' He later found out that she had agreed to go only for his sake, knowing how much he wanted to visit the USSR, and how difficult it was for an Indian communist to get a visa:

So I came to know that at this most critical moment of her life, when the slightest movement or noise distressed her, when she might collapse at any moment during a hazaradous journey, when even at the end of it there was no surety of cure, when parting from her loved ones and from India was perhaps a final farewell, in spite of knowing all this, Rashida was willing to take a sporting chance so that I might go to the Soviet Union. It was so typical of her. It was the way she had lived her life, with such astonishing courage and selflessness, making it always a bridge to the happiness of others. And it was my unique privilege to see her live it thus to the end. It is not possible to express the feelings one has at such moments: admiration, gratitude, pride, love, and indescribable anguish.

As for myself, I held to this decision so that, instead of sitting helplessly to watch her die, we might continue the struggle for her life. And to do that, I knew that we had to go to the Soviet Union, where alone this help was possible.[56]

Rashid Jahan left Bombay on July 2, 1952 and died three weeks later on July 29th. She undertook a circuitous journey, via Rome, Zurich and Prague. Though too ill to see the sights of Moscow, Mahmud narrates how one day, shortly after their arrival, she smiled contentedly and lay back on her pillow, sighing: 'I have heard the Kremlin chimes.' She had heard the Soviet play, *Kremlin Chimes*, and enjoyed it.

In Moscow, the Party had laid out the best possible medical facilities for her at the Kremlin Hospital. Though hampered by language she told the senior doctors treating her in her characteristically spontaneous manner: 'I would like you to treat me not only as a patient and friend, but also as a colleague.' Through the interpreter, Comrade Tanya, she said: 'Tell them not to be afraid. They can treat me as an experiment and do anything that they like if that will help to gain knowledge of this disease. And if I die, let them do a post-mortem if they have to.' On July 16, a collegium of eminent doctors met to discuss Rashid Jahan's case; unfortunately even the most

respected of Soviet doctors could hold out no hope.[57]
Thereafter, she gradually began to sink till even opening her
eyes or talking became difficult. Mahmud had to accept 'the
fact that Rashida was now beyond human help'. Just before
the end came, weak and far too ill to speak, Rashid Jahan's last
words, spoken with great feeling, were: 'I am sorry only for
one thing – that I did not live to see even one little corner of
India free.'[58]

Mahmud's travelogue had begun thus: 'Every journey has a
purpose. When I undertook this hazardous flight from Bombay
to Moscow with my wife Rashid Jahan, my purpose was to
find new life, for her, for me.' Within three weeks of his arrival,
his wife was gone: 'She passed away in the early hours of a
lovely summer morning in far away Moscow. And thus it was
that this book came to be written.' Mahmud stayed on for five
months in the Soviet Union, as he was 'anxious to see and
study as much as (he) could, having come so far'.

Rashid Jahan lies buried in a Moscow cemetery; the epitaph
on her grave reads: 'Communist Doctor and Writer.'

End Notes

[1] Exact date found in the Brochure produced by the Female Education Society, Aligarh.

[2] The CPI, set up in 1925 was banned in 1934; its members, therefore, led a shadowy existence. The visibility enjoyed by Mahmud and Rashid Jahan, both known Communists, was unusual.

[3] Prof Ali Ahmad Fatimi has written extensively on the influence of the October Revolution on Manto as well as the existence of communistic literature made available through the efforts of men like Abdul Bari. Manto himself has written an eloquent portrait of the man he held in great esteem as his mentor, entitled 'Bari Saheb' in a collection called *Ganje Farishtey* ('The Bald Angels'). Manto writes of his fascination for Russia, of looking at the world map with his friend Hassan Abbas, and planning to use the overland route to travel to Russia: 'We imagined the streets and lanes of Amritsar as Moscow, and we wanted to see the terrible end of tyranny.'

Also, it should be remembered that Amritsar's twin city, Lahore, was already a hotbed of communist activity. The *Inquilab* had been launched in 1922 under the editorship of Ghulam Husain who had earlier translated some of M.N. Roy's writings into Urdu. Known as 'the people's paper' the *Inquilab's* office soon became a hub of socialist activity in Lahore. Among those associated with it were Shams al din Hasan and M.A. Khan who, along with Ghulam Husain, were also office bearers in the North Western Railway Workers' Union which exercised tremendous clout all across the Punjab.

[4] M.D. Taseer and Faiz were married to two sisters: Christabel and Alys George. Taseer knew Zaheer and others in England and was among the core group that helped draft the *Manifesto* of the Progressive Writers' Association in London. Taseer also taught English at the M.A.O. College and was its Principal from 1938-41.

[5] Quoted in *The Unicorn and the Dancing Girl*, edited by Khalid Hasan (New Delhi: Allied Publishers, 1988), p. xxvii.

[6] Ibid., p. xv.

[7] Aulad Ahmad Siddiqui, younger brother of Ale Ahmad Suroor, narrated a conversation with the historian, Mohibbul Hasan in which the latter told him that *Mujhse Pahli si...* was written for Rashid Jahan. Apparently, Faiz counted himself as one of her many admirers and visited her Dehradun home. Mohibbul Hasan taught History at the MAO College and Alys Faiz refers to teaching him French and learning Urdu from him in an interview in . Sheema Majeed (ed.), *Coming Back Home: Selected Articles, Editorials and Interviews of Faiz Ahmad Faiz* (Karachi: Oxford University Press, 2008), p. 143.

[8] From *Naqsh-e-Faryadi* ('Imploring Imprints'); the collection was published in 1941 while Faiz was still in Amritsar, but written over a period of ten years).Translation mine.

[9] Hameed Naseem, a broadcaster in later years, who knew Rashida and Mahmud in Amritsar, recalls travelling to Lahore by car with the couple and Birjees who was then visiting. They went to Lahore to attend a meeting of the All India Students' Federation. Reference in Athar Siddiqui, *Khatun*, op. cit. p. 39.

[10] N.K. Sharma (also known as 'Panditji), theatre director and activist, told me how Rashid Jahan took his father, Ratanlal Sharma (elder brother of H.L. Parwana), then a trade union leader active in the textile area of Chhatta, deep into the jungle near Amritsar late at night to initiate him as a Party worker. Later, Rashid Jahan became very close to the Sharma family and N.K. Sharma's mother would refer to her with much affection.

[11] Hajra Begum, '*Kuchch Rashid Jahan ke Bare Mein*', *Khatun*, op. cit., p. 13.

[12] The English version of the *Manifesto* was published in the February 1936 issue of the *Left Review* in London. A modified version of the original *Manifesto* drafted in London was eventually adopted by the AIPWA in its Calcutta session in 1938. For a detailed discussion on the differences between the two versions of the *Manifesto*, see Ralph Russell, 'Leadership in the All-India Progressive Writers' Movement', in B. N. Pandey (ed.), *Leadership in South Asia* (New Delhi: Vikas Publishing House, 1977), pp. 104-127; and between the English and Hindi version in Carlo Coppola, 'The All-India Progressive Writers' Association: The European Phase' in *Marxist Influences and South Asian Literature*, pp. 6-10.

[13] Educationist and proponent of Hindustani as a link language.

[14] Sajjad Zaheer, *The Light*, op. cit., p. 7.

[15] Rashid Jahan knew several of these eminent people, as they came to her parents' home in Aligarh; for instance, she was instrumental in setting up a meeting between Maulana Abdul Haq and Zaheer. I suspect the Progressives banked upon her unusual appeal to charm unsuspecting writers and poets, especially the old-world ones.

[16] Sajjad Zaheer, *The Light*, op. cit., p. 23.

[17] Interview, Oral History Project, Nehru Memorial Museum & Library, New Delhi.

[18] Golden Jubilee Brochure produced by the PWA, found among the papers of Ghulam Rabbani Taban at NMML.

[19] Ibid. Mahmud's words contain a chilling portent of the attitude adopted by the hardliners among the progressives, especially when the controversy over the place of 'obscenity' in literature erupted over Manto and Ismat Chughtai.

We also get a foretaste of the divide between *jadeediyat* (modernism) and *tarraqui-pasandi* (progressivism) that would split Urdu writers into two warring camps, and how the word 'individualism'would become anathema to the proponents of *tarraqui-pasandi*. We hear echoes of the *Manifesto* in his condemnation of those who look back on past glories and the sort of dogmatic 'If-you-are-not-with-us-you-are-against-us' rhetoric that would prove to be the undoing of the progressives in later decades.

[20] The full text of Premchand's address, translated by Francesca Orsini, can be found in *The Oxford India Premchand* (New Delhi: Oxford University Press, 2004).

[21] During these days in the AICC, Zaheer organized a series of lectures at Swaraj Bhawan and invited Nehru, Acharya Narendra Deva, Jayaprakash Narayan, P. C Joshi and K. M. Ashraf to speak on different aspects of the contemporary situation in the country.

[22] Dr. Z. A. Ahmed was later member of the Central Secretariat of the CPI.

[23] A cousin of Mahmud, like him also a member of the extended royal family of Rampur, Hajra Begum (1910-2002) was a divorcee with a small son when she travelled to London to do a Montessori Teachers' Training course. She married Dr Z. A. Ahmed on May 20, 1936 and played an active role in the CPI as a full-time member. Her nikah was performed by Dr. Ashraf, and Zaheer was a witness. The very next day she and her husband went to meet Nehru to offer their services. Dr. Ahmed was put in charge of the economic department of the AICC and Hajra, instead of working with Vijay Lakshmi Pandit (Nan) as Nehru suggested, chose to set up the Railway Coolies' Union at Allahabad. In the NMML interview, she revealed how those with communist leanings had to work either with the Congress or the Congress Socialist Party and wait to be 'contacted' by the CPI during the period when the Party was banned. The transcript of her interview at the NMML, as part of the Oral History Project, revealed a fund of information on the workings of the CPI. Hajra Begum was the elder sister of stage and cinema actor, Zohra Segal. Hajra Begum also revealed how she was attracted towards communism thanks to Mahmud and other male relatives who gave her Bernard Shaw's *The Intelligent Woman's Guide to Socialism and Capitalism*.

[24] Born to a Muslim Rajput family, K. M. Ashraf (1903-1962) was the product of an eclectic education – from a madarsa in Moradabad to the MAO College to Jamia Millia Islamia and then back again Aligarh where his academic brilliance impressed the Maharaja of Alwar into funding his education abroad. In England, not only did he become an avowed communist but mentored many young Indian students including Zaheer and Mahmud. On his return to India in 1932, he plunged into the freedom movement, joined the Congress

Socialist Party and took charge of the minorities' cell in the AICC and the Muslim Mass Contact Programme. While his academic work was on the social and cultural conditions in Medieval India, Ashraf was a scholar with a wide range of interests, and his influence over the communists of his generation was profound.

[25] See Nehru, *Selected Works*, Vol. 14 (New Delhi: Orient Longman, 1981), pp.16-17 and pp. 523-547. Nehru dwells at great length on the 'self-contradictory role' of the CPI and the relations between Congressmen and Communists in an interview with Dr. Z. A. Ahmed, in a letter to Gerald Peel (an Australian Communist Party leader) and in a report dated January 1946 when he recommends that Zaheer, Ashraf, Sohan Singh Josh, etc. be expelled from the primary membership of the Congress. Before the sheen had worn off, both Zaheer and Mahmud had 'infiltrated' the Congress bastion at Allahabad. As part of the communist training imparted to them, they were required to devote themselves to legitimate activities such as making contact with 'unmarked' members of the intelligentsia (being writers helped), holding private study circles and openly aligning themselves with trade union and workers' activities.

[26] Zaheer, NMML, Oral History Project.

[27] Hajra Begum, NMML, Oral History Project.

[28] IOR/L/PJ/12/430.

[29] In the NMML interview, Zaheer stated that Mahmud lived in Anand Bhawan for almost two years while he worked for Nehru and he was joined by his wife, Rashid Jahan. Mahmud wrote a note on the election tour which Nehru undertook in 1937. We find a reference to it with Nehru pointing out instances where he disagrees with Mahmud. See *Selected Works of Jawaharlal Nehru*, Vol. 8 (New Delhi: Orient Longman, 1976), pp. 41-42.

[30] Hamida Saiduzzafar, writing in *Shola-e-Jawwala*, mentions that Mahmud travelled with his wife to England in 1936 to seek medical treatment for lumps in her throat.

[31] Several Indian trade unionists and three British communists were arrested in March 1929 and tried under Section 121A of the Indian Penal Code, on charges of a communist conspiracy to overthrow the British rule. The charges levelled against the accused caused widespread outrage and helped in strengthening organised communism in India.

[32] I found a reference to a manuscript written by Mahmud, possibly in the nature of a memoir, of his days with Nehru. However, this has not been corroborated by anyone; nor could I find any trace of the manuscript. It was listed among the books seized from him under the Sea Customs' Act when he landed at Bombay in 1936.

[33] Reference found in Khalilur Rehman Azmi, op. cit., p. 181. And in Sudhi

Pradhan (ed.), where the play is referred to by its English title. I have, unfortunately, not been able to find a copy.

[34] Published by People's Publishing House in 1954, this is an unabashed, almost naive, account of the author's complete adoration of all things Soviet. For a well-travelled man, Mahmud's unquestioning and child-like admiration for the Soviet land and its people appears a trifle over-the-top. He gushes over 'Moscow, the city of our dreams!' and its wide roads, modern architecture and energetic people. In the course of his five-month stay, he travelled to Georgia, the Black Sea, Stalingrad and Uzbekistan, visited institutions, theatres, art galleries, etc. in Moscow, attended the XIX Congress of the Communist Party of the Soviet Union (Bolsheviks) where he met several leading figures from the worldwide Communist movement.

[35] Being a full time party member, Mahmud had to go underground when the CPI fell foul of the new Indian government. Like scores of other comrades, he too went underground to evade arrest and continue Party work. My mother, Mehjabeen, recalls Mahmud and other communist friends of her father, A.A. Suroor, coming to stay with them, incognito. At such times, the family had to observe the utmost secrecy and not allow servants or neighbours to guess the identity of the mysterious guest who stayed locked up in a room for days, and whose food was delivered on a tray by the host himself! My mother's brother, S.A. Siddiqui, recalls the many fleeting appearances Mahmud made at their home during his 'underground' years. Usually appearing late in the night, he would often come in disguise with a fake moustache, overcoat, felt hat and muffler, shrouded in mystery, to have hurried meetings with his wife and other Party members in the home of A.A. Suroor who, though not a Party member, was nevertheless a known sympathiser.

[36] Naim Khan, who knew and worked with both Rashid Jahan and Mahmud and did the *kitabat* (Urdu calligraphy) for *Chingari*, recalls how Dehradun had emerged as a hub of communist activities and how, after the CPI was banned in 1936, the *khoofiya* (secret) police were to be found loitering in every street and alley of the city. Its proximity to Saharanpur, another important centre of peasant and farmworkers' activities, made Dehradun a hotbed of covert communist activities. Mahmud and Rashid Jahan, both known communists, operated from the family home and actively participated in these revolutionary activities. See Naim Khan's *Yaadein* in *Shola-e-Jawwala*. My uncle, S.A. Siddiqui, has drawn for me a vivid portrait of Naim Khan: a lanky figure dressed in kurta-pajama and waistcoat who also manned the People's Publishing House outlet near Rashid Jahan's clinic close to the Qaiser Bagh crossing in Lucknow. He remembers Rashid Jahan treating him and the other members of the family; and while she was gentle with children, most parents were in awe of

her and fearful of a tongue-lashing in case they slipped up with the medication.

[37] Her activities during this period are described by Hajra Begum, *Khatun*, op. cit., p. 13.

[38] I am grateful to Comrade Shamim Faizi who alerted me to the existence of a few copies of *Chingari* in the archives of Ajoy Bhawan. I was able to find some, especially those that carried plays and short stories by Rashid Jahan.

[39] Dr. Z. A Ahmad mentions some of his comrades and the time they spent at Deoli in *Mere Jivan ki Kuchch Yaadein* (Allahabad: Lokbharati, 2008).

[40] Naim Khan, *Shola-e-Jawwala*, op. cit. Naim also writes how he was sent away to a safe house by Rashid Jahan when a warrant for his arrest was taken out. He ran various errands for the Party during the underground years, receiving instructions via Rashid Jahan; one of his tasks was to get news about the inmates at Deoli.

[41] Dr. Hamida Saiduzzafar, *Shola-e-Jawwala*, op. cit., p.'d'. Mahmud dedicated *A Quest for Life* with the following words: 'To Rashid Jahan, who made this book possible.'

[42] I went to Dehradun to interview Dr. Sarvat Rahman on March 24-25, 2010. She was then a spry 87-year old living an intellectually and socially-charged life; I am fortunate that she was able to share with me a fund of memories about Rashid Jahan and Mahmud who were older than her, but as her family home, 'Shameem', was close to Mahmud's house (called 'Naseem', since been bought by the Welham Girls' School), she had occasion to meet them several times. Dr Rahman trained at the Lady Hardinge Medical College, and lived and worked in France for the better part of her professional life. After retirement, she returned to her home in Dehradun and became an energetic translator of Faiz, Majaz, among others.

[43] Naren Gupta recalls how Rashid Jahan told him about her uterine cancer in a blunt no-nonsense fashion. When she went to Bombay for surgery, she took him along.

[44] Priyamvada Gopal, *Literary Radicalism in India*, op. cit., p. 32

[45] Rajendra Raghuvanshi (1920-2003), from Agra, was a founder-member of IPTA, and vice-president of IPTA National Committee (1958-2003). This reference is from *Swagat Kathan (Aatm Katha Ansh), Natrang*, 71, September 2003. Mahmud's shervani was worn by Krishan Chand Khanna who enacted the role of a nawab in a play based on Amritlal Nagar's stories, called 'Nawabi Masnad'. Several of Rashid Jahan's more elaborate dresses were used for the dances in these plays and were worn by Shobha Sood.

[46] Interviews with Birjees Kidwai, Drs. Sarvat Rahman, Drs. Bano and Naren Gupta, Munibur Rahman and Mehjabeen Jalil paint a similar picture of a chaotic, disorganised household, full of hustle and bustle, which always had

several people, either friends or Party workers, living in it for indefinite periods of time.

[47] *The Light*, op. cit., p. 14.

[48] Lola Chatterji (ed.), *Autobiography: Hamida Saiduzzafar 1921-1988,* (New Delhi: Trianka, 1996), p. 61.

[49] Hamida Saiduzzafar, op cit., p. 18.

[50] *The Light*, op. cit., p. 14.

[51] Hamida Saiduzzafar, *Autobiography,* op. cit., p. 36.

[52] In *Quest for Life,* op. cit., p. 13, Mahmud narrates how, ill and dying though she was, when their Russian translator told Rashid Jahan that theirs (Mahmud and Rashida's) was a 'unique and wonderful friendship', 'There was such pride and happiness in her face. I saw that same expression a few days later when she herself introduced me to one of the doctors using the Russian word she had picked up, 'Doctor, he is my *mousch* (husband)!'

[53] I am grateful to the late Prof. Aulad Ahmad Siddiqui for giving me his copy of this out-of-print book.

[54] *A Woman of Substance*, op. cit., p. 100.

[55] First published in *Qaumi Awaaz,* August 15, 1952; later included in *Shola-e-Jawwala.*

[56] *A Quest for Life*, op. cit., p.1-2.

[57] Naren Gupta, who had seen the slides of her biopsy, told me that he knew that the cancer was vigorous and that it was 'too late'.

[58] This was in keeping with the official communist line of 'false freedom', i.e., the true freedom for the Indian masses was yet to come, even after the country gained freedom from imperial rule in August 1947.

4

Writer and Dramatist

Mujhse pahli si muhabbat mere mahboob na mang

Don't ask me for that old love, my love... .

– Faiz Ahmad Faiz

Rashid Jahan and the PWM

Let us first look at Rashid Jahan's post-*Angarey* writings in the light of her association with the PWA. She is believed to have written 25-30 short stories and 15-20 plays, many of them specifically for the radio which she considered a powerful medium for mass communication.[1] Unfortunately, the great bulk of this material has been lost. She wrote and directed many plays based on her own radio scripts as well as some based on the works of Chekov, James Joyce and Premchand. Taken together, her ouevre as it exists today in the form of *Aurat aur Deegar Drame wa Afsane* and *Woh aur Doosre Afsane wa Drame*[2] reflects one singular quality: more than anything else she was disturbed by the plight of women. Her experiences as a 'lady doctor were central to her work, and the influence of communism coloured her perspective. In this section, we will examine a third influence on her writing: that of progressivism and the company of progressive writers.

Meeting Premchand at the first All-India Progressive Writers' Conference in April 1936 had a lasting influence on Rashid Jahan. Premchand's inaugural address offered a new definition of literature, namely, 'the criticism of life'. It altered her own understanding of both literature and the role of a writer:

> We will have to change the standard of beauty. So far this standard has been based on wealth and love of pleasure... For them (artists) beauty lies in a beautiful woman, not in the poor and ungainly mother who is toiling hard after putting her baby to sleep in the hay. If our artists have decided that beauty definitely dwells in painted lips, cheeks and eyebrows, how can it have anything to do with tangled hair, cracked lips and sunken cheeks.[3]

After the Conference, over dinner at Zaheer's home while the others were downcast about the 'mixed signals from some of the participants (such as the debate over Hindi-Urdu initiated by Jainendra Kumar), Premchand and Rashid Jahan were clearly enjoying each other's company:

> He (Premchand) was roaring with laughter at Rasheeda's (sic) characteristic style of mockery: she compared the lengths of Maulana Hasrat Mohani and Dr. Aleem's beards, commented on the mathematical formulas in Ahmed Ali's paper, and derided Saghar Nizami's tight *sherwani* and even tighter *churidar pajama*. In his turn, Premchand began to level some friendly criticism at us, the young Progressives. He said, "I like to see you walking fast to achieve a quick revolution, but I am afraid if you begin to run heedlessly, you may trip and fall. And at my age, if I attempted to run with you and fell down, I could hurt myself seriously." And he chuckled. "But come what may, we will never let go of your hand," said Rasheeda, laughing.[4]

Premchand died shortly thereafter, on October 8, 1936. But in the few months of his association with the Progressives he did everything he could for their cause: he published the Hindi version of his inaugural address in *Hans* (July 1936), encouraged Hindi writers to join the PWM, talked about the movement

from public platforms, at Congress events or Hindi Sahitya
Parishad functions. Deeply moved by his contribution to their
fledgeling movement and keenly aware of a writer's need to
change with changing times, Rashid Jahan noted after
Premchand's death:

> One of the most exceptional qualities in Premchand's art is the
> influence of the changing times. There was a time for writing
> *Boodhi Kaki, Subah-e-Akbar* and *Bazar-e-Husn.* Times changed, the
> Congress came to power and with these changes the changing
> reflection of the socio-political scenario that one can find in
> Premchand, cannot be found in any other writer. The youth of
> today are different from the young people of ten years ago. If
> Premchand had been alive today, I am convinced his stories would
> have changed to keep pace with the changing world.....He left a
> lasting and sweet impression on us.[5]

Being a founder-member of the PWA, Rashid Jahan
remained in close contact with the association and took a lively
interest in its activities. Not only did she attend the PWA
meetings in Lucknow, she travelled to the bigger conferences
in different cities as often as her health permitted. She attended
the Fourth All-India Conference of Progressive Writers held
on May 22 - 25, 1943 at the Marwari Vidyalaya Hall in Bombay,
along with Rajendra Raghuvanshi, as secretary of the Lucknow
branch, and a host of Lucknow Progressives. In an atmosphere
of increasing militancy and politicisation, Comrade S. A. Dange
delivered a presidential address that was a far cry from
Premchand's inaugural address of 1936, and a new version of
the *Manifesto* was adopted.

We can well imagine Rashid Jahan in the thick of action at
such events, knowing how keenly she was involved in the inner
working of the PWA and how she was loved and feared in
equal measure by her colleagues.[6] She was a signatory to the
resolution passing the new *Manifesto* which Sardar Jafri, K. A.
Abbas and Zaheer were at pains to clarify, did not 'restrict but

widen the scope and appeal of our literary activities'. Emphasising that the document would 'serve as a basis for the united front of all Indian writers who claim to be patriotic', this core group of communists within the PWA, who constituted its ideological flank and decided the direction of its activities, adopted a sharply political tone. Also, Comrade Dange used the PWA's platform to defend the stand adopted by the CPI in its support of Britain in the Allies' War effort by dubbing it a 'people's war' in the following words:[7]

> Can we remain neutral and not be against fascism and belie our whole past, our greatest of poets, our whole national and patriotic leadership? We cannot. We stand against fascism and its complete destruction in this war. We choose to side against fascism and for the liberation of all nations and peoples of the world.[8]

The Bombay meeting was an important one for Rashid Jahan for yet another reason; the Indian People's Theatre Association (IPTA) held its foundation conference on the same occasion. With the young and energetic P. C. Joshi as its president and the Sri Lankan Anil de Silva as general-secretary, IPTA set itself the aim of using theatre and other traditional arts to portray the problems facing the country. Joshi had earlier begun the practice of gathering the country's prominent writers, journalists, artists, economists, historians, film and stage actors to rally around the party organ, *National Front*, and later *People's War* and *People's Age*. He commissioned Sunil Janah to take photographs of the Bengal Famine and document people's movements elsewhere, such as in Telengana. Joshi understood, and capitalised on, the need to use culture as a living tool, a need that found expression among a host of creative writers across the length and breadth of the country. Rashid Jahan returned from Bombay brimming with ideas of crafting a new kind of literature. Several of her plays were used by the IPTA and she even wrote some especially for IPTA.[9] While the catalyst for IPTA was the great Bengal Famine,[10] it continued to be active long after the PWA declined. In the early days, IPTA, PWA and the Bombay film industry had overlapping membership which shared a common socially-transformative agenda.[11]

With Mahmud's release from Deoli prison, Rashid Jahan moved back to Lucknow in 1942.[12] Till the late Forties, virtually till ill-health confined her to her home in the last two years of her life, she attended the meetings of the Lucknow branch of the PWA, some of which were held at Ale Ahmad Suroor's house and some, according to Zaheer, at Rashid Jahan's house, too.[13] Zaheer narrates with wry humour how she would crib about the mess left behind after each of these literary meetings:

> The trouble is that all of you merely pretend to be progressive. When it comes to practice... the expectation from women is that they should do all the uninteresting and dirty work in the house, keep your homes clean for you and make your tea for you, so that you can sit back as the masters of the house and create literature. Isn't that your view of women whom you claim to treat as equals?[14]

As a writer, her most active years were from 1938-42, when several of her stories and plays were published in *Naya Adab*, *Chingari*, *New Masses* and other literary and political journals of her time.[15] It is hard to know how many prose essays or journalistic pieces she might have written in addition to the stories and plays since many of the journals she wrote for have since folded up and she herself did not keep copies of her numerous articles.[16] Given her slender output and the marked unevenness of her work in literary terms, why then should we study it at all? Again, Hajra Begum offers a clue:

> We value Rashid Jahan today because she was the first short story writer in Urdu who fearlessly showed us those aspects of society which had traditionally been kept hidden and veiled. She was the first woman writer who showed us the mind of a rebellious woman, a woman who might have been defeated by life but whose spirit and strength refuse to accept defeat till the very

end.....Her talent lies in the fact that through her few stories she influenced scores of women writers who followed in her steps.[17]

Rashid Jahan can be credited with crafting a new lexicon for the Urdu prose writer, and using it with blithe confidence. Unlike the progressive poets who were conducting similar experiments in craft and technique, we see an unusual degree of freedom and a blasé disregard for tradition in her use of language; it is almost as though Urdu prose was like putty in her hands as she strove to make it express new and urgent concerns. With the genre of the Urdu short story being in its infancy, the absence of an evolved literary canon for the Urdu short story empowered her instead of intimidating or curbing her natural impulse for a new kind of self-expression.

Assessing the short stories

Moved by the abjectness of women who kept track of time only through pregnancy and childbearing, who were appendages of men at best and playthings at worst, and whose bodies were not their own, Rashid Jahan chose to bring together her experiences as a female doctor and as the daughter of a social reformer in her stories. Her desire to write primarily about women can be traced to her father's decision to start a school for girls: both show an inherent desire for education and the upliftment of women; in the father's case through a pioneering attempt to provide modern, scientific education to girls in a safe and secure environment; in the daughter's, through a more radical, more explicitly anti-colonial, reformist desire to 'expose' and thereby bring about change in the status of women. The only other reformers apart from Shaikh Abdullah – Rokeya Sekhawat Hossein in Bengal, Maulvi Karamat Husain in Lucknow and to a certain extent, the enlightened Begums of Bhopal – had concentrated mainly on women's education. No one, till Rashid Jahan burst upon the scene, spoke as openly about other matters that concerned women just as much as their education, namely, their reproductive health, sexually transmitted diseases, oppressive marriages, the inherent inequality between the sexes that was taken as a matter of course in most families and manifested itself through time-honoured and therefore unquestioned practices such as seclusion, parda, and so on.

Hajra Begum does not find it at all odd that Rashid Jahan should have written about women or their problems, though she does find it strange that she did not write about her own milieu; instead she chose to do so about women from middle or lower-income families. While not a creative writer or even a literary critic herself, Hajra Begum nevertheless possessed a keen eye and was quick to highlight the importance given to lower classes in Rashid Jahan's works. She was also perceptive enough to see the changes wrought in Rashid Jahan's literary life in keeping with her growing political consciousness. The post-1937 stories, she feels, reflect Rashid Jahan's increasing intellectual and ideological resolve; the stark realism of the early stories is overlaid by a sharper political awareness.

Being a woman and a doctor, she and the eponymous woman protagonist of *Woh, Mera Ek Safar, Chor* and many such stories, rejoice in their freedom to travel, to flit between the private and public realm, to delve into life behind parda, emerge and speak about the unbearable suffocation and oppression behind it.[18] These stories could not have been written if there had been no men like Shaikh Abdullah to allow women like Rashid Jahan to come to the fore. So, in a sense, Rashid Jahan was not only a pioneer in her own chosen field of writing, but also the direct result of her upbringing.[19] She can be seen as an 'organic intellectual'[20], one who rose from the ranks of the professional classes and came to represent the interest of the people she knew and interacted with.

Always in a hurry, always on the go with so much to do and

very little time to achieve everything, Rashid Jahan did not have the luxury to hone her craft or even polish and perfect her first drafts. Consequently, they sometimes display an incomplete-ness. Given her emphasis on content and considerably less attention to structure or characterisation, it seems that she herself viewed her stories as a means of education rather than literary expression. However, what they lack in skill and craft, they more than make up in the freshness and innovativeness of their approach and the zesty, everyday language employed by her characters. Rashid Jahan wrote as she spoke – freely and fearlessly. Without the slightest trace of coyness or false modesty she writes about venereal disease, lack of family planning, absence of a woman's consent for marriage, and false notions of 'manliness' in traditional Muslim households – written not so much to shock but to confront and expose issues that had always been conveniently concealed.

With her sympathetic portrayal of lower-income, working class people and critical commentary on middle and upper classes, she was following the largely didactic example of nineteenth-century French and Russian realists and her sources of inspiration seem to be much the same as Manto's.[21] However, from the stylised naturalism of the *Angarey* pieces, she began to move to a more unaffected, less self-consciously didactic style that went beyond the 'confront and condemn' model. Stories such as *Nayi Bahu ke Naye Aib* (The New Bride's New Faults), *Gharibon ke Bhagwan* (The God of the Poor), *Chhidda ki Maa* (Chhidda's Mother), and *Nayi Musibatein* (New Troubles) even managed to garner some praise from readers and critics who were growing weary of the propagandist element in the Progressives' relentless arsenal. Read almost half a century later, some of her stories are remarkable, not for any singular literary qualities, but in the choice of subject, tone, tenor and treatment of awkward issues that had been considered beyond the purview of literature.

In this regard, a short story *Woh* (That One) and a play *Aurat*
(Woman) (both published in the only collection that appeared
during Rashid Jahan's lifetime) deserve special mention. They
do so on grounds of image and representation, that is, the
image of the woman as sufferer – silent in *Woh* but outspoken
in *Aurat*. The action in *Woh* takes place in a newly-opened
space, a public space, where women from different social classes
meet, an encounter that was inconceivable even a decade earlier.
Two women – an educated working-class young woman from
a 'decent' background and another, a prostitute obviously
suffering from syphilis that has left her horribly disfigured –
meet for the first time in a public dispensary. The young woman,
a teacher in a girls' school, shocked and repulsed by the
diseased appearance of the other, nonetheless smiles, prompting
the other woman to ask her where she has come from. The
teacher gives the name of the school where she works and the
defaced woman, obviously a fallen woman who has caught
the dreaded disease from some nameless customer, turns up at
her college. Soon, the visits became a daily routine: the
nameless, faceless woman appears, mutely presents a single
motiya flower to the young teacher (whose name we are told is
Safiya, who puts the flower in her hair) sits for a while and
leaves.

The woman's face, disfigured by disease, her shockingly
revolting appearance and her obvious adoration of Safiya
initially cause mirth followed almost immediately by censure.
Everyone in the school, from the teachers to the principal and
the cleaning woman, disapproves of her daily visits; they wish
to have nothing to do with so repulsive, immoral and detestable
a creature. One fat, old lady teacher even says that they must
observe parda from such a one. Safiya, ashamed, embarrassed
and no less repulsed by these daily visits, nevertheless allows
the creature to come, accepts the *motiya* flower, puts it in her
hair and lets her sit briefly in the chair facing hers – a chair that

no one wants to sit in now and one which even the cleaning lady refuses to dust. So it would have continued had the nameless creature not wiped her snot on the office wall one day. The cleaning woman, already sore with the woman's daily appearance, pounces on the woman, forgetting the good manners dinned into her from decades of service among respectable folk. Beating, kicking, pummelling, she screams obscenities at her, accusing the woman of forgetting her place: a whore who sat in the chowk wanting to sit in a chair where respectable women sat, that too now that her flesh was rotting and falling away! The nameless woman, devastated by what she sees as a loss of respect, takes the beatings and goes away, sobbing: 'Now you know!'

More than the nameless woman's incredible naiveté in imagining that Safiya would not have known who she was or what she suffered from, our interest in the story stems from the fact that such an encounter occurred in the first place. Two women whose paths could not have crossed do so due to a chain of events set in motion by an imperceptible wave of modernity that was creating unexpected ripples in unlikely places (a hospital and a girls' school, in this case). Rashid Jahan, both the agent and product of change, was quick to seize the possibility offered by a chance meeting between two women who have absolutely nothing in common save their womanhood. That she chose to turn it into a tale of unsurpassed compassion and tenderness is a tribute to her humanity. In Safiya she gave us an unlikely heroine, one who wears her compassion like a badge of courage, and in the nameless 'that one' (who is also genderless in the Urdu *woh*) she gives us a most unexpected icon of suffering, one who suffers a most gruesome fate but who nevertheless continues to harbour in her ravaged detestable body the capacity for a love that is pure and undemanding.

Another story deals with a subject considered beyond the

preview of not just literature but 'civilised' conversation: childbirth. Premchand refers to the temporary importance enjoyed by the sweepress who delivers a zamindar's son in *Doodh ka Daam* (The Price of Milk) but no one had hitherto made such graphic references to the 'bloody' details: the sight of a midwife pressing down hard on a woman's belly, pinning the pregnant woman's thighs with her toes while she deftly pulls the placenta and then cuts the umbilical cord, the cleaning-up of the after-birth, the tying of a long bandage-like strip of cloth around a woman's abdomen to keep the tummy flat – all these gory descriptions were new to the Urdu short story. As a doctor, they came naturally to Rashid Jahan and she made ample use of her own experience in countless labour rooms to make several penetrating observations in *Asif Jahan ki Bahu* (A Daughter-in-Law for Asif Jahan): the role of the midwife as she presided over the delivery like a 'master of ceremonies'; the complete lack of privacy on such occasions with a gaggle of female relatives crowding the room; the use of unsterilised thread and a rusted knife to cut the cord; the grubby hands and unhygienic practices of midwives and their fear that new-fangled lady doctors ('mems') would rob them of not just their livelihood but their moment in the sun when their expertise and experience saved the day; and the festive atmosphere with much to-ing and fro-ing of relatives, *domnis* singing *zachchagiris* and the feasting that accompanied the birth of a child.

The condition of women, especially those who lived in seclusion, was of especial interest to Rashid Jahan as was the importance given to marriage in traditional households. *Bezuban* (literally 'tongue-less' but translated here as 'Mute'), is a penetrating look at the institution of 'arranged' marriages, the compulsions and conditions of parents wishing to hold on to the time-honoured ways of sharif families, and the ignominy of those girls who find themselves still single beyond the so-called 'marriageable' age. Inordinately proud of their lineage, poor unwed Siddiqa Begum's parents reject the proposals – few and far-between though they are – on some ground or the other: 'Sometimes there would be a dispute over the dower money; sometimes over the amount to be spent on the entertaining. Sometimes a flaw would be found in the groom's parents; sometimes an impurity would be found in his grandmother's lineage.' The perfect daughter, Siddiqa, is described by her mother as someone who would 'not dare to even let out a squeak in front of [her] father ... she sits where she is made to sit, she eats what she is given'. Helpless, she can only watch in mute and growing frustration as her parents find fault with everyone and declare proudly that they 'would rather buy two-paisas worth of arsenic and give it to Siddiqa to swallow and put her to sleep forever' than agree to the 'modern' practice of 'showing' the girl to prospective in-laws. The story ends with yet another proposal disappearing into thin air because this time the boy's family subscribes to a new and altogether unpleasant tradition: that of accepting money from the bride's family.

Rashid Jahan also explored the relationship between men and women both from the lower strata of society as well as the educated middle class. In an unusual story that comprises entirely of a dialogue between an unnamed man and woman, *Mard wa Aurat* (Man and Woman), a man proposes to a woman but instead of a happily-ever-after ending they come upon the stumbling block of her job, which she refuses to abandon for the sake of matrimony. The man makes snide references to it only fetching a measly Rs 100, to which the woman says: 'Whatever it may be; it is the key to my freedom' and 'freedom implies standing on one's own feet'. From the question of job and salary, the disagreement goes on to other issues that plague all marriages: who to meet who not to, who one likes and who one doesn't, to sit at home and 'look after the house' or go out

and have a life; the dialogue ends with the man asserting his
natural superiority over the woman. He throws the age-old
dart that all men have invariably thrown at working women
'...while you draw deep gulps of your freedom, your children
will suffer'; to which she says that the children should be raised
jointly by both husband and wife. A short, sharp story, like
many others written by Rashid Jahan, it raises age-old questions
about men and women making it at once ageless and universal.

Gosha-e-Aafiyat presents a lighter, humorous take on
marriage, where a group of husbands form a club or band to
escape nagging quarrelsome wives. What with an elderly
character declaring that one day in the future there will be no
'husbands' and no 'homes' in the traditional sense, it is also a
spoof at the vacuous, club-going newly-westernised Indians
freshly introduced to the delights of dancing with the wives
of other men and enjoying greater social interaction between
the sexes. The satire is sharper in *Sauda* (translated here as
'Sale' but it can also mean 'Deal') about a group of sharif men
going to an isolated spot by a river for a good time. A party of
three men and one woman obviously means that the men must
take their turn and so a deal has to be struck on who goes first:
'The woman was quiet. In the bazar when three or four dogs
chase a bitch with such passion and restlessness, even the poor
bitch hides her face and runs away from so many impetuous
customers. But the woman – who had been reduced to a state
worse than that of the bitch in the bazar by wealthy men and
their respectable wives – simply stood by the open door of the
motor car.' *Sauda* is the only piece of writing by Rashid Jahan
that has any overt reference to romantic love and some fairly
explicit scenes of bodily hunger between the sexes, as for
instance: 'Warm, quick breaths enflamed my face. I lifted my
face up. My eyes were fixed on his eyes. My resisting body
grew limp in his.' And elsewhere, 'Bodily proximity creates a
sensation like a flash of lightning, a quicksilver madness, a

heat that courses through and causes a state when one has lost all control over oneself and no one exists in the whole wide world except him and me.'

A nother story, *Buri Sohbat* (Bad Company), is about a judge whose rebellious son is drawn towards communism (shades of Sajjad Z aheer, maybe!): 'I pulled myself out of a pit, gave my family a leg-up in the world so that he, my son, can go around with K arl M arx tucked under his arm.' The son, for his part, wants prosperity for not one or two successful people but for everyone to partake equally of progress. The judge saheb and his successful elder son, a collector no less, conclude sagely: it is only bad company which is responsible for such mistaken beliefs! *Iftari,* on the other hand, is a rambling story of a young man who was once drawn towards the idea of social change but after marriage and the birth of a child, becomes a petit bourgeois. H is wife, untutored though she is, retains the shiny idealism she had once shared with her husband. Seeing the change in him, she treats him with silent condescension but holds on to her belief in a better tomorrow. H idden amidst the many jibes at religiosity – the sort that believes in the outer tokens such as *roza-namaaz* (fasting and prayer) but not the true generosity of spirit which is the bedrock not merely of Islam but all religions – *Iftari* is also a telling statement on the loss of ideals in some (the 'paper tigers') and the steely, persistent resolve in others. W hen her son asks her why she, N asima, is not fasting when everyone around them is doing so during the month of R amzan and whether she is scared of going to hell, the young mother tells her son that hell is all around them: 'There... where that blind beggar is standing. There... where the weavers live. There... where the ironsmiths and the dyers live.' H er answer is virtually lesson in M arxian dialectics: 'The fire of hell, my son, is the fire of hunger. O ften, you don't get anything to eat in hell and when you do, it is very little and of very bad quality. O ne has to work very hard in hell. And the clothes that the people in hell wear are old and tattered. Their homes are small, cramped and dark, filled with lice and bugs. What is more, my dear Aslam miyan, the children in hell do not have toys to play. Heaven, on the other hand, is 'here where you and I live with your aunts and uncles. It is here in this large, clean house where we get to eats lots of delicious things such as butter, toast, fruits, eggs, meat, milk. Children have good clothes to wear and a motor car to play. In answer to the child's innocent query as to why everyone doesn't live in heaven, Nasima says: 'Because, my dear, those who live in heaven do not let others come in. They get these other people to do all their work but then they push them back into hell.' The story ends with the mother telling her child, fiercely but with utter seriousness, that when he grows up he must banish this hell, and, upon his insistence, she promises to help him.

Not all of Rashid Jahan's stories deal with Muslims; *Garibon ka Bhagwan* and *Punn* expose the hypocrisy of religious figures and the inequality they foster. Another very short story, a mere two pages long, packs quite a punch like the equally brief *Dilli ki Sair*. Called *Insaf*, it begins a bit like Premchand's *Doodh Ka Daam* where a poor low-caste boy gets to play and study with a high-caste Raja's son. But in Rashid Jahan's hands the story acquires such velocity and sting as it hurtles towards its devastating denouement that it allows no scope for Premchand's laborious character-building and plotting. The poor Ram Singh consistently does better than the Raja's son yet scores lower marks. When he goes to the Raja seeking justice, the wily pandit who teaches both children paints a classic scenario straight out of a feudal nightmare: If Ram Singh becomes educated he will get a good job and become equal to Pritam, the Raja's son, even get posted as an officer and Pritam might have to bow before him. The Raja is quick on the uptake; he dispenses justice immediately and brutally. It is best to discontinue the boy's education, the Raja decides, for: 'As it is, these low-born people are rising. Education is responsible for spoiling them.' And poor Ram Singh, who had gone expecting justice, gets the boot instead. For all his anger against this gross injustice, he is helpless and forced to abandon his studies.

In story after story Rashid Jahan displayed her strength in the depiction of the lower classes, people she met in the course of her work and those she knew as servants and hangers-on in her extended family. *Chhidda ki Maa* is a story about a woman who was employed in her aunt's house to pull the fan, and Chhidda tended her uncle's horses. The story is a pithy account of the cruelty women heap on women and the tension that exists between a mother-in-law and daughter-in-law: 'Does one see a daughter-in-law's face or her traits? If a wife does not bear children, it is like keeping her and feeding her for no good reason. A wife is good only as long as she bears sons and a buffalo is good if she bears calves.' However, instead of portraying the mother-in-law as a relentless villain, she points out the insecurity that lies at the heart of all of women's problems and their dependence on sons and husbands to claim their space in the social order.

In stories like *Chor* (Thief) while there is anger against the system that produces thieves who milk the system dry but do not get caught, there is also an earnest desire to bring about change. The story's protagonist, a woman doctor, finds herself confronted with the thief who robbed her home, but is now facing her as the father of a critically sick child. Should she turn him over to the police or tend the child who clearly needs her immediate attention? She decides not to turn him in since all around her thieves are roaming about in the guise of clever charlatans. She acknowledges that there are different types of theft: stealing, picking pockets, burgling houses, armed robbery, black marketeering, and big countries annexing smaller ones. In stories like *Chor*, we see very little attempt at psychoanalysis.

Steven Poulos offers an interesting reason why this could be so:

> Rashid Jahan never bares her characters' souls not only because her stories were short and purposeful, but because the trend toward a psychoanalysis of one's characters was not part of her training and was only starting to become influential in Indian literature during the twilight of her career.[22]

For a writer like Rashid Jahan, travel became a leit motif; travel could be a literal journey by train or a figurative one from an enclosed/cloistered space to an open/uncloistered one. Her own experiences of travelling in the course of her studies, work and other activities afforded ample opportunity to travel by train. We have already seen her depiction of a woman from Faridabad who travels to Delhi in the *Angarey* story, *Dilli ki Sair*; in *Mera ek Safar*, the protagonist is not a burqa-clad, suburban housewife dependent upon the mercy of a negligent husband; instead of the woman as appendage being *taken* on a trip that turns into a fiasco, here we find an empowered, educated, enlightened woman who could well be a younger Rashid Jahan herself. Written in the form of a letter to a friend, *Mera ek Safar* is about a young woman travelling home from college. She has short hair, wears a sari, jumps over steps and runs to catch the train – much to the amusement of onlookers who have never seen such a sight. She finds herself in an over-crowded third-class 'ladies' compartment where her fellow travellers do not know what to make of her.

Seeing the bindi on her forehead, a Hindu woman makes space for her to sit beside her. Asked about her caste, the young woman laughingly replies: 'Chamar!' Since the young sari-clad educated woman does not 'look' like an untouchable, her interrogator is not amused, and says: 'Just because you are educated, you think you can fool others.' What follows is a sympathetic portrayal of the minutiae of social interaction between the majority and minority religious groups by one who, as we later realise from her name is Muslim yet can view the antics of both groups as an objective bystander. The over-crowded, pressure-cooker-like train compartment becomes a microcosm for India and the women display the best and worst instincts of poor, illiterate, ignorant people who live in close proximity and view the other with suspicion and mistrust. The trailing dupatta of a Muslim woman touches a Hindu and sparks a near-riot resulting in torn clothes, scratched faces and an exchange of insults and abuses. The narrator (whose name is Zubeida) stands up and hectors the warring women into submission and shame. The story ends with the Hindu and Muslim women, who had earlier been at each other's throats, hugging each other and weeping as their journey comes to an end. The women emerge as naive, child-like pawns in a game they have watched others play but who have no real understanding or interest in its dynamics. As in the play, *Padosi* (Neighbour), Rashid Jahan seems to imply that women, unlike men, can rise above petty differences and bridge the communal divide.

By writing the story in the form of a letter and beginning it with a description of the narrator's confidence and education that clearly sets her apart, making her almost a novelty, Rashid Jahan consciously adopts a distance from the women she describes. It is only the train journey that brings them together for a few hours, otherwise they have nothing in common. We are reminded of the distinction post-colonial scholars of subaltern studies, like Gayatri Chakravarti Spivak[23], make between 'speaking for' in the sense of political representation and 'speaking about', or 're-presenting' as in portraying. In *Mera ek Safar*, Rashid Jahan is clearly doing the latter.

Evaluating the plays

During her most active years as a writer, from 1938-1942, Rashid Jahan wrote several radio plays which were broadcast from the Lucknow and Delhi radio stations; several of them directed by Rashid Jahan herself.[24] Hajra Begum believes that the bulk of her long plays, apart from *Aurat* and *Parde ke Peeche*, were written after 1941 or 1942; this was when she moved to Lucknow and began spending more time with literary luminaries like Mulk Raj Anand, Anand Narain Mulla, Ale Ahmad Suroor, Firaq Gorakhpuri, Majaz, etc. Compared to her stories, her plays are longer allowing her to devote some attention to setting and prop details. They also move away from the expose-and-condemn model of her earlier work.

Contrary to *Parde ke Peeche* which ended on a high note with no resolution or hope for improvement in sight, in *Aurat,* Rashid Jahan turned the image of the suffering woman on its head and made her a votary of progress. Fatima, a childless woman, is married to Atiq, a maulvi who is bent upon marrying again, ostensibly to beget an heir but actually to get a younger wife, the daughter of a 'devotee' who will also be more pliable. For all his ostentatious piety and dispensing of charms and amulets to the needy, Atiq is a wily, greedy, typically chauvinistic man who does not think twice about cursing and beating his wife when she questions his authority and wisdom. The format of the play, longer than most of her short stories, allows Rashid Jahan to develop her characters and give freer rein to the idiomatic, earthy language that enhances the naturalness of her writing. Its length allows her to take up several issues she had only touched upon in the *Angarey* play, *Parde ke Peeche*.

Unlike *Parde ke Peeche*, however, the wronged woman in *Aurat* is no longer willing to accept her lot. Where Muhammadi Begum was content to bemoan her fate and share her misfortune with a confidante who could offer little more than clucks of sympathy, Fatima finds a receptive, more proactive support group: her (male) cousins offer unconditional support and her tenant's wife expresses outrage and indignation at Atiq's behaviour. Fatima's educated cousins, Qadeer and Aziz, tell her to go to court to claim ownership of the house she and Atiq live in for it belongs to Fatima not Atiq. She is sensitised to the fact that she owns property and can prevent Atiq from bringing a co-wife to live in her house. Also, one of the cousins has had a test done on Fatima and discovered the reason for her persistent miscarriages: she has venereal disease, passed on no doubt by her pious husband. The play ends with Fatima threatening to hit her husband back if he raises his hand against her: 'Careful! You better back off if you want to keep your honour intact. If you dare to raise your hand one more time, I will not be responsible for what happens.' From Muhammadi Begum to Fatima is a woman's journey from passive submission to a self-aware, intelligent questioning of authority and standing up for one's rights.

Aurat is remarkable for the several pointed observations that Rashid Jahan slips in: the widespread notion that young Muslim men who adopted western-style suits instead of the traditional shervani-kurta-pajama were aping Christians; similarly, Muslim women who wore saris were guilty of forsaking Islamic practices and imitating kafirs. She makes Maulvi Atiq mouth several inanities and falsehoods that were widespread among Muslim families of her time: a husband is the worldly god of his wife and she is duty-bound to please and obey him ('without doubt or delay') in every way; a woman who disobeys her husband is 'sinful and terrible', paving her way for hell; women must observe parda from their male cousins, even those they might regard as younger brothers; Allah has 'commanded' men to marry four times and therefore there is no shame in it; women who are fatherless, brotherless and barren to boot have no safeguards in a marriage; and hitting a woman is the right way to teach her a lesson for her insolence.

We also hear the feminist in Rashid Jahan when one woman character in *Aurat* says:

A man thinks as long as he has given a woman food and clothing, he has done enough. The more conscientious husband would think he is being fair if he spends one night with one wife and the other with the second. As though wives are mere toys for their husband, he can play with either one he fancies. And who is to blame? What if the two women were to unite? What would the man do then?

Commenting on the unequal status of women sanctioned by religion, she makes the unfortunate Fatima observe ruefully: 'Those who create religions, write shariahs and laws – they are all men after all! They write everything to suit men; what would they know about a woman's heart? Had they been women, they would have known!' Fatima's cousin, Qadeer, who is the sanest person in the play, speaks for Rashid Jahan when he stops Fatima from wallowing in self-pity for being a helpless woman: 'As long as a human being does not have confidence in himself and does not become his own heir, no one in the whole wide world can help him.'

In *Kaantewala* (The Lever Man) the action revolves around the man who operates the lever at a railway level crossing. Two poor women talk about the rule of the English which was infinitely better than the natives' what with spiralling prices, hunger, malnutrition, closure of ration shops, retrenchment of workers, hoarding, black marketeering, and worse still, communal riots. In a conversation between a lever operator and a track checker and their wives, there are references to prohibition that allows only soldiers and leaders to drink; the end of the white man's raj that has brought corruption, inefficiency and sloth in its wake; and the rampant food shortages caused by corrupt public distribution networks. Rashid Jahan airs her communist beliefs when she makes these illiterate and poor men talk of the wretched leaders who have betrayed the workers and how the latter must be united if they are to fight for their rights. She recalls for them, and for us, the railway workers' strikes that had crippled the country in the late 1920s and brought the government to its knees. She talks scathingly of a government that shuts down fair price shops and instead talks of giving measly increments: 'There was a time once when the government used to talk of giving us our rights, eliminating hunger and poverty; now it is worried about safeguarding the interests of the Birlas and Dalmias.'

When Barsati, the lever operator Dhuli's son, comes home, injured in police firing on a mob of hungry workers who have gone to the city to get grain from fair price shops, Dhuli's rage and frustration boil over. He demonstrates his defiance of an unconcerned system in the only way he knows: he refuses to operate the track lever and shows, for the first time in his entire career, a red lantern instead of the green flag that allows trains to change tracks. Dhuli's red lantern is a sign of the pent-up anger in the working classes against a system that is as oblivious and uncaring as the rail engine that moves on, blithely blowing clouds of steam, unmoved by the misery of those who live in wretched hutments beside the railway tracks.

Padosi (Neighbour) is a powerful statement of empowered womanhood. Beginning with a depiction of domestic politics and vicious in-fighting between sisters-in-law, it goes on to make a larger statement about the good that women can do if they learn to stand on their own, organise self-help groups, rise above petty distinctions of caste, class and religion and form a sisterhood. Rashid Jahan's attention to detail is as minute here as it was in the stage setting for *Parde ke Peeche*. The play opens with three sisters-in-law from a typical middle-class Hindu family engaged in a conversation with their maid and sweepress; what emerges from the dribs and drabs of petty family disputes is a powerful commentary on caste taboos, communalism and religious hatred. The maids who work in the homes of good Hindu families are prohibited from working in the homes of Muslims for they pollute and defile, but the sweepress refuses to abide by such rules; not only does she work in the home of a Muslim neighbour but in times of trouble helps the Muslim family and plays an active role in bringing the women of the two families together. If it were not for her, the two neighbours would have remained isolated, cut off from each other by fear of the alien-ness of the other. The sweepress acts as a catalyst in helping the two families see each other as human beings, and eventually it is the women who show more courage and humanity than their men. They avert a communal riot and help bring peace to their neighbourhood. Gandhi, too, finds mention as one who wanted to wipe the tears from everyone's eyes – be it the sweepress Champa, the Muslim woman, Kulsum or the widow Sita. The play ends with the hope that five-year old Billo will not grow up with a warped view of inter-communal relations as, thanks to the sweepress's initiative, her family's isolation has diminished and a window has opened for her to view the world in its totality.

Rashid Jahan also wrote of 'experimental' marriages; inter-caste and inter-community, that would stir the pot of multi-cultural, multi-ethnic India to produce a new, pluralistic society. In *Hindustani,* she has Suresh marrying Razia and Ashraf marrying Sita, indicating the way to a more heterogeneous India, one that is hopefully more tolerant. Like the majority of her stories, these plays are not great in literary terms; instead of testing them on the touchstone of great literature, they should be seen as visionary statements, as creative suggestions for a better tomorrow.

End Notes

[1] Apart from All India Radio (AIR), Radio Tashkent was extremely popular with Indian listeners; its signal was even stronger than the BBC's. It undoubtedly exercised great influence on those who wrote for radio. Most progressive writers were associated with the newly set-up AIR in some capacity or the other. For a study of the setting up of AIR, see P. C. Chatterji, *Broadcasting in India* (New Delhi: Sage, 1987).

[2] Lahore: Hashmi Book Depot, 1937; New Delhi: Maktaba Jamia, 1977. Taken together these two volumes include the stories in *Shola-e-Jawwala*, and can be said to be representative of her entire published work. This does not, of course, take into account her unpublished radio plays. *Shola-e-Jawwala* (Lucknow: India Publisher, 1974) was published posthumously by her sister-in-law Dr. Hamida Saiduzzafar and Naim Khan, who worked with both Rashid Jahan and Mahmud; it also included some reminiscences about Rashid Jahan. *Selected Short Stories and Plays*, translated into English by Atia Abid, comprises sixteen short stories and seven plays. It was published by The Female Education Society, Aligarh in 2005. Shakil Siddiqui's *Rashid Jahan ki Kahaniyan* published by Vani in 2011 introduced her to Hindi readers; and Humaira Ashfaq's *Nasr-e-Rashid Jahan: Afsanon, Dramon aur Mazamin ka Intekhab* (Lahore: Sang-e-Meel, 2012) introduced her to Urdu readers.

[3] Premchand's address, translated by Francesca Orsini, *The Oxford India Premchand* (New Delhi: Oxford University Press, 2004).

[4] Sajjad Zaheer, *The Light*, op. cit., p. 74.

[5] Article entitled '*Munshi Premchand aur Tarraqui Pasand Adeebon ki Pahli Conference*', in Humaira Ashfaq (ed.), *Nasr-e-Rashid Jahan* (Lahore: Sang-e-Meel, 2012), p. 283. The article corroborates Zaheer's description of the first AIPWA meeting in April 1936, the arrangements being made for it, and Premchand's interactions with the young progressives. It is a delightful piece of reportage in its informality and ease of expression. Ashfaq does not mention its source; possibly it was written for *Chingari*.

[6] It must be pointed that despite being bold and non-conformist, Rashid Jahan never experienced any alienation or exclusion at the hands of the progressives. Unlike Miraji, Manto and Ismat Chughtai, who suffered varying degrees of osctracisation within the PWA, she was extended nothing but warmth and friendship. Was it because of something in her own personality? Or was it the fact that as a writer she was no threat to her peers?

[7] The CPI's stand was blindly accepted by Party workers, though in later years many among the rank and file pointed it out as one of the reasons for the Party's poor showing in later years.

[8] Sudhi Pradhan (ed.), *Marxist Cultural Movement in India* (Calcutta: National Book Agency, 1979), pp.118-119.

[9] There are stray references to Rashid Jahan's involvement with IPTA; that her plays were used by IPTA was corroborated by S. M Mahdi, former member of IPTA, whom I interviewed in Aligarh. *IPTA ki Yaadein*, a SAHMAT publication, edited by Rajendra Sharma (2012) mentions Rashid Jahan in several IPTA meetings.

[10] Poets and writers wrote in white heat about an oppressive colonial system that caused food shortages, and awakened the Indian public to an essentially unjust system of governance. The Urdu poet, Wamiq Jaunpuri, wrote *Bhooka Hai Bangal* which became a rallying cry for the common man and focused attention on the hunger that was stalking the Bengal countryside, once known for its lush paddy fields.

[11] For a study of 'The Progressive Tradition and the Film Industry', see Talat Ahmed, *Literature and Politics in the Age of Nationalism: The Progressive Episode in South Asia, 1932-56* (New Delhi: Routledge, 2009), pp. 164-171.

[12] Rashid Jahan worked briefly as a lecturer in the Dept. of Gynaecology at King George's Medical College, Lucknow, before devoting herself solely as a private practitioner. She suffered prolonged bouts of ill health from 1942 to 1950, including three major surgeries, See Hamida Saiduzzafar in *Shola-e-Jawwala*, op. cit., p. 'Kh.' Sometime in the late 1940s, she began to show advanced signs of leukoderma, too.

[13] My mother recalls the PWA meetings held at her father, Ale Ahmad Suroor's house at 7 Barrow Road, where Rashid Jahan came along with the who's who of Lucknow's literary firmament: Abdul Alim, Ehtesham Husain, Mumtaz Husain, Shaukat Siddiqui, Mohammad Hasan, Anand Narain Mulla, Salam Machchlishahri, Hasan Shahir, Manzar Salim, Kamal Ahmed Siddiqui, Noorul Hasan Hashmi, etc. By the early-1950s, the group of progressive writers in Lucknow had expanded to include younger faces: Ratan Singh, Abid Sohail, Sharib Rudaulvi, Arif Naqvi, Agha Sohail, Iqbal Majeed, Hasan Abid, etc. D. P Mukerjee or Munibur Rehman would join them whenever they came to Lucknow as would Kali Parshad, head of the psychology department at the University. My mother remembers sitting in at numerous such meetings where the likes of Prithviraj Kapoor would show up and read a story or a play. She also remembers the home-made delicacies prepared for these regular meetings that turned their house into a festive place, with much to-ing and fro-ing of important writers and litterateurs who nevertheless took time out to talk to her and her siblings. A luminous account of these PWA meetings of the Lucknow branch is also to be found in Arif Naqvi's *Yaadon ke Chiragh* (New Delhi: Modern Publishing House, 2005).

[14] Sajjad Z aheer, *The Light,* op. cit., pp. 231-32

[15] H ajra Begum, *Khatun,* op. cit., p. 16.

[16] A sampling of six prose pieces in H umaira A shfaq's volume gives a sense of the range of her concerns: *Munshi Premchand aur Tarraqui Pasand Adeebon ki Pahli Conference* (M unshi P remchand and the F irst Conference of P rogressive W riters*), Hamari Azadi* (O ur Independence), *Adab aur Awaam* (L iterature and the P eople), *Urdu Adabiyat mein Inquilab ki Zaroorat* (T he N eed for R evolution in U rdu L itearture), *Aurat Ghar se Bahar* (Wom an O utside the H ome), and C handar Singh G arhwali, the last being an essay on a soldier of the IN A who lost his life fighting for the country.

[17] H ajra Begum, op. cit.

[18] L ike R ashid Jahan, Ismat C hughtai, too, delved into her experiences as teacher, principal and inspector of schools to write stories where the narrator was a woman professional. Being a working woman, a novelty in itself, was an enabling experience for this new breed of women writers. It afforded them opportunities to travel without male permission or patronage and appropriate spaces that had hitherto been inaccessible to women raised in parda. Ismat had to fight against heavy odds, first to go to the school at A ligarh, study up till BA at IT C ollege, and then take up employment.

[19] It must be mentioned that R ashid Jahan's other sisters chose to chart their own destinies, too: two became educationists, one a popular film and T V actor and a fourth married early and chose not to work. Just as R ashid Jahan was reviled for writing the *Angarey* pieces, K hurshid (who joined the H indi film industry as R enuka D evi) was attacked for transgressing the limits of respectability for sharif M uslim women.

[20] A ntonio G ramsci has made a distinction between organic and traditional intellectuals. See Q uentin H oare and G eoffrey N owell S mith (ed and trans), *Selections from the Prison Notebooks* (N ew York: International P ublishers, 1980).

[21] See my book, *Liking Progress, Loving Change,* for a detailed study of the E uropean and R ussian influences on M anto's work.

[22] Steven M . Poulos, 'R ashid Jahan of *Angare*: H er L ife and Work', *Indian Literature* (N ew D elhi, Sahitya A kademi.)

[23] G ayatri C hakraborty Spivak, 'C an the Subaltern Speak?' in C ary N elson and L awrence G rossberg (eds.) *Marxism and the Interpretation of Culture* (L ondon: M acmillan, 1988).

[24] H amida Saiduzzafar, *Shola-e-Jawwala,* op. cit., p. 'kh'.

Shaikh Muhammad Abdullah and
Begum Wahid Jahan

A doctor at work

Dr. Rashid Jahan

As a young bride

Mahmud and Rashida – the golden couple

Mahmud and Rashida with friends and family

*Rashid Jahan with Fakhra Masuduzzafar on her right and
Jahanara Habibullah (both cousins of Mahmud) on her left*

Dr. Rashid Jahan

2. Stories & Plays

That One

I met her in the hospital. She had come to get some medicine, as I had. All the women present there moved away from her. The doctor, too, expressed her disgust by closing her eyes. I was repulsed by the sight of her but, somehow, I managed to look at her and smile. She smiled too; or at least, she attempted to. Her nose had completely disappeared; in its place were two large, red gaping holes. An eye was missing, and with the other, she could barely see without craning her neck.

A short while later I met her again at the window of the dispensary. Deferentially, she asked me, 'Where do you live?' I gave her my address. She took her medicine and left. Without my asking, the compounder began to tell me all about her, 'She is a wicked woman ... a prostitute. She is rotting away. Now that she is dying of disease she has come for treatment. The doctor is quite mad to write a prescription for her each time; such a vile creature should just be thrown out.'

A teacher at a girls' school, I had recently graduated from College. The world lay at my feet. The future was like a garden before me, filled with roses and sweet-smelling jasmine. The world appeared to me like a night drenched in moonlight. I seemed to be floating on a river that was gently flowing one moment and rushing in a cascade the next moment. I was happy.

I knew neither sorrow nor pain. My teaching job was no more than a way to pass the time; the universe appeared to me to be suspended in a moment of waiting.

The curtain parted and I saw her enter the office in my College. Surprised, I shot to my feet and, out of force of habit, without thinking, I said, 'Please take a seat.' She appeared to hesitate, but then she sat down. She carried a twig of *motiya* in her hand. She placed it on the table in front of me. It is true that I felt a sickening revulsion at picking it up but, somehow, I controlled my feelings and put the flower in my hair. She smiled, got up and left. No words were exchanged.

It became a daily occurrence. Every day, when classes got over, she would raise the curtain and enter my office. I would ask her to sit down. She would do so and every day she would place a flower in front of me. My colleagues began to tease me about her. But no one would sit on the chair she had sat on. There was something so repulsive about her appearance. I myself could not bear to touch the chair she had used. The old cleaning woman, Nasiban, would grumble every day after the woman left: 'This new teacher is an odd one; why does she meet such a filthy, vile creature? Why should I have to clean and dust a chair that she has sat on?'

The Principal, too, raised her eyebrows to show her displeasure. 'Why do you call her here? Surely, the parents of the girls will complain one day that a wicked whore comes to visit you.'

Next day, again, the woman showed up. Again, I said, 'Please take a seat.' Now she had begun to sit for some time, gazing at me all the while. We never talked to each other. Did she think I didn't know the truth about her? She would only look – with the one crooked eye and the repulsive, noseless face turned towards me. Sometimes I suspected that her eye was swimming with tears. What does she think? I wanted to ask but I didn't know where to begin.

Often it would happen that my fellow teachers would get up and leave as soon as she appeared in our room. On their way out they would tease me, in English, 'Come, let's go; Safiya's 'that one' has come. We will go and sit in the Library. Look at the wretch's face.'

Another would say, 'You know, Safiya, I can't even eat after seeing her. The sight of her revolting face makes me want to throw up.'

'But she has chosen the best 'un; she is the number one among all of you. We should observe parda from that vile creature,' one fat old teacher said acidly.

I sat and continued doing my work while that one kept watching me. Soon, I became restless. What can she see? What does she think? Was she once like me? My hair stood on end at the thought.

Why does she come here? Doesn't she know that people hate the sight of her and find her nauseating? Slimy mucous constantly dripped from the gaping red holes that were her nostrils. Every day I would tell myself that I must ask her not to come here. After all, the Principal is right; moreover, the girls, too, had, begun to grumble. The teachers go about vomiting all over the place. But when she would show up the next day, I would once again offer her the chair and say, 'Please take a seat.'

Does she not have a mirror? Does she not know that she is paying for her sins? Why does someone not tell her? Does she even have someone? Where does she live? Where does she come from? Does she really think that I merely regard her as an ill person? I have turned into a strange sort of joke in my College. And not merely a butt of jokes but, increasingly, of ridicule. Yet every time she places a flower in front of me, I put it in my hair. She smiles her frightening smile.

Why does she look at me like that? Who is she? Who was she? Where was she born? How did she reach such terrible state? What does she feel when she comes near me? Is she relieved or pained?

One day as she was going out, she bent, blew her nose and wiped the snot on the wall. Nasiban, who was putting a fresh lick of fowler's earth on the writing slates of the smaller girls and had been nursing her ire against that one for a long time, leapt to her feet with the agility of a woman half her age. She delivered a hard whack on the woman's waist with the wooden slate. The woman was rattled.

All the good manners that living with educated folk and working in a school for twenty years had been drilled into Nasiban, all the good manners that Nasiban was forever trying to instil in the young girls, were forgotten in an instant. Nasiban became the street urchin that she really was. Out poured a volley of abuses: 'Bitch... whore... coming here and sitting on a chair. Till yesterday, she was sitting like a common whore in the chowk, and now that her flesh is rotting and falling away she has come to sit here like a begum...'

A hard kick, then another, followed by a punch...

I ran and held Nasiban. 'Hai, hai... what are you doing?'

Girls swarmed around us. Teachers too came running to join the commotion. Nasiban was beside herself with rage.

'You are the one who has given her these airs. She is a pebble from the drain; you have picked her up and brought her inside. Look how she has dirtied up the wall. I have been working here for twenty years... In all these years, I have never heard of whores coming to the College. I will not stay here anymore. Call someone else who can...' and Nasiban leapt towards the woman with renewed ferocity but people held her back.

I bent and helped the woman get up. She was crying bitterly. I held her by the arm and took her towards the main gate. Blood was trickling from her temple; but she seemed unaware of it. Hiding her face and her tears from me, she mumbled, 'Now you know.' And then she went away.

A Tour of Delhi

'**M**y dear sister, let me in,' the voice could be heard from the outer courtyard. At the same time a girl appeared, wiping her hands on her kurta. Among all her acquaintances, Malika Begum was the only one who had sat in a train, and that too, travelled from Faridabad to Delhi for a day. All the women from the neighbourhood had gathered to hear the story of her travel.

'Ai hai, come if you have to, for my jaws hurt from speaking so much! May Allah stop me if I am lying, but I have told this story thousands of time. I sat in the train from here and reached Delhi, but there he met some wretched Station Master. He left me sitting on top of our luggage and went off with the man. And I just sat there wrapped in my burqa. In my wretched burqa, and on top of that those awful men! Men are no good in any case and the minute they see a woman sitting alone they begin to circle around her. I could not even eat a paan. One of those wretched fellows would cough, another would pass comments. And I, I was nearly fainting with fright, not to say such terrible hunger that only God could help me. The Delhi station, my dear, is so big that a fortress could not be bigger. The station stretched from here till there, till as far as the eye could go; all you can see are the railway tracks, engines and goods trains. What terrified me most were those jet black men who lived inside the engines.'

'Who lives in the engines?' someone asked.

'Who lives there? God knows... they wear blue clothes, some have beards, others are clean-shaven. They jump onto moving engines by holding the railings with one hand. Those who watch them jump on like that are terrified by the sight. And the sahebs and memsahebs, there are so many of them at the Delhi station that they cannot be counted. They walk about, hand in hand, speaking in their *git-pit* lingo. While our Indian brothers stare at them wide-eyed. It is a wonder that their eyes don't pop out! One of them said to me, "Show us your face." I immediately... '

'So, why didn't you show him your face?' someone teased.

'Allah-Allah, had I gone there to, show my face to these wretches?' And then, with a sudden change in her tone and tenor, 'Listen if you want to, and don't interrupt.' A sudden silence descended. After all, one didn't hear such delightful talk in Faridabad. Women came from far afield to hear Malika's tale.

'And the vendors... they aren't like the ones we have here. They are all dressed in clean khaki clothes, some wear white. But their dhotis in some cases were dirty. They carry baskets around, selling paan, bidi, cigarette, dahi bare, toys. Toys and sweets. They leap out from moving trains. When a train arrives there is such a din that you feel your ear-drums will burst. The coolies shout their heads off, the vendors scream in your ear, and the passengers fall over each other. And I, I poor thing, sat on top of my luggage in the middle of it all. I must have been bumped into and pushed around a thousand times. All the time, out of sheer nervousness, I was mumbling to myself: *jal tu, jalal tu, aai bala ko taal tu.*

'At long last, just as the train began to move, fights broke out between the passengers and the coolies. I will take one rupee. No, you will get only two annas. The squabbling lasted an hour and only then did the station empty itself. But it was never completely empty; the local goons loitered about.

'Two hours later he showed up, twirling his moustache without a care in the world, and said, "If you are hungry, I could get you some puris. Will you eat? I have eaten in a hotel." I said, "For heaven's sake, just take me back to my home. I have had enough of your wretched tour of Delhi. I wouldn't want to go to Heaven with you. What a trip this has turned out to be!" The train to Faridabad was ready to leave. He sat me down in it and sulked, "As you wish! If you don't wish to see the sights, don't!" '

A Daughter-in-Law for Asif Jahan

Asif Jahan's husband was a wealthy Deputy Collector and her only son, Nur-ul Islam, had been born after the death of several babies. He was everyone's favourite. There was no one who would not have happily given their daughter in marriage to him, but Asif Jahan had set her heart on getting Kubra's daughter for her son.

She was a woman who believed in doing what was right. She wanted to bring Kubra's daughter home, because Kubra was not only her husband's youngest sister but a sister-in-law as well, because she was married to Asif Jahan's brother. It was precisely because of such far-sightedness that Asif Jahan was much loved in her family. Had she fixed her son's marriage among her own people, her in-laws would have made faces, and had she done so among her in-laws, then her family would have been saddened. With Kubra's daughter, both her own family and her in-laws would be happy!

By the grace of God, Kubra Begum produced a child every year or so and by the age of twenty-five was the proud mother of five sons. Her luck was the talk of the entire family: may every girl have good fortune such as Kubra's, everyone agreed. Each time you saw her, she had a baby boy playing in her lap; after all, one wouldn't wish a daughter even on one's enemy.

Each time Kubra produced yet another boy, the world drew its breath with envy. If anyone was unhappy it was Asif Jahan. While she was happy at Kubra's good health, for giving birth is a little like dying, when yet another boy was born, Asif Jahan could not stop her tears.

'What can anyone do? It is my bad luck. I saw my Nur-ul Hasan's face after nine dead children, and now I can't see my dearest wish come true for him. Wherever you look, you see nothing but daughters, so many daughters that there aren't enough grooms to go around. But for my poor boy, Allah Miyan is not sending a bride.'

Kubra Begum had been lying in the last throes of her delivery for three whole days. The family midwife sat beside her. The house was filled with a gaggle of older women, sisters-in-law from both sides of the family as well as their children. There was such a din that you couldn't hear a thing. The house looked like it was getting ready for a bridal party. The women were arguing among themselves whether or not a lady doctor should be sent for. Labour pains came, wave upon wave, yet the baby showed no signs of popping out.

After all, women give birth all the time but no one had ever heard of such a prolonged labour. A sacrificial lamb was offered, grain was distributed among the poor as alms, amulets and talismans were brought – in short, everything that could be tried was attempted. Kubra Begum lay faint with pain and exhaustion. Asif Jahan spread out her prayer rug on the takht and busied herself in prayer: 'O Lord of all the World, have pity on Kubra's small children and free her from this pain. O Lord, hear me this time and send me my daughter-in-law. Five times I have been disappointed... hear my pleas this time,' Asif Jahan pleaded. Hope in God's mercy dripped from every pore on her face.

The sound of Kubra Begum's screams and whimpers reached Asif Jahan's ears. 'Hai, Apa... I won't live this time... Allah!

Have pity on me!... I'll die... I'll die...'

'Ai hai, don't say such things, Kubra.'

'Water... hai...'

'Gulshabbo... ari o, Gulshabbo... where are you, you wretch! Look, the bowl is lying empty...' someone screamed from inside.

A short while later, Kubra Begum's screams reached a new crescendo and the women's voices, accompanying the screams, grew louder. 'Good girl... give another push ... push harder... that's it...' and Kubra Begum let out such a horrifying scream that Asif Jahan froze in fright. The few seconds that passed thereafter seemed like years. And then the sound of a baby's crying could be heard; Asif Jahan let out a breath of relief and returned to complete her prayer thus: 'O my dear Lord, whether it is a girl or a boy depends on nothing but Your will. But I am thankful to You that You have saved Kubra's life...' And with these words she fell down in prostration. She had barely raised her forehead when a little servant girl came running out, 'It is a girl, Begum Saheb, it is a girl...'

With her head still bowed, Asif Jahan's face was wreathed in smiles. She raised her head, pulled out a purse from her bodice and placing a rupee on the servant girl's palm, walked towards the delivery room. Already there was a crowd of women inside. Every married woman in the family was present there. As soon as Asif Jahan entered, a woman said, 'The placenta is yet to fall.'

Kubra's cousin and sister-in-law sat at the head of the bed, and at the other end sat the midwife with her feet still planted on Kubra's thighs. The sister-in-law got up to stand among the crowd of women and gave her place on the bed to Asif Jahan.

'Poor Kubra was in such agony this time, but all because of your good fortune, it is a girl. Even though it nearly cost its mother her life,' Kubra's cousin said to Asif Jahan.

'God heard the prayers of all of you, for I had nearly lost

hope this time. Whatever happens, happens for the good. What would a Mem have done? She would have inserted all kinds of objects and instruments. The slightest delay and you people start asking for a Mem to be fetched. Did women not give birth when these wretched Mems were not around?' The midwife began to mutter loudly in a peeved tone.

'Ai hai, there is a limit to how late. It has been two nights and three days. She has been writhing in pain and you didn't know how long it would take. After all, have we not given birth to children? Don't we know how long it normally takes?' Kubra's sister, Aisha Begum, answered.

'All right, so now you have muttered enough; tell us when the placenta will come out.'

'Life and death are in the hands of God, Biwi. No one knows when the Time will come. The baby has been born; there is still life in the umbilical cord. Look, look... how it is quivering!' The midwife was holding the cord in her right hand that was loaded with grimy silver rings and bangles, and with the other hand she was mopping up the mess. Aisha Begum was pressing down hard on the pregnant lady's belly; she was known in the whole clan to be the best at holding the abdomen just so to let the afterbirth slither out.

'Dulhan, do you feel the pain coming?'

'No,' answered Kubra in a half-dead voice.

'There is very little quivering left in the cord,' said the midwife, holding it between her toe and left hand as she began to massage Kubra's belly with her right. By now Kubra was ashen with pain and fatigue.

'Ai hai, Masitan, don't cut the cord yet; the afterbirth hasn't come out,' said one of the women standing near the bed.

'Ai, Biwi, you are a mere child of yesterday. I am the one who brought you into this world; now you are teaching me what to do? Do you think my hair has turned white in the sun? By God, Badi Begum, these girls can drive the sanest of us crazy! Am I mad that I will cut the cord before the placenta has been expelled?'

Masitan kept tugging at the placenta and the women began to narrate their different experiences – what happened during their own pregnancies or during that of some woman in their neighbourhood, or about the midwife who comes to the house of their in-laws, or about a certain woman who died during childbirth and how the placenta remained stuck inside her.

'You remember what happened to the wife of Ashiq Husain,' asked one of the women. 'The placenta did not come out, evening fell and the midwife kept trying. Till finally, even she had to admit defeat and declare that the placenta was stuck inside; there was nothing more she could do. The poor thing had to be taken to the hospital where the Mems pulled it out. But, Bua, I have heard that the woman's liver too got pulled out. She died three days later, leaving behind three little mites...'

'A lady doctor had to come and pull out my sister-in-law's placenta; she was ill for a long time afterwards but at least she was saved.'

The midwife could not remain silent as the conversation veered towards Mems and lady doctors. Sounding annoyed, she said, 'No one should die young. Is this the time to be talking about such awful things? Do you have nothing to say except talk about Mems and lady doctors? Just look at them, Badi Begum...'

'She is right. Qaiser, talk of something else,' Badi Begum said.

'Yes, yes,' said the midwife sounding more peeved than ever. 'Aisha Bibi, press harder. The placenta is about to come out.'

Aisha Begum, who was already holding her sister's belly in a vice-like grip, half rose to her feet as she kneaded her fingers harder than ever. The pregnant lady yelped with pain, 'Apa, for the love of God, stop it! I will die at this rate...'

'We are nearly done; you are about to be free of it.'

The midwife inspected the placenta. 'See, Badi Begum, see for yourself. It is all there; don't say later that some of the afterbirth got left behind.' And so saying, she extended the placenta towards Asif Jahan and all the women present in the room took turns to examine it and offer their views and comments.

'Ai, Bibi, don't let go of her tummy just yet; she is bleeding heavily. Hold her tight,' said the midwife. And Aisha Begum clamped down with all her strength.

'I will cut the umbilical cord now. The bleeding will stop soon,' and the midwife once again held the umbilical cord between her toes and began to push down nimbly with her fingers. Then, picking up a sewing thread that had been lying beside the bed, she tied up the umbilical cord. Once again, looking around, she picked up a rusted knife from the floor and cleaned it. The haemorrhage showed no sign of letting up. Masitan got off the bed with a victorious air. She got to her feet and then, stretching her body, said, 'Ai hai, you move away, Badi Begum; you will not be able to lift her. Come and help, Sabira Bibi, you and Qaisar.'

Sabira and Qaisar slipped their arms under Kubra and, without paying any heed to her cries of protest, raised her about eight inches above her waist as Masitan began to wrap a six-yard long strip of cloth tightly around her lower abdomen. The bleeding had stopped somewhat. But by now Kubra was as white as a washed sheet and looked as fragile as a torn shred. The child was delivered, the placenta expelled, and if Allah were to show His mercy, her strength would return.

At long last, Asif Jahan turned towards the baby and, with one look at her face, remarked, 'She is dark of complexion.'

'Ai, this is hardly the time to talk of her complexion. Would I have abandoned her even if she was pitch black? Ai, Masitan, will you bathe the baby or not?'

Masitan bathed the baby, and despite Asif Jahan asking to hold the little girl, refused to hand her over. 'Bibi, she is the answer to many prayers. I will not give her to you like that; I will first take what is my due.'

'Ai, what is this new tradition that you have started? I have already put what is your due in the *kunda* in which you have thrown the placenta.'

Grinning widely, Masitan asked eagerly, 'In the name of Allah, how much...?'

'Five rupees... what else?'

'Badi Begum, I will never accept five rupees!'

'Have you gone mad, Masitan? People put one taka when a marriage has been fixed at birth in the *kunda* along with the afterbirth. Is this the time to be handing out gifts? Take what you want when the marriage takes place.'

'Yes, Bibi, you are right! I will be alive when she gets married, won't I? You ladies don't think twice before spending lakhs of rupees, but when it comes to giving what is one's due you always quibble and quote custom and tradition. The sweeper will get her due; Gulshabbo, the gardener's daughter will get hers, everyone will get something. I tell you, Bibi, I will not accept these five rupees.'

Masitan was the family midwife. She had been present at the birth of nearly everyone. She knew she could fight for her due. Asif Jahan opened her purse and threw another two rupees atop the placenta lying in the *kunda*. Masitan, who had been expecting five, was none too pleased with the two rupees. Nevertheless, she washed the money and tucked it away. All the women assembled in the room gave a little something to Masitan: someone gave fifty annas, someone a rupee. Masitan picked up the *kunda* and said to Kubra, 'Dulhan, I tell you, this daughter of yours has come after more prayers and pleas than any son. I swear, I will accept nothing less than gold bangles.'

'Ai wah, when did Kubra pray for a girl? You take whatever you want from Mumanijaan; she is the one who has been praying for a girl. We will give you what we have given at the birth of all other babies in this family,' Aisha Begum replied.

'Do you hear, Badi Begum?' Masitan appealed to Asif Jahan.

'Why don't you go now, go and wash up, eat a paan or two. You can think of nothing except "give-give",' Aisha Begum responded with some annoyance.

Aisha Begum was known to be sharp and quick. As soon as she settled her sister, she sent for the *domnis*, professionals who came to sing on festive occasions. The house that was already full of hustle and bustle began now to resound with the sound of drums and songs. Amid all the pranks and laughter, no one spared a thought for the sleep or comfort of the woman who had just delivered a baby.

All the women joked among themselves and teased Asif Jahan. The *domnis* sang a medley of songs: *zachchagiri, suhaag, gaaliyan*. They also enacted scenes from a delivery room by strutting about with their bellies sticking out. 'Ai ji, which month is this?' asked the one who was pretending to be the husband, while the other who was supposed to be the wife, answered, ' 'Seventh' or 'Eighth'. All the unmarried girl who had been rounded up and penned into a separate courtyard during childbirth, moved about freely now. Some young boys, too, sneaked into the zenana. The twelve-year old groom was among the cluster of boys, crouching at the back and listening and watching the goings-on when, suddenly, one of his older girl cousins chanced upon him. The girl pounced and caught hold of him. 'Look here, everyone, the groom is here!'

Peals of laughter rang out.

The groom tried to wriggle away and pleaded with his captor, 'Please, Baji, please... let me go.' And as he tried to escape towards the male quarters, his cousin called out loudly behind him, 'Ai, what kind of groom are you? Come inside, come and see what a moon-like bride you have!'

One of My Journeys

Shakuntala,

You girls have such a rotten sense of humour! You turned my watch back! What if I had missed the train?

I got so late leaving the college that by the time I reached the railway station, though the train was still standing at the platform, the guard was blowing the whistle again and again. Only I know how I managed to catch that train! I hitched up my sari and ran all the way from the overhead bridge. Believe me, if you had been with me, we would never have caught the train. You should have seen the railway staff – they were gaping at me with their mouths wide open. I looked neither left nor right but simply galloped as fast as I could. I was still some distance down the bridge when the train began its slow crawl away from the platform. I increased my speed and took two and three steps at a time. The guard was a sweet man; he looked at me, smiled but blew his whistle yet again.

I am sure I presented such an odd sight that whoever looked at me could not but help laughing. My hair was undone. You will say: What's new about that? Your hair is always all over the place! No, but seriously, yesterday I was in a real mess. All my pins had fallen out and my hair covered my face. I could barely see the stairs I was flying over. My sari was trailing behind.

My breath was sounding like the air whooshing out of an ironsmith's bellows. And I – all I could think was putting one foot before the other! There were only two more stairs left. In my hurry, as I tried to jump over those, me feet got entangled in my sari, I tripped and fell flat on my face!

People rushed to help me to my feet. But in a flash, I was up on my own. Panting, my face flushed a bright crimson, I pushed the hair away from my face, gulped a deep breath of air and screamed: 'Train!'

The guard was smiling. So was everyone else on that platform who had seen my ignominious fall. I could hear peals of laughter all around me. Why should I hold it against that poor guard if he too was laughing at me? Anyhow, he managed to control his laughter long enough to say: 'I have halted the train. (more laughter) Please hurry up; the train is already late by five minutes.'

I began to run again. This time, I managed to get into the first coach in front of me. It was a men's coupé. I sat there, looking out of the window, surrounded on all sides by smiles and laughter. When I got my breath back, I went to the washroom and straightened my hair. Then I returned to my seat and began to wait for the next station. When the train halted I got off, bought a ticket and went into the ladies' coupé.

The coupé was jam-packed. Being a third class compartment exclusively for women, it was packed with children and luggage. There wasn't even space to stand. I put my face in the window near the toilet and began to peer outside. Those of you who only travel first or second class cannot imagine the sort of smells that assailed me from my vantage point near the toilet. As I stood there with a handkerchief stuffed in my nose, a Hindu woman made a little space for me on her seat and said, 'Behenji, come and sit here.' I sat down next to her. There were four benches in the coupé. Hindu women and their children sat on two and Muslim women and their offspring occupied the other two. No doubt I had been asked to sit near the Hindu women because of the red bindi I sported on my forehead. I thanked the bindi for coming to my rescue, the red dot that so offended my grandmother and made her angry, not so much with me as with my parents!

'Behenji, the three of us are going to get off in another hour or so; you can sit properly, then.'

I thanked her and said, 'I will also be getting off in an hour.'

After a while she asked, 'Do you study?'

I said, 'Yes.'

'Are you married?'

'No.' My 'no' displeased her so much that she puckered her face and brows and turned to look the other way.

Another woman piped up, 'What is your caste?'

'Chamar!' I answered and laughed loudly.

I was so pleased with myself at having caught the train that I wanted to rock with laughter, shout and jump around with sheer joy. I was sitting there with some measure of restraint when their questions began to tickle me and I could not help but laugh out loud. But, the woman who had asked the question took offence.

'You are a chamar? Just because you are educated, do you think the rest are fools?'

The Muslim women who were sitting on their benches and chomping paan after paan, seemed just as illiterate. Moreover, they seemed to belong to one particular biradari. The Hindu women, though uneducated, looked as though they belonged to different castes such as bania, thakur and brahmin. But I have always found that, while travelling, everyone becomes a brahmin, and in all my travels I have never found anyone belonging to a caste lower than a thakur, at the very least!

A Muslim woman, wearing a tight black pajama, a pink dupatta and laden with silver jewellery, got up from her seat. Her nose-ring, worn as it was on her septum and not her nostril, was so large that it hid her paan-stained lips and teeth darkened with *missi*. I am sure that, once upon a time, some man, fed up with a talkative woman, must have invented the nose ring so that a woman's voice would remain trapped in her mouth. And women are such silly creatures that they turned this invention into tradition. No wonder then that every religion teaches that women have feeble minds.

Anyhow, listen! The Muslim woman picked up her *lota* and began to move towards the toilet. Hindu women quickly huddled away. One poor woman, who was sitting on her luggage, got onto her suitcase with her shoes on in her haste to get out of the way. The Muslim woman passed blithely on – her dupatta trailing behind her like a blanket of benevolence passing over the Hindu woman on the suitcase and another who sat beside her.

The two Hindu women squealed with rage and turned to the others: 'Did you see? Did you see how odd she is? She went past us with her clothes touching us.'

'How else could she go to the toilet? Why are you sitting in the way?' A middle-aged woman spoke up.

'Who has stopped anyone from going? But she could at least draw her dupatta tight around herself when she walks past us. Why must she touch us with her clothes?' my neighbour asked with a crackle in her voice. She was holding a Hindi newspaper in her hand.

'If you sit in the way this is bound to happen,' another Muslim woman spoke up with deliberate carelessness.

'If we don't 'sit in the way', where should we sit? On your head? Look at you, sitting there with your legs sprawled while we are so cramped. And, still, this bothers you! As though the train belongs to your father and you are the only ones who have bought tickets.' Turning around and gesturing with her hands, a Hindu woman spoke to the Muslim woman.

'Yes! The train belongs to our father. And we will sit with

our legs sprawled like this. Do what you can. And, one more thing, if you speak any more rubbish, it won't be good for you.' The middle-aged Muslim woman spat a stream of paan juice in the middle of the compartment and scolded the Hindu women.

'Won't be good for us? What will it be, then? Are you a Collector that you will have us tied to canons?' the Hindu woman retorted and, turning towards her own 'party', she asked me, 'Are you listening, Behenji? Ever since these Musalmaniyan have entered this compartment, they have been creating havoc.'

By now I had understood why these two 'camps' were sitting separately. A battle between Hindus and Muslims was raging inside this compartment. These women from poor households seldom got a chance to fight on the streets. Now, by a stroke of good fortune, they found themselves confined together in a third-class railway carriage; and so decided to make the most of this rare opportunity to vent spleen at each other.

I sat up and began to listen more carefully to what was going on around me. A young Muslim woman spoke loudly, obviously for the benefit of her Hindu audience: 'Ai Chachi, why are you bandying words with these low-born types? These people are not fit to be spoken to.'

'What did you say? Low-born? Mind your tongue, or are you bent on spilling blood?'

The woman who was sitting next to me spoke up haughtily, 'Do you know who I am? If you utter another word, I will have you witches taken off the train right now.'

The Muslim girls let out a raucous peal of laughter. 'Did you hear that? There sits the Latsaheb's wife!'

My neighbour pushed me aside and got up in a flurry of excitement. Just then the door of the toilet opened and the woman with the enormous nose ring came out. She was still standing by the door when the woman atop her suitcase called out, 'Look here, you, watch where your clothes go when you walk.'

'I will walk as I please,' she said as she sauntered back carelessly with her dupatta trailing behind her. Again, her dupatta touched the woman sitting atop her suitcase. Gritting her teeth, the woman with the luggage tugged the dupatta sharply so that the woman with the nose-ring fell down. Her *lota* tumbled away; most of the water inside it splashed on two Hindu women and drops fell on many more. All the Hindu women shouted in unison: 'Ram! Ram!' The woman who had pulled the dupatta let it go and began to examine her own dhoti for signs of pollution. Meanwhile,the woman with the nose-ring picked herself off the floor. The entire episode had happened so suddenly and quickly that her companions were still getting to their feet when she flung her dupatta aside and stood straight. Then, looking neither this way nor that, she planted a sharp blow on her enemy's bent head. 'Haramzadi! What do you think of yourself?'

A strange wave of frenzy and fury coursed through the compartment. Each woman glared at the women of the other party, eyes popping with rage. I bent my head to peer out of the window to see if a station was approaching, so that it might serve to distract these women. But this was an express train; it left behind all the small stations and had a long way to go before it came to a halt.

After being assaulted and drenched, was it possible for these women to remain silent? Those who were in wet clothes were willing to fight till death. Now, they fell upon the woman with the nose-ring with combined fury. Help came from the other side too. Four or five women grappled with each other in that cramped space. One grabbed a tuft of the other's hair while her own ear-ring was being yanked.

They fell on their luggage, got up quickly, only to fall down once again. As the Hindu women lunged for the nose-rings and ear loops, the Muslims yanked their braids. They dug their teeth into whatever piece of flesh they found on the enemies' bodies. And if they managed to land one punch, they followed it with a flurry of blows and kicks. In other words, kicking-scratching-biting-punching Furies were writhing over the luggage and the floor of the compartment.

The lady who sat next to me shifted her luggage to one side so that she too could get into the thick of the battle, but she couldn't find an inch of space to stand in. Maddened beyond control, she stooped and landed a couple of blows on an eight or ten year old Muslim girl. At this, a couple of Muslim women who had so far been content with indulging in verbal warfare, jumped into the fray and landed plumb into the enemy's territory. On this side too, Hindu women who had so far been on the fringes of the battle, got to their feet. The wrestling bouts, so far confined to one side, now began on both sides. I shrank further into my corner. My neighbour saw my faint-heartedness and invited me to join the fray with the following exhortation: 'Behenji, why are you sitting there and watching? Will you get beaten by these *malech* women?'

A middle-aged Muslim woman glowered at me with her terrifying eyes. I quickly averted my gaze and began to look out of the window to convince her that I had no desire to be a party to this slaughter and mayhem. I noticed that some children were cowering in a corner and taking in the scene with terrified eyes, and others were bawling at the top of their lungs. And the mothers... such was their enflamed communal frenzy that they were oblivious even to their offspring. The only thing missing here were cries of 'Allah-o-Akbar!' and 'Sri KrishanMaharaj ki Jai!' Instead, cries of 'Whore!', 'Slut!', 'Bitch!', and such other words rent the air. I cannot even write some of those words; you must imagine the rest.

An old Muslim woman who had so far been sitting in a corner and shaking her head came up with a new ploy. Perhaps her intentions were good; the outcome was disastrous. She opened her packet of food and began to shower pieces of meat and dollops of mince on the other party. The Hindu women paused for a minute then changed tack. One picked up the *lota* that had fallen on the floor and threw it out the window. The Muslim women lunged for the luggage of the Hindus and in the blink of an eye, each side was sticking on the other's luggage like glue. If one party was trying to prise it away, the other was hell bent upon saving it. This snatching and pulling of luggage assumed monstrous proportions. Already, a few small items had been flung and were lying somewhere in the fields yonder. By now I was scared that after they were done with the luggage they might start hurling the children.

A woman infuriated to the point of madness is worse than an enraged bull. And here, there were so many women, and all had reached a terrifying stage where they were beyond sorrow and joy. I sat there wondering what I could do to stop these women when my neighbour lost her wrestling bout and fell on top of me, and a middle-aged Muslim woman's punch landed blindly on top of my freshly-combed hair with such force that it knocked the wind out of me and darkness fell before my eyes. With one shove, I pushed the neighbour off my lap and stood up. I smacked them so hard with my right hand that both the neighbour and the middle-aged woman struck their heads in a mid-air collision, and I leapt to pull the chain.

Shakuntala, how I wish you had been there! I have seen lots of catfights, especially fights breaking out among women in trains over space or religion or children or littering... in fact, over all sorts of things. But I had never witnessed such a scuffle before. Someone was bleeding from her nose, another from her earlobes, someone's clothes were torn to shreds and a clump of hair was clenched in someone's fist. A poor woman's sari had come undone in the mêlée but she was supremely unaware of it as she grappled with the mob.

Look at me, getting carried away with my own lecture! How I wish you were there! You would have seen how Zubaida too can speak!

I got hold of the chain and screamed at the top of my voice: 'Will you stop fighting or not? Shall I pull the chain and call the police?'

The squabbling women paused, looked at me, saw my hand holding the chain, and came to their senses. Their hands loosened their grip on each other. I seized the moment and thundered: 'Just look at yourselves! Look, you are practically naked!' Immediately, the woman with the dishevelled sari pulled the cloth to cover herself; perhaps she had just realised that she had been nearly nude. 'Your ears are bleeding.' Immediately, several hands went up to their ears. 'Your kurta is torn to shreds. Tell me... are you women or animals?'

I had my hand on the chain all the while. But I sensed that if I stopped speaking even for a moment they might get back at each others' throats. So I went on babbling. I said all sorts of things. And now, I can barely speak. I turned to look at my neighbour and said, 'Do you think this is a wrestling pit that you must display your tricks and throws? You may be the Station Master's wife and possibly you have studied at some kanya pathshala, but aren't you ashamed of yourself? You hit an innocent little girl.'

The woman had barely opened her mouth to answer when I launched forth again, 'Quiet! If you have an ounce of shame, you should drown in it!'

Then I turned towards the old woman and, clenching my teeth, hissed at her, 'Badi Bi, if you were not old enough to be my mother, I would have throttled you with my own hands. People like you should be buried alive. What did you mean by flinging the meat about like that? Is it the festival of Holi that you are throwing colours around?'

The old biddy turned her puckered mouth and wrinkled eyes towards another woman and asked, 'What is she saying?'

Incensed, I shouted, 'You wretched deaf old hag! Must you think of jihad in your old age?'

The scene was worth viewing. Every woman sat stock still, her hair all over the place. I had the upper hand. Every eye was turned in my direction and I, I was trumpeting like an enraged elephant. 'You... Why did you pull the dupatta of that woman who walked past you? So what if it touched you? Are you an untouchable? You fancy yourself as Gandhi's disciple if you start wearing a khaddar sari?'

Suddenly, I realised I was talking like these women. All sorts of words and expressions were tumbling from my tongue. I was amazed at how articulate I was.

'Why must you walk like this? Does the train belong to you? If there are others present here who don't want to be touched by you, why must you touch them? What is the meaning of this forcible intrusion on others?'

Bit by bit, my anger was lessening and the women too were finding their wits again. This time, I tried a new trick.

'Let the next station come... I am going to lodge a police report. It will serve you right when you are caught and put in chains.'

One woman gathered enough courage to say, 'Let it be, Miss-sahebji. After all, fights do break out between people. Don't report us to the police or there will be no end of trouble.'

'I *will* tell the police. You are welcome to fight amongst yourselves, but why did you fall on top of *me*? Why did you pull *my* hair? I am not going to let you go so easily.'

'Miss-saheb, the honour of our daughters and daughters-in law is in your hands. They have been wrong; let them be now,' the middle-aged Muslim woman began to speak ingratiatingly.

'Why should I let them go? All this is your doing. You are the one who has been inciting these girls all this while. Had you scolded them even once, things would not have reached such a pass. You silly, foul-minded, quarrelsome woman! You pulled my hair! I am not going to let you go so easily.'

My Hindu neighbour let out a loud laugh when she heard

me and bent to say something to a woman sitting nearby when I burst in, 'Do you think you are any better? You are the one who dragged me into your fight. When I refused to get up and join your forces, you fell down on me deliberately, just so I would be forced to become a part of you. You too have been inciting the Hindus for all this while. If you are so fond of being a leader, go to the bazar and show your leadership there. I can see it written on your forehead. Must you get into a brawl the moment you spot a Musalman? You may be the Station Master's wife or anybody else. I will make sure I include your name in my complaint to the police.'

All this while, as I had been standing, every now and then I would clutch my head and let out moans of pain. Now I sat down. The Hindu and Muslim camps broke up in disarray. The women looked only at me. Some of them stared at me mutely, some tried to speak fawning words in honeyed tones. They were trying to convince me not to tell the police and to calm down. Finally, I decided that the middle-aged Muslim woman, my Hindu neighbour, the woman with the nose-ring and the Hindu girl who had been splattered with water should apologise to each other and promise not to repeat their actions. And, yes, the old Muslim woman must stand up and apologise to the Hindus with folded hands. The middle-aged woman lived in a village and, in her entire life, had possibly never apologised to anyone for anything. She didn't know what to do. When she continued to sit without uttering a word, I threatened her: 'All right, as you wish. Don't apologise. You know very well what I plan to do. What is the point of telling you again and again?'

She looked at her Muslim sisters in an attempt to shore up her flailing courage. But the scene had changed. Their wounds and cuts forgotten, they were eagerly taking in this new development. And I, I was as unsmiling and resolute as Death. A few girls nodded their heads in encouragement. The middle-aged woman stood up. Like a child who has forgotten his lesson

stands up sheepishly and then sits down fearfully on his seat in
the classroom, she too looked around helplessly and then sat
down. I turned to look at her. She shot up from her seat with
great alacrity and said: 'Forgive me, forgive me, forgive me.'
    I said, 'Wait! Have all of you forgiven her?'
    There was a chorus of 'Yes! Yes!' from all sides.
    I turned to my neighbour, 'Shrimatiji, it is your turn now.'
    'Why? Are you the gor-na-ment?' she tried, once again, to
raise the banner of revolt.
    'It is a great pity that I am not the government. Clearly, you
are not ashamed of your behaviour. Anyhow, when I lodge my
complaint against you, I will also mention your husband who
works for the railways. I am sure the police will take good care
of him after my report.'
    She seemed to waver at the mention of her husband's name.
When a Hindu woman piped up, 'Behenji, stand up, won't you?'
she shot to her feet. In a half-dead voice she said, 'Sisters,
please forgive me for my wrongs!' and sat down quickly.
    Now my gaze fell on the woman with the nose-pin. Her
nose was bleeding and she was already on her feet. She extended
her hand and said, 'Sister, it is a two-minute journey; what is
the use of these fights and riots? If my dupatta is untouchable,
you are not likely to touch my hand. Anyhow, please forgive
me. It was my fault.'
    And then something strange happened; something that I could
never have imagined! The Hindu woman, who was dressed in
a coarse khaddar sari, embraced the Muslim woman with the
nose-ring and began to cry.
    Women are strange creatures! One moment they are
something, and the next moment something else! A short while
ago they were fighting because the dupatta of one had touched
the other; now they were clinging to each other and weeping.
    The station was approaching. They began to collect their
luggage which had scattered during their fight. But these two

girls hung around each other's neck and kept crying. And I was so engrossed by the sight of them that I forgot all about the old hag.

Look at me! I had sat down to write a letter to you and I ended up describing the whole train incident. Anyhow, I will tell you whatever I had to say when I meet you. I had a lot to write, but this will have to do for now. I think of the College all the time, especially the basketball match. Do write soon and tell me what I can bring for all of you from here.

Yours,
Zubaida

Mute

Siddiqa Begum's marriage was proving to be a very difficult one to arrange. She was a true blue Saiyyedani. Her father, Hamid Hasan, was reasonably well placed. What is more, she herself was one among thousands when it came to beauty. Yet, Siddiqa Begum was still not married and already twenty-three years old. Her mother, Ahmadi Begum, could not sleep at night worrying about her. Siddiqa Begum was the youngest of her siblings. Two elder sisters were married and had faced no problems in finding grooms. The elder sister had been seventeen when she was married and the middle one barely fourteen. Siddiqa Begum was twelve years younger than the middle sister, so her childhood was spent as if she was the only girl in the family.

By the time Siddiqa Begum came of age, there were no suitable boys among the immediate relations, and the few who were of marriageable age were so poor that they could not be considered. One or two who were reasonably well off did not have a good character and those who were educated wanted to marry outside the family!

The proposals that came from outside the family were no good; either the boy was not of pure Saiyyed stock from both sides or the groom was too old or already married with children.

The few who passed the test had conditions of their own. Some would insist on first seeing the girl before making a formal proposal. In some cases, matters did not progress due to Siddiqa Begum's lack of education. In short, there was something or the other wrong in each case. Everywhere you looked, you saw boys and girls getting married; yet Siddiqa Begum remained unmarried.

A new wave is said to be coursing through every nook and corner of Delhi; yet you will still find homes where no storms brew and no earthquakes tremor. The same age-old traditions, the same men's quarters in the outer part of the house where a crowd assembles each evening and the same confines of the women's seclusion. School education for girls was not possible in a home such as Hamid Hasan's; even boys in his family were given only religious instruction. Hamid Hasan's eldest son first memorised the entire Holy Quran, then learnt Persian and when he was a little older, went to the seminary at Deoband for training to becoming an *alim*, a learned man. He returned and took responsibility of the entire household as well as the property. He had married into a good and wealthy family, and with the grace of God, fathered four children. Hamid Hasan was a well-respected man; his family was ranked among the highest. Yet his daughter, SiddiqaBegum remained unmarried so far.

Hamid Hasan vigorously opposed the education of girls. Siddiqa Begum had read the Holy Quran and one or two religious tracts. Anything more was anathema for her father. As someone who was ready to lay down his life for his ancestors, he followed traditions with as much devotion as a Deputy Commissioner might to obey the orders of a Khan Bahadur. Where the bounds of religion ended and tradition began – he never bothered to investigate this grey area, nor did he ever wish to. The standard of *sharafat*, or civilised behaviour that his ancestors had set, was the bar against which he measured everything. He kept himself totally aloof from the new ideas that were bubbling around; his world comprised of a few like-minded friends who met, smoked their huqqa spoke of the good ol' days and shed a tear or two over the wickedness of the present time.

Hamid Hasan was a lucky man. He had a wife who shared his beliefs. She was a living, walking, talking embodiment of the Delhi of 1857. She would not allow a lad nine years old to enter the zenana; in fact, not all women were allowed entry either. She thought it was a bad practice to socialise and go to the homes of all sorts of people.

She fought with her brother because she believed girls should not even be tutored at home, and broke off the engagement of her son with her niece because she was against girls being taught English; after all, one wanted to bring home a daughter-in-law, not a Memsaheb!

So intractable were her beliefs and such was her pride that for fifteen years she refused to meet her only brother. No wonder then that Ahmadi Begum had raised Siddiqa Begum in an inviolate bower. Some of their closest relatives had not even seen the girl's face. Siddiqa Begum was made to observe parda from even the ladies among her acquaintance. She insisted that Siddiqa Begum live in exactly the same way as she had done in her youth: as an unmarried girl she had to plait her hair without a parting; forget using ittar, she was forbidden to even touch flowers. Every possible attempt was made to make sure she remained a child and an unknowing one at that. Siddiqa Begum was not allowed to make friends, meet people, or even go out. Her days were spent in listlessness. She might occasionally take up some sewing; that was her sole occupation. She had sisters, but they were so much older and both were married in distant Hyderabad. There was a niece, younger than her, but already married and therefore free to sit with the older women. How she envied them their freedom, how she chafed at the bars of her cage. Siddiqa Begum prayed, 'Ai Khuda, cut my bonds and set me free.'

Occasionally, when Razia Begum, a distant aunt, visited them she would be more frightened than ever. 'What if I meet the same fate?' Siddiqa Begum shuddered at the thought. Razia Begum was unmarried at sixty. Despite her age, she had a strange awkwardness. Girls and newly-married young women gossiped and giggled at the sight of her. Razia Begum appeared to be aware of her singular lack of fortune and avoided going out much.When she did, she made every effort to look for the most inconspicuous spot where she could remained unnoticed.

At other times, Siddiqa Begum would think of another aunt, Zakia Khatoon, widowed within a month of her marriage. She moved about fearlessly and said whatever she wanted to.. She was unfortunate, yes,but every time Siddiqa Begum compared the two, she much preferred the life of her widowed aunt to that of the unmarried one.

Whenever she heard her parents whispering among themselves or overheard a snatch of conversation between her mother and sister-in-law, Siddiqa Begum sensed something was in the air. Whenever these whispered conversations ceased, she concluded that the proposal had been rejected. How she raged against her mother at such times! Her unwed aunt's sad and apologetic face swam before her eyes and she would ask herself why, oh why, must her mother place so many conditions for her marriage? There would be a dispute over the dowry money; sometimes over the amount to be spent on the entertaining. Sometimes the groom's parents had a flaw; sometimes an impurity would be found in his grandmother's lineage. But who could Siddiqa Begum share her feelings with? The mother was, after all, a mother and not a friend. She was mortally terrified of her father. She was distant and fearful of the brother and the brother's wife was an outsider. The maids who worked in the family were old family retainers going back to a hoary past. Who could she confide in? Or speak to? What was she to do?

Once again, Siddiqa Begum found herself standing with her ear to the door of her room, craning to hear the conversation between her mother and SughraBegum.

Sughra Begum was a widow from an impoverished but genteel family. Helpless in the face of her poverty, she had gradually adopted the vocation of fixing marriages. Because she came from a sharif family, she had the freedom to go from one respectable household to another which, no doubt, helped in arranging marriages.

Siddiqa Begum's fury mounted as she heard her mother. Ahmadi Begum was speaking in a peeved voice, 'Ui, Bibi, this must be some new-fangled custom that people should go around inspecting brides! We don't follow such practice. I wasn't married without anyone coming to 'see' me and, may God help me, so weren't my two daughters. Neither did I inspect my daughter-in-law before bringing her to my house. Have the sharif families disappeared from this country? Go and ask the boy's mother if she has washed off all traces of respectability and shame? She can parade her daughters all she wants, strike deals and bargains. Our daughter may be pock-marked and squint-eyed but she is still the daughter of Hamid Hasan and the grand-daughter of Amjad Husain. Our family has lived in this city for fourteen generations. We are not some lowly sort that people have to first find out about us. Where can they find a girl from a family such as ours? It is only the fortunate few who can cross the threshold of our home. We are proud of our name... yes, yes, I know everything. I can see the boy for what he is... He is the only son. He gets four hundred rupees as rent. He earns another two hundred fifty as salary. He comes from a good family, he is respectable.... I can see all that but why should I agree to their first coming here to see the girl before making a proposal. Supposing the women of his family

come here to see her and say we don't like her... what then?
Nothing will happen to them; they are the boy's side. But I will
not be able to show my face anywhere. I am willing to let my
daughter stay unwed all her life but I cannot agree to this
bargaining.'

'Ai hai, Begum, you don't want to listen...'

'What is there to listen to?' Ahmadi Begum interrupted. 'I
cannot be as shameless as Afsar Jahan. She is related to me
but the less said about her ways the better. I believe she
'showed' her middle daughter at least four or five times before
her marriage was fixed. No, Bua, I cannot do this. I will not
show her to the boy's mother or his sisters.'

A maidservant appeared and announced that passengers had
come in a palanquin and the bearers were asking for pardas to
be put up. She hurriedly plucked a couple of sheets off the
beds and moved towards the outer part of the house.
Meanwhile, Ahmadi Begum too straightened herself, and said
to Sughra, 'Have I turned my hair white in the sun?'

Four women crossed the courtyard and came towards them:
the two middle-aged ones, who appeared to be sisters, were
accompanied by two younger ones. They embraced each other
and sat down on the *farsh*. One of them spoke up as she was
still settling down, 'Why didn't you come for the *milad* on
Friday?'

'My grandson was feeling poorly and the Mughlaniji who
looks after him has not been coming. She has been gone for
over a month, supposedly to wed her nephew and there has
been no sight of her since. Siddiqa too has been a bit under
the weather; she has a headache and has been lying down... Ai
Hashmat, why are you becoming thinner by the day? You have
just got married... this is the time to be happy.'

'Well, Sughra Apa, what brings you here? Have you brought
a match for Siddiqa?' asked Hashmat's elder sister, Mussarrat.

'Ai, Bibi, a house that has a ber tree will attract pebbles,'
Sughra Begum answered with alacrity.

'So, Khala jaan, what have you decided? We have been longing for Siddiqa's marriage,' Mussarrat said.

'Marriage is no joke, especially these days. For one thing, none of the old families are what they were; everywhere there is some flaw and impurity. No, Bua, I am not speaking of any one in particular. In this city of Delhi, a new illness is going around: that of showing daughters. After all, we also got married. Now people are saying – even Sughra Bua agrees – that there is no harm in showing your girl to prospective in-laws. Harm? I ask you! Have we been holding on to our centuries-old respectability for this day? These days, there is no regard for family or tradition. All people seem to want is money and this new-fangled git-pit lingo. After all, my sister agreed to show Hashmat; but is Hashmat any happier for it?'

'What is wrong with Hashmat's husband? If she is not happy, it is her fault. What is she lacking in? She has a husband who loves her, cares for her and is wealthy too; what else does she want? She tells me not to talk about her. She says I have done what I had to do. She says I don't know what it means to live as a second wife. Her husband says he doesnot even want to look at his first wife; it is Hashmat who feels bad for the poor thing. Have you heard, Bua, of something so strange?' said Mussarrat's mother.

'Amma, why must you talk about me where ever we go? Khala jaan, tell us about Siddiqa's proposal.'

'Nothing has been fixed yet. Whenever a suitable boy comes along, this business of seeing and showing crops up. What is worse, they say they will first see and only then make a formal proposal.'

'Ai, Bua, you are pointing a finger at me for showing Hashmat. At least, I only showed her discreetly to the women from the boy's side; what about those who show their girls to the men?'

'Ai, Bua, who are these people?' Ahmadi Begum asked with horror.

'Who are these people? Don't you know Safdar Jahan? She even showed her daughter to the prospective groom. She got him to peep from the door in front of her.'

'Really? Really?' and with this Ahmedi Begum pounded a fist on her chest and swayed, 'And did the earth not split wide open to swallow her? I could never do such a thing; I would rather buy two-paisa worth of arsenic and give it to Siddiqa to put her to sleep for ever... Ai, did they make them sit face to face? Is there no end to shamelessness? Making a girl sit in a room and getting the boy to peer at her through the doorway! It is a good thing the boy agreed to the match; if he hadn't agreed, would they have got people to peer at her twice, thrice? My hair stands on end when I hear such things. Tauba, Tauba!'

'Ai hai, Begum, which world do you live in? Show me a home where girls are not being shown? Safdar Jahan only did what thousands of others are doing. The methods that are being adopted these days to fix marriages are enough to drive you round the bend. The proposal for Mahmud Khan's son was sent to a certain family. But the son was adamant that he would not marry the girl without seeing her first. The girl's family didn't think it was appropriate to call him home, so they took the girl out to one of these new English-style shops to show her to the boy,' Sughra narrated.

'And that silly wretch promptly showed her face?' Ahmedi Begum retorted with some displeasure. 'Yes, Bua, after all, why not? When the mother did not feel any shame in taking her daughter to a shop to show her, the daughter is after all educated. If that is so, Bua, then what is wrong with the Mems? They go around hand in hand with men. If God shows His infinite mercy, the same will happen here.'

'Ai, have you heard of the shameful manner in which they fixed the marriage of their middle daughter?'

'I wouldn't be surprised by anything they do. Sending their unmarried girls far from home to study in schools like boys...

letting them ride about on bicycles. Could such a girl have lasted in my home? That is why I chose to break all ties with my brother. But, tell me, how did the wedding go?'

'Everything happened according to the girl's wishes. She declared that she would marry only that boy. The mother and father were happy. I have heard that the boy used to visit their home; the marriage took place a whole year after it was fixed.'

'Bua, if someone were to ask me, I would say that's the way it should be,' Hashmat said with a long sigh.

'By parading the girl around? Have they no shame? Don't ever talk like this in front of my Siddiqa. No wonder, I don't want her to talk to married women. ... And, Bua, when I hear such stories, I feel a pain in my heart. How my poor father's spirit must be suffering at the sight of his grand-daughter's misdeeds! I knew what my sister-in-law would be up to from the early days. It has been sixteen years now and I haven't seen their faces and may God never show me their faces as long as I live! How I control myself when I hear of their lowly antics. If my father had been alive, would these people have had the courage to behave in this fashion? I believe now my nieces have taken to going about with their faces uncovered. How can one blame the offspring? They will do as they have been raised... Look at my children... They will not dare to even let out a squeak in front of their father. And Siddiqa... she sits where she is made to sit, she eats what she is given to eat.'

Ahmedi Begum made paan for everyone and, kept the conversation going, 'Nowadays, I see people being in such a hurry to get rid of their daughters, as though they are getting rid of the garbage in their house. In our time, parents would make the boy's family plead for years before they agreed to give the girl in marriage. And, Bua, now, apart from giving the daughter, there is the new custom of promising to give money too.'

'Yes, sister, you are right. The widow of Hafiz Jalaluddin

has come to stay near our house. She has seen at least twenty
girls and in each one of them she has found some fault or the
other.'

'Which Hafiz Jalaluddin?' asked Siddiqa's mother in some
alarm.

'They are Saiyyeds. The family is good, too. The boy isn't
bad either. But the mother is something else. And our Sughra
Apa here has shown them about six or seven girls already.'

'Ui, Bua Sughra! And you got their proposal to my house?
You have a nerve!' Siddiqa Begum's mother expostulated,
displaying a mixture of anger and disbelief.

'Ai hai, Begum, you believe everything...'

And Siddiqa Begum, who had been listening to each and
every word with her ear pressed to the door, heard her mother's
tone of voice and understood everything. She got up and flung
herself on her bed and began crying piteously.

Sale

Memory is a strange thing! It troubles you at the oddest of times. Whenever I take that road, old conversations, faces, the same old memories come alive. All of us had gone for that drive. Prakash's car is like Prakash. You can tease him, pull his leg but he will never go beyond a limit he has set for himself. Perhaps he was once in love with someone. He looks like he can smoulder. But why should I bother? He is not going to come alive for me, nor am I interested in fanning his hidden fire to life. But, really, sometimes he makes me so mad! And I want to get to him. I want to get under his skin and see for myself if there is anything else there apart from ice and flint.

Anyhow... five of us had decided to meet that night and go for a drive. We were young and happy. There were four women and Prakash. Despite our fun and laughter, none of us was actually all there. In that beautiful, dark, star-spangled night – the sort of night that can drive you wild – each one of us had sent our real selves far, far away. I could be wrong. But I was certainly not there. Perhaps the air, water, silence and beauty of that dark night had awakened the others in much the same way as it had brought me to life.

As we reached the river bank, we sat on the small bridge across the river and began to chatter. I lay back in the car. I was not feeling too well in any case; and this place, the sound of the water, the bridge – all of it had another significance for me. It was a night like this, dark and glittering with stars; the same sound of water, and the same place but with just the two of us – him and me.

We were both on that pleasurable but dangerous path of love where even the smallest impediment appears like a mountain, nay an ocean, a joyous obstacle to cross. Aah! How beautiful, delicate and how close to nature that time is! One completely loses control the moment one sets eyes on the other person. Bodily proximity creates a sensation like a flash of lightning, a quicksilver madness, a heat that courses through and causes a state when one has lost all control over one's self. No one exists in the whole wide world except him and me.

Fishermen were busy casting their nets. I ran down to them, and began to lend a hand in their work. A young and beautiful woman, even if she has driven up in a big car on such a beautiful night, will make some impression on the fishermen.

They forgot their work and let me play with the nets.

He, too, got off the car and came down to the river bank.

'Why did you come down here?' he asked accusingly.

'Why not? What was there to do up there?' I teased. Right there, in front of everyone, he scooped me up in his arms and began to caress me.

'I was up there... what else? Come, let's go back. Why are you wasting time here?'

'For heaven's sake, leave me alone.' I spoke angrily and tried to wriggle out of his lap.

Those eyes, that face, it came closer and closer still. Warm, quick breaths inflamed my face. I tilted my face. My eyes were fixed on his eyes. My resisting body grew limp in his.

'Are you embarrassed to be seen with me? I don't care about the world; let them see us. I can take you from this end of the world to the other.' And, slowly, he put me down.

Was I embarrassed? I too hardly cared. Forget the fishermen, if the entire world had gathered there to watch us, I would have been proud of my love; not ashamed of it.

Again, the same night, the same face bent with passion and love, was ablaze before my eyes. But this time that woman was not me. There is movement even in love as there is in life; it is not a dead thing that can be buried in one place. When it changes its place during its dance, it becomes stronger, more intense, more beautiful than before. Yes, it leaves memories in its place which, with the passage of time, creates restlessness and pain. But what is a life without that?

I was miles away from myself that night. I was making mental paintings, and destroying them when a motorcar came and stopped near me. At first I was scared. I was alone and I didn't know who might be in the car. But I was reassured when I saw a woman. I ducked and lay down out of sight. Our car was parked in such a way that I could see them but they could not see me. A man I knew by sight and whose young wife and little children I knew was standing in the patch of light between the two cars; he was dishevelled, drunk and too far gone for any civilised behaviour. He was frantically waving with one upturned hand and with the other compulsively rubbing himself.

'Someone please turn off this light! Hey, what is this?' His voice was hoarse.

The doors of the cars opened. Three burqa-clad women came out.

'Darling, take off your burqa here. Who is there to see you?' One of the five or six men in their party spoke up.

'So, my lovely, will you give me a kiss?' That harsh sound reached my ears after some time.

'Why not? I will give it if you take it!' answered one of the burqa-clad women, her voice sounding completely dead and insensitive.

There were three women and five or six men. Obviously, someone would have to wait. Two of the men were possibly richer and more important than the others, because two women were handed over to them without the slightest ado. And those two couples disappeared into the bushes.

Now one woman remained, and three men. They began to argue; wrangling broke out over who would go first, who last.

'Yaar, I'll go first; I'd told you so earlier.'

'Masha Allah, and why ever not? Why will you go first? So that you have a great time while all my enthusiasm is deflated?'

Another one spoke up angrily, 'Why didn't the fourth lady show up?'

'All right! Let's draw lots.' This time the gentleman's voice had anger as well as anxiety.

'And hurry up; how long can one hold out?'

In the dark, the three men seemed to be swaying constantly. One woman and three men and all three were so keyed up and over-wrought it was hard for them to reach a decision. Their voices were quivering with lust, their bodies twitched uncontrollably.

The woman was quiet. In the bazaar when three or four dogs chase a bitch with such passion and restlessness, even the poor bitch hides her face and runs away from so many impetuous customers. But the woman – who had been reduced to a state, worse than the bitch in the bazaar, by wealthy men and their respectable wives – simply stood by the door of the open door of the motor car.

'All right, dearie, so you tell us who should go with you first?'

She laughed loudly. 'Arre, any one of you can come; all you bastards are the same for me.' And so saying, she ran towards the bridge and one of the men ran after her.

A few minutes later, a strong beam of a torch flashed. My friends were trying to go down to the river. Those few seconds of strong light revealed two naked bodies. As soon as the torch lit the darkness, the man – scared of being recognised and uncaring of his naked body – hid his face in the woman's burqa.

Evidently, it is not a sin to commit a sin; it is a sin to get caught.

Suddenly, peal after peal of the girl's dead laughter rent the air. She was laughing at the dogs.

I did not go to that spot by the river again.

Man and Woman

Woman: Arre, you have come again?

Man: Yes.

Woman: But weren't you to be married yesterday?

Man: Yes.

Woman: Then?

Man: Then what?

Woman: I mean, where is your bride?

Man: You really want my life to be ruined.

Woman: But when did I say anything of the sort?

Man: Then what do you mean by troubling me so?

Woman: Meaning?

Man: Why do you pretend? You know exactly what I mean.

Woman: I see. But I have been ready to marry you for over a year; you are the one who declines.

Man: Oh, you mean you are ready to get married? But what about your job?

Woman: That will remain, too.

Man: But I cannot accept that my wife should go about working for others. And instead of looking after the house or her children, she should charge off every morning.

Woman: Won't you also leave for work every morning? Am I supposed to sit at home all day and swat flies?

Man: There are always enough chores to do in the house, such as housekeeping, etc.

Woman: Right... so while you go to your office I should spend the day peering into every corner of our home.

Man: I didn't say that but surely there is enough to do in the house.

Woman: Such as?

Man: You know, looking after the house... After all, our mothers did that, didn't they?

Woman: You mean I should keep the hearth going?

Man: I didn't say that.

Woman: Then what do you mean by looking after the house?

Man: Look here, I don't know. You have made it a habit to pull my leg whenever I come to meet you.

Woman: All right, if you don't like the sound of my voice, I will stay quiet then... Tell me, are you really getting married or did you say that just to impress me?

Man: I will get married one day; after all, your highness is not the only woman in the world. Tell me, why are you so worried about me?

Woman: Because I love you very dearly.

Man: Well said! If you really loved me, would you have been so adamant for a year and would you have argued with me?... 'I won't leave my job'... After all, what is so special about your precious job? It isn't as though you are earning a thousand rupees. All you earn is a hundred rupees, no more.

Woman: Maybe, but these few rupees hold the key to my independence.

Man: You mean your independence lies in a mere hundred rupees?

Woman: Hundred, two hundred... that's not the point. The real test of independence is the ability to stand on your own two feet.

Man: You don't have the slightest faith in me. You think I will give you no money.

Woman: Not at all, but I wouldn't have earned that money by my hard work.

Man: How does it make a difference who earns it – a man or a woman.

Woman: Oh, of course it makes a big difference. You must have heard that old folk song: the male sparrow bought a grain of rice, the female bought a grain of daal and together they made khichdi.

Man: I don't want your grain of daal.

Woman: I won't be able to eat plain rice.

Man: Indeed, you will want chutney, papad, pickles.

Woman: Indeed, I will.

Man: Whenever I see you, you are surrounded by a flock of admirers – like moths to a flame.

Woman: Obviously, you will not let them enter the house.

Man: Never.

Woman: But you know they are my friends.

Man: Yes, indeed, very dear friends.

Woman: Does that mean they will not be able to come and meet me?

Man: I hate them intensely.

Woman: Can I ask why?

Man: Each one has his or her own temperament.

Woman: So why don't you make sure I sit in parda?

Man: I wish I could do that, but will you agree?

Woman: There are many other things that I wouldn't agree to either.

Man: Anyhow, you may or may not agree to other things, but I will not be able tolerate the flock of your admirers.

Woman: So, who will be permitted visit our home?

Man: Only common friends, that is, those who are common to both of us.

Woman: Hmm. Mr and Mrs Sethi and Mr Safdar.

Man: Why? Why can't they come?

Woman: Because I can't stand them.

Man: But why? Why do you dislike them?

Woman: I just do.

Man: Surely there has to be a reason

Woman: Each one has his or her own temperament.

Man: You talk like a child.

Woman: And you?

Man: I always talk sensibly and rationally.

Woman: Yes, of course you do. According to your argument, you hate my friends so they cannot enter our house but if I hate your friends... too bad! They will come and go without restraint.

Man: All right, Bibi Saheba, you work from morning to evening and when I come home tired after a long day and want to enjoy a moment with you, you find that your wife returned home with a drove of friends. So this is the map of married life you have in mind?

Woman: Can I ask what sort of map you have in mind of our life after marriage? In the morning when you are setting out for work, your wife should get you ready – all dressed up like a doll! Then, after you have gone, she should stay home – turning the beads of a rosary, taking your name and do the housework. This life of forced imprisonment is called 'looking after the house'. And, then, when you return home, tired and irritable, your wife should please you and later fawn over Safdar sahib and Mrs Sethi.

Man: I didn't say anything of the sort.

Woman: Then what did you say?

Man: All I meant was that you should stay home like all the other women and look after the house...

Woman: Again, 'look after the house'?

Man: Yes, look after the house.

Woman: I cannot quit my work and sell my freedom.

Man: Your freedom?

Woman: Yes, my freedom.

Man: Indeed! While you draw deep gulps of your freedom, your children will suffer.

Woman: It is not as though the children will be born immediately after marriage.

Man: Well, they will be born some day; unless, of course, you even object to their birth.

Woman: No, I have no such objection.

Man: Will you quit your job when the children are born?

Woman: No, not even then.

Man: Can I ask you, then, who will look after the children?

Woman: You and I, together.

Man: A woman's first duty is towards her children.

Woman: And a man's first duty is to be deserving of children.

Man: What do you mean?

Woman: I mean a woman is always being ordered to raise children, but who do the children belong to?

Man: The father.

Woman: Then why should I raise them? He should raise them who owns them.

Man: You say the strangest of things!

Woman: What's so strange about this?

Man: What isn't strange about this? Now you are refusing to even raise children.

Woman: I may or may not refuse to do so; you clearly are refusing to do it.

Man: My job is not to raise children; my job is to earn money.

Woman: I will earn money, too.

Man: Hmm... Such pride over a measly hundred rupees! God alone knows the havoc you would have created had you earned more.

Woman: All right, for the sake of argument, imagine that your salary is a hundred rupees and mine is eight hundred. In that case, who should leave the job? You or me?

Man: You.

Woman: Why?

Man: Because I am a man.

Woman: You mean you consider yourself superior, no matter what the situation?

Man: I am not the only one who thinks so; the universe has created me superior.

Woman: I don't think you are better than me. You should get married to a woman who worships you day and night.

Man: Yes, I will. After all, you are not the only woman in the world.

Woman: Then, go your own way. Why do you come here every day and bother me?

Man (after a moment's silence): You claim to set much store by love.

Woman: So do you.

Man (after another silence): So, tell me, when will you marry me?

Woman: Whenever you say, but I won't leave my job.

Iftari

'Those who have kept the roza may help others open their roza! May you be blessed by Allah!' the voice could be heard from the deorhi. The Begum Saheba of the Deputy Saheb was short tempered at the best of times. 'God knows where they are all day long. They appear from nowhere at this time and don't let one open one's fast in peace.'

'May you be blessed by Allah!' the quaking voice once again penetrated deep inside the house.

'Nasiban, ari o Nasiban, go and see ... .there are some jalebis lying from two days ago; go and give them to the beggar.'

'Anything else?' asked Nasiban.

'What else? Do you want to give the rest of the house along with it?'

Adjusting her dupatta, Nasiban went indoors. Begum Saheba sat on a takht in the verandah. A dastarkhwan was spread out in front of her; placed on it were various items that had been prepared for iftari. Some items were still being fried. She would look at the watch after every minute, waiting to break her fast and eat her paan and tobacco.

Begum Saheba's temper ran high at the best of times; during Ramzan it became a byword among her servants. And poor Nasiban bore the brunt of it. She had been raised in the family,

and had no one in the world except Begum Saheba; and Begum
Saheba satiated her maternal instincts by beating up Nasiban
often and thoroughly. Though the hot weather had departed,
nevertheless a hand-held fan was placed beside Begum Saheba
which, as and when the need arose, would also be used to take
swipe at of poor Nasiban.

'Arre, have you gone there and died? Why don't you come
out?'

Nasiban wiped her mouth quickly and moved towards the
deorhi with the jalebis.

'Show me how many are there.'

Nasiban extended her outstretched palm. There were only
two jalebis on it.

'Two?' Begum Saheba shrieked. 'But there were more! Come
here, you... did you eat the rest?'

'No, no,' Nasiban whimpered. But Begum Saheba's x-ray
vision had spotted a piece of jalebi sticking to Nasiban's teeth.
Enraged, she picked up the fan and fell on Nasiban.
'Haramzadi, so this is your roza! You wicked girl... you couldn't
wait another half hour? Wait... I will teach you to enjoy the
joys of pilfering.'

'Never again, Begum Saheba, I won't do it ever again...
Allah.... Forgive me, Begum Saheba, please... please...'
Nasiban begged and pleaded.

'Never again... never again... You wait and see... I will
beat the living daylights out of you... I will teach you to break
your fast...'

'May your children prosper! Help a fasting man break his
fast!'

Tired and out of breath, as the Begum Saheba began to
pant, she pushed Nasiban and said, 'Go, you wretch! Go and
give these jalebis to the beggar! He has been shouting for a
long time. Give him this daal, too...'

Begum Saheba added a little bit of daal to Nasiban's palm.

Whimpering and sobbing, Nasiban reached the deorhi and gave the two jalebis and handful of daal to the beggar.

The 'New Road' must have been new once; but now it was old, in a sorry state and lined by houses on both sides. Except one or two houses in good condition, most of the houses were old, decrepit and bore ample testimony to the hard times that had befallen the neighbourhood.The road was a wide one, its pavements encroached upon by a motley group of dyers, washermen, weavers and ironsmiths who used it as a part of their extended courtyard. In fact, during the summer months, there would be so many beds spread out on the road that an ekka would find it difficult to pass by.

Apart from the houses, in this predominantly Muslim neighbourhood there were three mosques. A contest appeared to be going on among the mullahs of these masjids. Each competing with the other to see who could fool more people among the poor, illiterate inhabitants and how best to fleece them of their hard-earned money. From teaching the Holy Quran to young children, to giving amulets, talismans and casting spells, the mullahs were masters of all tricks by which to hoodwink the poor ironsmiths and weavers. The families of these three good-for-nothing and idle mullahs lived in the midst of these hardworking people like termites in the middle of a thickly-forested jungle that, bit by bit, eat up the tall thick trees. The mullahs were white-collar folk and those they fed on were dirty and grubby. The mullahs were Saiyyeds and considered part of the sharif class, whereas the hard-working people were supposedly mean and lowly.

In the neighbourhood, on the lower floor of an old dilapidated house was a junk dealer's shop. On the floor above, about fifteen or twenty Khans lived. The upper floor faced the road. The Khans were natives of the north-western frontier and were all money lenders. They were all exceptionally dirty, too. Everyone in the neighbourhood was terrified of them.

For one almost everyone owed them money; for another, they were known to leer at women. A lone woman dare not walk past that house.

All day long the home of the Khans remained locked. In the evening when they returned, they would boil some meat in a pot and with some naan bought from the bazar, they would eat straight from the pot. Digging their hands into the cooking pot they would picked out meat pieces, and toss sucked-out-clean bones on to the street below. Close to their dinner time, many dogs would gather. Their growling and barking could be heard for a long time.

After eating their fill, the Khans sat with their ledgers and settled their accounts. Some spread out their blankets, lit their huqqas and retired for the night. A few among them would set out for a night of revelry in the city.

These Khans, who made a living out of usury, considered themselves to be devout Muslims and were very particular about observing rozas and offering namaz. Even though their religion expressly forbids taking interest on lent money, they simply called it profit, and offered it as their devotion in the court of their Almighty. Since it was the month of Ramzan, all the Khans were fasting and hurrying back home for iftari. To pass time, they stood on the roof of their house, looked down on the street below, and if perchance a woman were to pass by, they would comment loudly. The house across the road from theirs kept its windows shut all the time. Occasionally, from a sliver of light it became evident that a new tenant had come, but then carriages and tongas would appear and the house would be emptied yet again.

One day Asghar Saheb reached the neighbourhood in search of a house on rent. He saw this house, too. It was at a time when the Khans were away. Asghar Saheb liked the house, especially the rent. After having it cleaned and painted, he moved in with his mother, wife and child. His wife, Nasima, liked the house very much. So what if the neighbourhood was dirty and run down, she said, but where could one find such a large house for a mere twenty rupees. She resolved to set about decorating the house instantly. In the evening, she stood at the window looking out at the children running about on the road when her mother-in-law, standing beside her let out a sharp breath and stepped back.

'Ai, look at those fat louts, look at the way those Khans are looking at us. May their eyes be poked out... see how they are looking here and laughing!'

Nasima turned to look. She saw several Khans standing on the roof of their house and grinning in her direction. The moment Nasima looked in their direction, she noticed a perceptible ripple in their ranks as they began to talk loudly among themselves. Fortunately, the two houses were at a certain angle to each other; nevertheless, there was an ample view.

'Ai, Dulhan, close the window and move away. What sort of parda-less home has Asghar chosen for us? I can't live here for two days.'

Nasima made no reply; instead she stood there and kept staring straight into the eyes of the Khans. Her mother-in-law went away, grumbling: 'What can one say to men when women have no shame?'

Asghar and Nasima's life had known its share of obstacles. They had been engaged in their childhood but as they grew older and the rigours of parda increased, they learnt ways to dodge it and meet as often as young people in Muslim families do under such circumstances. Things had reached such a pass that they would even exchange letters.

When Asghar was studying in College he, like other youth, was afflicted by the ache for freedom and independence for his country. He was famous for his rousing speeches and inflammatory articles on the cruelties perpetrated by the English, the injustices inflicted by the zamindars, the hard times faced by the farmers, the plunder of the capitalists and the trade unions of the working classes. Being a good speaker, he was quite famous among students. The world had many hopes from Asghar, and Nasima had even more! Asghar wrote all about college life to Nasima and when Nasima read about him in the newspaper, she would raise her head high with pride. No one from among her circle of friends or even a friend or fiancé of any of her friends was involved in the freedom struggle. Nasima had begun to ready herself for a new life with Asghar.

An intelligent person needs but a signal. Nasima was a smart girl; she could well understand the ills that plagued her society. At the same time, she began to conjure schemes in her mind, schemes to improve the state of affairs. She began to ready herself to make all sorts of sacrifices for the sake of her country, its freedom and wellbeing. It was almost as though she was in love with the idea of its freedom; such was her love that she could even lay down her life for her country.

They were married as soon as Asghar completed his B.A. and when they began to live together, she discovered that Asghar's open-mindedness was confined to a small circle. He did indeed introduce his wife to a few of his friends. In fact, meeting these people helped Nasima realise that she would have to step forward and do things on her own if she truly wanted to make a change in the world around her.

Nasima's fervour and passion for change was increasing, but Asghar's was declining by the day. He said something, and did something else. However, he could not lie to Nasima with the same ease with which he made excuses to his friends. First he would say that they were expecting a child and after the child was born his excuse was that the child was still small. Then, he said he must complete his law studies before jumping into the fray; as soon as his law degree was over, he took up a job and that too a government one, which took him further and further away from his friends.

For how long could he hide what lay in his heart from Nasima? To the world outside, he could seek refuge in the excuse of his wife and child, but what could he say at home? Nasima too understood that her husband was not likely to do anything; he was just a paper tiger. If perchance he met any of his old friends, he would start the oratory and verbal pyrotechnics, and present his apolitical life as something of a necessity that had been foisted on him. He would let his friends believe that Nasima was the reason why he had gone astray. This opportunism formed a knot between the two. Nasima became increasingly resentful and silent.

Asghar's friends were now mostly from the legal profession. Some were lackadaisical government employees including some from the Central Intelligence Department. Asghar felt uncomfortable alone with Nasima because, in his heart, he was guilty of a theft and Nasima knew who the thief was. So much so, that he began to imagine every word she uttered to be a taunt. Her frigid silence irritated him and he wished he could slap her hard across her beautiful face. Had Nasima fought with him, hurled insults or pierced his heart with barbs, he would have possibly felt less hurt than he did by her silent condescension.

The time for iftar was drawing near. The Khans were huddled near their window. Some were standing, others brewing their tea. Nasima too was peering out of the window holding her son, Aslam. It had been almost two months since they had moved to this house. The Khans had grown accustomed to her face and her brazenness in showing it. They had stopped paying any notice to her even if she stood by her window for hours. At this hour, their eyes and ears were glued to the mosque nearby.

With just a little time to go for the iftar, a beggar appeared from one of the lanes and began to walk on the street; the way in which he was walking, as though feeling every step of the way, made it amply evident that he was blind. His body was trembling. He could barely hold the stick he was using as support and guide. He was holding something in his fist which could not be seen because of the quivering. Moving slowly, he eventually reached Nasima's house and stood leaning against her wall.

'Look, Amma, look what the beggar is holding in his hand.'

Nasima peered and said, 'It looks like something to eat.'

'Then why doesn't he eat it?'

'Perhaps he is fasting, too. May be he is waiting to hear the azan.'

'Amma, you don't fast?'

Nasima smiled at her son and said, 'No.'

'Why did Abba tell the Daroghaji that he is fasting; was Abba lying?'

Nasima thought for a minute and then said, 'Why don't you ask him yourself?'

'So, Amma, why don't you fast?'

'Because you don't,' Nasima teased her son.

'That's because I am little. My grandmother says those who are old enough and still don't fast will go to hell. What is hell, Amma?'

'Hell? Why, there it is!... Right there in front of you!'

'Where?' asked Aslam, turning his head to look in all four directions.

'There... where that blind beggar is standing. There... where the weavers live. There... where the ironsmiths and the dyers live.'

'But my grandmother says there is fire in hell.'

'Yes, there is fire. But it isn't the sort of fire that will light our hearth. The fire of hell, my son, is the fire of hunger. Often, you don't get anything to eat in hell and when you do, it is very little and of very bad quality. One has to work very hard in hell. And the clothes that the people in hell wear are old and tattered. And their homes are small and cramped and dark, filled with lice and bugs. What is more, my dear Aslam miyan, the children in hell do not have toys to play.'

'Kallu doesn't have any toys, Amma; it is because he also lives in hell, isn't it?'

'Yes.'

'And heaven?'

'Heaven is here where you and I live with your aunts and uncles. It is here in this large, clean house where we get to eat lots of delicious things such as butter, toast, fruits, eggs, meat, milk. Children have good clothes to wear and a motor car to play with.'

'Then, Amma, why does everyone not live in heaven?'

'Because, my dear, those who live in heaven do not let others come in. They get these other people to do all their work but then they push them back into hell.'

'And they become blind too?'

'Yes, my son, there are a lot of blind people in hell.'

'Then how do they eat?'

The sound of the azan could be heard and simultaneously a shot was fired to indicate that it was time for iftar. The Khans leapt towards their tea and the old beggar quickly drew the jalebis close towards his mouth. The blind man's trembling grew worse. His hands began to shake terribly and his head began to bob up and down. With some difficulty he managed to bring his hand close to his mouth and as he was about to transfer the jalebi from his hand to his mouth, it slipped and fell to the ground. The old man fell to the ground, too; and kneeling on all fours, he began to search for the jalebis with his hands. At about the same time, a roving dog appeared and pounced at the jalebis and ate it. Tired and dispirited, the old man sat down on the ground and began to cry like a baby.

The Khans saw the scene and let out loud peals of laughter.

They began to hold their sides and laugh at the spectacle of the old man and his sorry state.

Frightened by what he had seen, little Aslam clung to his mother and said, 'Amma.' His young mind had seen the true picture of hell for the first time.

Nasima looked at the Khans angrily and said, 'These miserable wretches!' Again, Aslam said in a low voice, 'Amma.'

Nasima stooped to pick him up and looking at him straight in the eyes, spoke in a forceful voice, 'My darling, it will be your job to remove this hell when you grow up.'

'And what about you?'

'I? Where can I go from my prison?'

'Why not? You are not as old as grandmother that you cannot walk,' young Aslam answered echoing the serious tone of his mother. 'You must come with me, too.'

'All right, my darling, I will also come with you.'

Thief

It was ten o'clock at night. I was sitting alone in my clinic, reading a medical journal, when suddenly the door opened and a man entered carrying a child. I was angry at my nurse for having left the door open. My time for seeing patients was long over. So, I spoke harshly: 'The time for seeing patients is over. Either come tomorrow or go to some other doctor.'

The man was short statured but had a lithe, muscular body. The child in his arms was taking fast, short breaths. Evidently, it had pneumonia. Its head lolled to one side and it looked virtually at death's door. The man spoke arrogantly; 'Memsaheb, take your fees; what else do you want?'

I may have softened at the mention of fees but his arrogance annoyed me. 'No doctor sees a patient without fees. I don't see patients at this time. You should know that this is the time for doctors to take a break. Moreover, your child is very sick...'

'That's why I have brought him to you. My sister-in-law's child was even more ill; you made him all right,' his voice had mellowed now and he seemed to be pleading.

I spoke angrily, 'If you wanted me to treat your boy you should have brought him earlier.'

'There was no one else who could have brought the child, and I couldn't come any sooner.'

There was the sign of a deep wound on his temple. Such an uncouth fellow could only have been injured in a scuffle.

The child began to whine. I was instantly filled with pity at the sound of it, and got to my feet with my stethoscope in hand. I examined the child and said, 'I will give him an injection right away. For the next four days, he must get this shot every four hours. Make the arrangements.' I took one look at his poverty and said, 'There is no need for fees. I will only take the cost of the injection. You can buy the other medicines from the market.'

Once again, he answered arrogantly, 'Saheb, I don't want your treatment as charity,' and so saying he put his hand inside his kurta and withdrew a ragged bundle.

Suddenly, the telephone rang. As I picked up the receiver my gaze fell on the man. He was untying the bundle. There was no end to my surprise as I watched him take out a thick wad of notes; there must have been almost five hundred rupees in it. And keeping a ten-rupee note on the table, he asked, 'Is that enough, or do you need more?'

I spoke into the telephone, 'Yes, yes,' and then looking at him, asked, 'What's your name?'

'Kamman,' he said and looked a bit uncertain.

'Kamman!' the name was familiar. Yes, I remember when the Darogha had come to my home to enquire about the robbery, he had taken the name 'Kamman'; he had also mentioned that the man had a scar on his temple. I looked closely at him. He was looking disinterestedly in the other direction. As I began to prepare the injection, I asked him, 'What do you do?'

He was about to answer when I said, 'You used to drive a tonga, didn't you?'

'How did you know?' he asked in surprise. 'Where did you see me? I haven't come here before.'

I drew the medicine into the syringe and said, 'Kamman,

you are forgetting. Just two months ago, you had come here in the middle of the night and cleaned my house out. Why do you steal?'

He looked me straight in the eye and spoke to me as an equal, 'Memsaheb, we each have our own professions.'

Now it was my turn to be surprised.

He asked, 'But, tell me, who told you my name?'

'The Darogha Saheb did... when he came to make enquiries. He and his men were talking about your daredevilry among themselves. I heard then; and, didn't they go to search your house?'

He began to shower the choicest abuses on the policemen. 'These mother-** policemen! They take their cut first and foremost, then we get our share in the end. Sister, they needlessly bring us a bad name. They tell the thieves to rob and to the householder they say, look, your house has been robbed! I'll settle that Darogha... Y'know, Memsaheb, the police comes to search my house scores of times in a year. And the same policemen alert me in advance. After all, I have fixed a monthly stipend for all of them. A warrant has been out in my name for the past five years continuously and thanks to the good lord I have not been caught once,' he bragged.

I held the boy's leg to give him the injection, but the man kept mumbling. 'They come and tell me themselves when they are about to come for a search, Memsaheb. If the police were not with us, we wouldn't last even a day in any neighbourhood. Then why do we get a bad name?'

'Don't let the child move his leg.'

'The buggers eat up more than half; what's left for us? We do all the hard work. We are the ones who get caught, we are the ones who end up doing hard labour in jail. These mother-** end up getting fed while they sit at home and do nothing.' His face became red and he seemed oblivious of the whimpering child. I made the child lie down and tried to quieten him. I could sense that the man was beginning to open up with me. I wanted to talk to him. This was my first meeting with a thief, that too a thief who had burgled my house! I said to him, 'Why do you steal, Kamman? Don't you feel sorry for the people you rob? You stole every single thing from my home. I didn't have even a set of clothes to wear. How much do you get for a set of spectacles? Dammit, you even stole my spectacles.'

'Nothing goes waste.'

I looked at him in surprise and asked, 'And what about the dupatta that was the only thing I had left to remind me of my dead mother? You even took that!'

I should get him arrested, I thought.

'Which one?'

'It was white net and had embroidery. Why would you remember it? God knows how many more thefts you have committed since then? You are hardly likely to remember anything.'

I was trying to keep him occupied by talking to him. 'So, how did you begin your career as a thief?' I was thinking... should I ring the bell to summon my servant?

'The same way everyone does... I learnt from my teacher.'

'Teacher? You have teachers too?'

'Why not? How did you learn to become a doctor?'

'I went to college to study medicine?' Should I ring the bell or not?

'We have our college, too,' he smiled. 'My college was the jailhouse. I was sentenced to six months after a brawl. That's where I met my teacher...'

The child began to cry. That's when the door opened and my younger brother appeared, dressed in his army man's clothes. He was a young man, a lot more powerful than Kamman; what's more, a revolver was slung from his waist. Kamman saw him and was shocked for an instant, then he picked up the prescription and began to head out of the door. Shall I have him arrested? Should I? I thought quickly. I could not make up my mind in time. He left the room.

'Apa, what's the matter? Why do you look worried?'

'Do you know who that was? That was the man who robbed my house.'

'How do you know?'

'I spoke to him.'

'You spoke to him, and you let him go?' Saying that, my brother leapt towards the door and looked out. The road was deserted. He ran a few steps and paused at the turn in the road. There, too, no one was in sight.

My brother returned and spoke angrily to me, 'Apa, you really are the limit! You met the thief and you let him go! Why have you kept this Gurkha servant? Why didn't you call him? And when I went after him, then too you stayed quiet?' Rubbing his hand angrily over his revolver, he said, 'I would never have let that bastard go.'

My brother is a seasoned hunter. At that moment, he had that look of chagrin that a hunter has when his prey eludes him.

'Has anyone heard of allowing a thief to get away like this?' I stayed quiet.

'You are very emotional. You must have melted at the sight of his child. Look at the man's nerve! He has left behind twenty rupees; these too are no doubt ill-gotten gains.'

'He had about five hundred or six hundred rupees on him.'

'You know, Apa, you may be elder but you are really very silly.'

Soon, my acquaintances came to know that the man who had robbed my home had come with his sick child for treatment and I could have had him arrested, but I let him go. Everyone was making fun of me. No one made any attempt to understand my dilemma. Till today, I have not been able to figure out if I made a mistake, or not.

A friend of mine is a police officer. When he heard about the incident, he said, 'Do you know, you have committed a legal offence. The man had a warrant in his name; it is a crime not to get such a man arrested.'

I wonder what will happen to those other thieves who neither have a warrant, nor ever will. There are several types of theft. Petty thievery, picking pockets, robbery, larceny, black-marketing, exploitation, filling your home with the money earned from the labour of others, swallowing up someone else's land or country. After all, why aren't these included in theft?

I am not bothered about what people say but when everyone around me began to make fun of me, I felt a twinge of conscience. Had I truly committed a crime by not having the thief arrested? I am a law-abiding citizen. I have certain societal obligations. By not getting that thief arrested, had I shown a lack of civic sense?

I looked around me. I saw that some of the biggest thieves walk around dressed up as saints, and live in large mansions. They travel in aeroplanes and have either gobbled up large tracts of land or are preparing to do so. And to safeguard their own interests, have gone a step further than poor Kamman who only bribed the police. They have the entire police and armed forces on their payroll. Kamman was speaking arrogantly to me, pretending to be an equal, on the basis of a mere five or six hundred rupees, whereas these others... they are not merely arrogant, they sit high above us on a pedestal and rule over us.

Chhidda's Mother

I had gone to my Mamu's house to spend my summer vacations. His syce's mother, whom all of us called Chhida's mother, was employed to pull the fan. She would sit there pulling the rope for the fan and kept talking. One day, she told Mumani jaan, 'Huzoor, please give four days' leave to Chhida. He will go to the village.'

'But he had just been. Why does he want leave so often?' Mumani jaan, who had dozed off, asked angrily. 'Why is he going?'

'What can I tell you, huzoor? My husband's younger brother has come; he insists that Chhida bring home the widow of his Chhajju. It is better if a woman of the family stays in the family.'

'How many women is this Chhida going to keep in his house?'

'It isn't Chhida's fault; his fate is blighted. The last wretched one...'

'All of them are bad according to you. You find fault with all your daughters-in-law. You don't let any of them stay,' Mumani jaan said. 'Go and tell Chhida, he won't get any leave.'

Chhida's mother fell silent, but just as Mumani jaan's eyelids began to droop, spoke up again, 'Begum Saheb, I am telling you the truth: that awful girl did not wash her hands after going to the toilet. I must have beaten her at least ten times over it.'

'And got your son to beat her another hundred times over it, too!'

'Oh no, Begum Saheb,' Chhida's mother simpered. When she spoke like this, three yellow teeth protruded and her ugly face looked more frightening than usual.

'And what was wrong with the one from Iglas[1]? That poor thing had such a lovely face!'

'She had a squint, Begum Saheb. You took fright if you saw her at night.'

'Yes, and you are as beautiful as a fairy! Have you seen your face in a mirror, you witch?' Mumani jaan laughed. 'You have a face like a she-devil. Children get scared at the sight of you. You are a fine one to criticise others. I tell you, Aisha, that girl had such a sweetly innocent face.'

The old woman laughed, and changing the rope pull for the fan to the other hand, said, 'Huzoor, does one see a daughter-in-law's face or her traits? If a wife does not bear children, it is like keeping her and feeding her for no good reason. A wife is good only as long as she bears sons just as a buffalo is good if she bears calves.'

'The poor thing lived with you for a bare three months; how could she bear a child? Anyway, let me sleep now.'

Chhida's mother returned to her query, 'So, huzoor, is it all right if Chhida leaves tomorrow?'

Mumani jaan got up. She poured herself some water from the surahi, drank it and went to lie down once again. 'You have had Chhida married at least eight or ten times in the last few years. Then you find fault in all the brides. If you had your way, you would not bring a daughter-in-law into your house. You bring one out of fear of your community, but you don't let any of those ill-fated creatures stay. You are more envious of them than any mistress!'

Getting angrier, Mumani jaan asked, 'After all, what is your problem? You listen to me carefully and tell Chhida too that this time if you throw out the girl, I will throw you out of my house.'

The old woman switched the rope-pull to the other hand and simpered, 'Begum Saheb, how can you let go of your own boy for the sake of some daughter-in-law. Chhidda is like your son; he will leave your doorway only when he dies, like his father did before him.'

Mumani jaan was pleased to hear this; removing her hand from her eyes, she asked, 'So when will he go?'

Knowing that she had won the battle, the old woman said, 'Whenever you let him go.'

'My brother is coming tomorrow; we will need the carriage. Let him go the day after. He will not get leave for more than two days. If he takes longer, I will cut his salary. I don't like these frequent absences. I don't know how many women he has wed and you, witch that you are, don't let any of them stay. Chhidda is like a sparrow made of clay; he does whatever the witch asks him to do...'

The old woman swelled with pride and said, 'Oh no, huzoor, the first one he got was no good. All the other girls who came as brides at the same time as her had at least two babies in their lap in as many years whereas she could not produce even a baby mouse!'

'The curse of that poor wretch has fallen on you. It is a good thing your house was robbed. How you used to beat that poor girl!'

'To tell you the truth, Begum saheb, I would never have turned out that one. Her father deceived us; he came to take her away in the month of Savan and never returned her. He married her off somewhere else.'

'Good thing he did that! The poor girl was saved from you. Narnia's wife was telling me she has a baby now,' Mumani jaan said.

'I met her at the fair in Waripur; she saw me and turned her face away. I would have had her and her father sent to jail. But her father gave me a hundred and fifty rupees. And only then did I let the community elders speak to her family. After all, it is no laughing matter!'

'And what about that one? What was her name? That tall one?'

'That one! Huzoor, don't even take her name. She bit my Chhidda's father to death as soon as she came.'

'Why? Was she a snake?' I couldn't resist asking.

'Bibi, there is a cure for snake bite but there is no cure for a witch.'

'How did she bite him to death?' I asked curiously.

'Bibi, what would you know of such things? You study in a school. She was a witch, I tell you, a witch. Three days after she came to our house, Chhidda's father got such a high fever that it never came down. He died within three days,' Chhidda's mother answered wiping her tears and puckering up her face.

'You are nothing but a witch,' Mumani jaan spoke, half asleep.

'How did he die then if it wasn't because of her? He got a pain in his gut the moment she crossed our threshold. For the next two or three days he thrashed about in pain and then the fever rose. It wouldn't come down no matter what we did. Begum Saheb even had him shown to a doctor at the hospital. We showed him to all the witch doctors in the city; everyone said a witch has got hold of him.'

'Go away, old woman, witches are not so stupid; if she had to eat someone, she would have eaten you. Why would she eat that poor man? He had enteric fever. How I told these stupid people to take him to a hospital! But do you ever listen to anyone? It was nothing but enteric fever.'

'No, Begum Saheb, you are a high class person. You are our master; whatever you say is right. But I am telling you, he didn't have 'enteric-penteric' fever; he died of the bite of that witch.' And drawing a long breath, she sighed, 'Oh Bibi, you wouldn't know about these things. When the fever wouldn't come down, the witch-doctor asked him if he could see anything, he said he couldn't. She was such a cruel witch; she had even sealed his mouth. In the last few days, things had become so bad that he would rise from his cot and begin to scream the moment she entered his room. What did I know? I knew nothing; I would tell her to go and fetch the milk. The moment she got the milk, he would fling his hand and throw the pitcher away. And when I gave him milk, he would drink it quietly. And he would scream with terror if she even gave him water. And, Bibi, I tell you, she had cast such a spell on my Chhidda that he was blindly in love with her. He did nothing but sing her praises all the time. I would say: You have bitten one to death already; how many more do you want to kill? I couldn't sleep at night, worried as I was. One day, without telling Chhidda, I went to Matru. He is a very clever witch-doctor. I fell at his feet and I begged him to save my son's life. He took one rupee right away. I told him, "The day this witch leaves my house, I will give you another rupee." '

'How did you get rid of her, then?' I asked.

'Oh, how hard I had to work on that one! It was with great difficulty that I got Chhidda to come around and believe me. Even now, whenever he remembers her, he is ready to start a fight with me.'

'Tell us what you did.' I had never heard such talk; for me the old woman's stories were like the tales of Alif-Laila.

'Oh, Bibi, what can I say?'

'Tell, tell,' I pleaded.

'I did whatever Matru asked me to do; what else could I do?' Chidda's mother tried to be evasive.

'After all, what did Matru ask you to do?' I persisted.

The old woman laughed and said, 'He told me to make an offering at the shrine of Badh-badh Shah. He also gave me a surma and told me to give it to Chhidda without telling him what it was for; the surma would make him see her in her true form.'

'Unfortunately, the witch put the surma by mistake and Chhidda became more devoted to her than ever before. Worse still, he began to beat me instead! I went running to Matru again. He said this witch wouldn't leave so easily. He gave me some powder and told me to make sure Chhida ate it. And, Bibi, the moment Chidda ate it he got a severe pain in his stomach and began to throw up blood. Matru also gave me a rag doll; it had needles stuck all over.Matru had told me to hide it in the house when no one was looking and, at the right moment, take it out and raise an alarm. Then see how long the wretch stays, he had said. Chhidda's fever rose and the vomiting showed no sign of letting up. I entered the house and staged a drama. Look, people, she is a witch, she knows black magic. She has found one prey; now she is about to kill another. All the servants gathered around. They stood about looking at the rag doll. They told Chidda, "Son, don't keep such a woman in your house." That time even Chhidda was scared. He sent the woman back to her parent's home with his uncle.'

'Just listen to her tales, Aisha. She is a first-class crook! She poisoned her son with her own hands. He was virtually at death's door. It was only when your Mamu jaan threatened to call the police that she agreed to take him to the hospital.'

'He was there for two weeks. I speak the truth, Begum Saheb, Chhidda was in the hospital for fifteen days,' Chhidda's mother spoke as though Chhidda had stayed inside a grave for two weeks.

'How far was he from death's door? He was brought back only because of your Mamu jaan's efforts.'

'No, Begum Saheb, how could he die? Matru had told me everything in the beginning,' the old woman answered with complete confidence.

'You wait and see, you awful creature; I am going to tell Chhidda all about you. All this while, I didn't know that you had poisoned your own son,' said Mumani jaan angrily, who took great interest in the personal life of her servants.

'Chidda came to know a few days ago. In fact, he beat me
and went running to fetch her back. But by then she had already
gone to live in some other man's house.' The old woman
laughed.

'Tell me, is she a wicked witch, or was that woman a poor
wretch?" Mumani jaan asked me.

'To tell you the truth, Begum Saheb, it was this Chhidda
who mooned over her. He went to her village, hung around
her house. He even tried to give money to her father but that
bitch refused to come. He is still ever-ready to pick up a quarrel
over her with me. I have told him: "You can beat me all you
want but I will not let that witch stay with you." '

'But why is she a witch? I still haven't understood,' I asked.

'Bibi, you can't understand this; she was a witch.'

'But why?'

'Why are you wasting your time arguing with this illiterate
woman; go to sleep now. Or else, you will take forever to wake
up in the evening,' Mumani jaan scolded me.

Four days later, Chhida's new wife came home. She had a
nicely filled out body. Though her face was scarred by pock
marks, she was a cheerful girl. Chhidda's mother brought her
to Mumani jaan the very day she arrived, so she could offer
her salaams. Mumani jaan gave her a rupee and said, 'I can
give no more to someone who gets three brides a year. You
will make me bankrupt at this stage. Now let this one stay,
you wretch!'

'Uh huh, Begum Saheb, the things you say! Do I get rid of
them or is it their own doing?'

Now Chhidda's wife began to pull the fan in the afternoons
in his mother's place. She and I were poles apart; our worlds
were strangers to each other. She heard my stories about college
and expressed wonder. And listened to her tales about her
village with surprise. Only when I met Chidda's wife, I realised
how little I knew about my country despite living in India. She
and I whispered to each other and not let Mumani jaan sleep

all afternoon. Disturbed in her slumber, Mumani jaan would mumble, 'Hmm hmm... let me sleep.' We would stay quiet for a few minutes and start whispering again.

I used to enjoy listening to her.

One day when she came, her eyes were blood-shot and her face was swollen. Her bangles were broken. I could see bruises and blood stains on her arms. When I asked her what had happened, she began to cry bitterly and said that Chhidda had beaten her. For the past few days, the old woman had begun to scream at her and carry tales about her to her son. She would add salt to the cooked dal, or wipe the rotis with her soiled fingers. She would spoil something or the other every day. When the son did not react to any of this, she tried a new tactic. As soon as Chhidda entered the house, she began to beat his wife and said, 'The slut was talking to Eidu.' Enraged, even Chhidda began to beat his newly-wedded wife over this.

Chhidda's wife cried for a long time. For the next three or four days, she was very quiet. The happiness that had awakened inside her and shown itself in the beaming smile on her face ever since she had shed the sorrow of widowhood and become a married woman, had disappeared completely. She was terrified by her mother-in-law and her face grew pale. Every day, the mother-in-law would spin yarns and present them before Chhidda with such cleverness that he would believe her; every day, the new bride would be beaten mercilessly.

I returned home as soon as my college reopened. I forgot all about Chidda, his mother and his wife. I couldn't meet Mumani jaan either for a very long time. At the time of my brother's wedding, Mumani jaan came to our house. One day, just like that, I was reminded of Chhidda's wife and I asked about her. Mumani jaan laughed and said Chidda had sold her long ago.

When I asked her how she could employ such a person, she said, 'How many people can I sack? The washerman has left several women. It is the same with the gardener. Eidu has divorced two women. It isn't considered a shame among these people; what can I do if women are so cheaply available in this country? Chhidda was born in our house; moreover he is good with the horses.'

I asked, 'And how is that witch of a mother of his? Is she alive or dead?'

'She is not the sort to die! But this new wife that has come recently has set her right.'

Mumani jaan went on, 'The old woman started her old ways but she has found her match in this girl. One day she beat the living daylights out of the mother-in-law and finally avenged all the previous daughters-in-law. She told her, "I am not going to leave this house. Those who came before me and left were made of some other mettle; god knows who they were and why they went. If you want to stay in this house, you had better mend your ways; if not, you can leave... "'

'For the next three days, the old woman hung around my house; she tried every spell and talisman that she knew. Now, she lives with them like a pussy cat and is so terrified of her daughter-in-law that sometimes I feel a twinge of pity for her.'

'And Chhidda?'

'He is a slave to his wife. That is precisely what is so hard for the mother to accept. But, you know, the truth is that all women are not the same.'

End Note

[1] Iglas is a township in Aligarh district. The original story has Chhida's mother speaking in a rustic dialect and using words and expressions spoken in the rural areas around Aligarh city. The story reflects how closely Rashid Jahan must have noted the dialect of the lower classes who worked in the women's college and in her parent's home as well as those she would no doubt have met and interacted with in her capacity as a doctor. Much of the story is a dialogue between Chhida's mother and the protagonist's aunt (Mumani jaan) and the protagonist herself (Aisha Bibi). The original Urdu version shows the difference in the language spoken by the *sharif* class (to which Aisha and Mumanijaan belong) and the lower classes who, despite working in the homes of the *shurfa*, retain the rustic flavour of their dialects.

Bad Company

'Abba jaan, Saeed Bhai is leaving.'

'Hmm!' said Chief Justice Sir Ataullah, hiding the blotter quickly.

'So, you have thrown him out yet again?' said Zakiya, with the spark of hatred and rebellion flaring in her eyes.

'What do you know about these things? Go, and do your work,' said Judge Saheb, sounding annoyed.

He wanted to tell her too to go away, but she was a girl, after all. He looked at her and, swallowing his anger, simply said, 'Go away, Zakiya, I have work to do.'

Judge Saheb rested his elbows on the table. His eyes were on his file. But his mind was elsewhere. He was so angry with Saeed: it was bad enough that he was good for nothing but now he was ruining Zakiya too. And the girl had a nerve: she had come to pick a bone with him, her father! Saeed was twenty-eight years old and he lived the life of a vagabond. 'At that age, I had achieved so much,' said Judge Saheb to himself. 'A good life makes one slothful. When my father had died leaving behind young children, my mother had taken on sewing jobs, and done all sorts of hard labour. I had begun taking tuitions from the age of thirteen. Uff, how it pains me to recall those years of poverty and hardship and today my son has the temerity to look me in the eye and ask me what I have done in life? How did my becoming rich help anyone? 'I pulled myself out of a pit and put my family up there on the skies so that he, my son, can go around with Karl Marx tucked under his arm.

'Our home was a dark, unlit hovel with a tiny courtyard. We somehow kept it standing all through the monsoon rain with the lick and polish of our hard work. We slept three to a cot. Today, sleeping in the comfort of a well-sprung bed, Saeedsaheb thinks he can change the world. He asks me if my children get well-placed jobs, how does it benefit humanity? Those who were with me in the old days don't stand to gain anything; if anything, they get an addition to the number of their enemies. After all, what possible sympathy do you have with those who continue to languish in the same old state of poverty, he asks me? You protect the laws that uphold the old order, he accuses me.

'I changed my lot. Did I tell others not to change theirs? I had the intelligence and the courage to forge ahead. The others were mean and idle; how could they change their lot?

'He tells me all the hard work I put in in becoming the Chief Justice has gone waste, completely waste. In fact, he didn't use the word "waste"; he said I have betrayed my hard work. Am I the traitor, or is he? He wants to decry all my hard work. He has been living for all these years in my house as an untrustworthy traitor. I am the one who has worked hard to reach this niche in society. Who is he?'

'Ibrahim, go brother Ibrahim, go and get an ekka!' the voice came from the other side of the house.

Judge Saheb heard the voice and grew angrier still. 'Now His Highness will leave in an ekka... to humiliate me... knowing very well that respectable people come here to visit me in the evenings. How many times have I told him... go and live in some other city if you must behave like this, but he won't listen! He says I will live where I am ordered to. Who

will order him? Whose order will he abide by? He doesn't listen
to his father. Of course, his is a stepmother. He doesn't listen
to his grandmother, either. So whose orders will he listen to?
The Party's? And what the devil is the Party? Nothing but a
group of convicts and bad characters who cannot bear to see
anyone progress or do well! They claim they will redistribute
the wealth of a handful, but have any of them ever known the
hardship with which wealth is collected?'

And drawing a long, deep sigh, Judge Saheb continued his
reflections: 'Is there any job that I cannot get for him? After
all, I have placed the three elder boys. The eldest, by the Grace
of God, is a Collector. The second is in the railways and the
third in the police. And this one refuses to take up employment.
Whenever I have tried to tell him: Stop this idling and take up
some work, what answer do I get? The answer is: 'I want to
take the whole world with me on the staircase on which you
have climbed to the top.' How can everyone be equal? To top
it all, he is so shameless... He had gone to Kanpur... Barely
six months later, he contracted typhoid. His friends, whom he
calls comrades, could not tend him for even two days. They
deposited him at the hospital. And he? Instead of taking offense,
he does nothing but praise them. He defends them by saying:
'They are not doctors or nurses. Moreover, they have no money.
Had they not taken me to hospital, I would have died.' He is
the apple of his grandmother's eye. She cried buckets and nearly
drowned the whole house. Now that he has recovered his
health, he has started this new...'

'Arre, Ibrahim Bhai, have you still not gone?'

'So, he is still here? Where is the sense in taking up a life of
such hardship? Where is the intelligence in taking up all the
sorrows of the world and gathering them in your heart? Each
one should look out for himself. If one can't hold one's peace
and sit still, at least one shouldn't go around bothering others.
This senseless boy stands forever with a mirror before me.

The whole world praises me. My name is a byword for success and prosperity, whereas for my son, my life is useless, purposeless, pointless. What does he know about hardship? But ever since he has returned from jail, he thinks he has come back from the Haj!

'I started to work from the age of thirteen! I educated myself, and then put my younger brothers through school. With great difficulty, I had passed my 'Entrance' exam and taken up a job for thirty rupees. When we left our hovel and moved to a house with a courtyard, how my mother had clasped me to her chest. I promised her that one day I would keep her in a palace with two maids waiting hand and foot on her. And what does my son say? He says, 'Ask those two maids how they feel about working in your house like slaves?''

'Wajid! Wajid! I had told Ibrahim to fetch me an *ekka*, but he's still not got one.'

'Ibrahim isn't here.'

'So you go and get one, brother.'

'I have been commanded by Lady saheb that I should not go anywhere at this time.'

'If you can't go yourself, then can't you look for Ibrahim?' Zakiya scolded Wajid. 'Saeed Bhai, if I were you, I would never have stayed here this long. Even the servants don't respect you. Really, you have no shame! If Hamid Bhai had told him to do something, he would...'

Saeed laughed and said, 'Is there any comparison between Hamid Bhai and me? He gives them tips and extras. He is a Collector.'

'Who stopped you from becoming a Collector?' said Sir Ataullah as he picked up the thread of his thoughts. 'I toiled for all those years to see my children prosper, to be respected. One is a Collector, the other is in the Police: how it pleases my heart to see them. But this good-for-nothing son of mine says I hanker for a good name; that is why I give donations, he says.

That's why I keep maids for my old mother. He does not have the slightest sympathy for me. Yesterday, when in a fit of rage I slapped Faiyazi, he got after me. Do I have no rights over my servants? How will I get by if I can't beat my own servants?'

'Does he know the difficulties I have endured? How I have suffered at the hands of arrogant superiors and how I have toiled to please them? There are so many things one has to do that one cannot even admit to one's self, for if one refuses to do those things one will languish forever in a pit. If I have been dishonest or stooped low ... who is it all for? Was it not for the day that my children and I could live peacefully and comfortably? And he looks me in the eye and says...'

A motor car comes to a stop outside Judge Saheb's window and Sir Ali Beg's elder son gets out. 'Arre, Saeed, whose luggage is this?"

'Mine.'

'Where are you off to?'

'I'm going to the Party office.'

'Arre, what is this nonsense that you're involved in? Why don't you leave all this? What if you end up going to the jail again?'

Saeed laughed and said, 'I am not fond of going to jail. I want to stay out and work; but we are dependent on the goodwill of officers such as yourself; you can send us in whenever you wish.'

Judge Saheb heard the conversation outside his window and said to himself, 'Yes, sir, you are right! Is there no end to your obstinacy and foolishness? I send thousands of people to prison every year. One movement of my fingers sends people to the scaffold. Is it not the ultimate offense that my own son should go to prison? I don't wish to set eyes on him. Thank God he is leaving today.

'But will I ever know any peace? On the one hand, my mother will cry and plead to get him back; on the other hand,

my wife will accuse him of instigating Zakiya and ban his entry
to the house. This time let Amma say what she will and let
Zakiya throw as many tantrums as she pleases, I will not let
Saeed Miyan enter this house. In any case, when I do send for
him, it isn't as though he will come back with his tail between
his legs. He will carry on as before. He calls my money the
nation's money. He spends my money heedlessly and argues
all the time. He weighs everything I say or do in his own scale
of justice... But what does he know about weighing? I know; I
have experienced it. I have fought for a few grams of flour
with the grocer. I sacrificed every wish for the future.

'Then I met my wife. What an awful woman she was! Not
for a day did I know any companionship. Saeed is the spitting
image of his mother. She was as careless about advancement
as I hankered for it. She had no love for money. People say she
was lucky; my legal practice picked up from the day she came
to my house. But she couldn't care less! After her death, it has
been such a long battle for me to marry Sughra. Had my first
wife been alive today, would she have been equal to the grace
and honour of my present position? Would she have been a fit
and able Lady Saheb? I shudder at the thought... Tauba, Tauba!'

The telephone rings. Judge Saheb frowns, picks up the
receiver and says, 'Hello... Who is it?'

'...'

'Arif... which Arif?'

'...'

'Yes, you had come that day...'

'...'

'You are a sub-inspector now, aren't you?'

'...'

'Yes, I remember now.'

'...'

'Yes, you had mentioned your son's wedding.'

'...'

'But you must excuse me... I cannot come today.'

' ... '

'No, not even for five minutes. I have a dinner in my home; I cannot come.'

' ... '

'Yes, I am happy. Please accept my congratulations.'

' ... '

'No, I hadn't promised. I had just said that if I am free I will come.'

' ... '

'Yes, Hamid is here but he has to be present at the dinner, too. All right then, Khuda Hafiz!'

As Judge Saheb raised his eyes, he saw his eldest son, Hamid, standing in front of him. Hamid asked with a laugh, 'So who was that?'

'A certain Maulvi Syed Hasan who used to be our neighbour once upon a time. He had taught me the Holy Quran when I was a child. This gentleman is his younger son. He was a Constable; now he has become a Sub-Inspector. His son is getting married. He has already come three or four times to invite me and now he is calling...'

'I don't know why these people are such block-heads! Why don't they understand on their own? Why do they force the other person to concoct lies? Just imagine... the Chief Justice is going to attend the wedding of a Constable's son! It is preposterous!'

Judge Saheb turned a fond eye towards his worthy son who was, with the Grace of God, a Collector. He lorded over lakhs of lives and had taken four days' leave to visit his father. Love and understanding for his father brimmed in his eyes. He had never tried to portray his father as a liar, traitor, or useless.

The clatter of the ekka could be heard. Judge Saheb looked at the sheet of blotting paper on his desk where, among the pencil markings, he had written: 'That boy says my life is a waste. In fact, not just a waste, it is a zero from beginning till end.'

Then he raised his eyes towards Hamid and said, 'Saeed Saheb is leaving. He acts as though he has done us a favour by staying here... that lazy, good-for-nothing fellow...'

Hamid spoke in the tone of one who was wise beyond his years, his voice dripping with concern, 'Bad company, you know...'

With a nod of his head, Judge Saheb accepted the sympathy extended by his able and worthy son.

Behind the Veil
(a one-act play)

A room covered in a white farsh. In the middle of the room a sozni is placed over the farsh and a lady is reclining against the gaotakhiyas placed on it. She appears to be sad and tired. Beside her is a small surahi, its mouth covered by a katora, resting on a copper plate. Facing her is another lady who appears to be about forty years old; she is busy cutting betel-nut into a kasna. A small chest is placed on one side of the woman and an ugaldan on the other. There are two doors in the wall as well as niches and almirahs containing crockery items. A hand-pulled fan is hanging from the ceiling, edged with a pink ruffle. A bed with a bedcover is pushed against one side of the room.

Muhammadi Begum: Ai hai, Apa, what can I say about myself... I have lived the better part of my life and what is left will soon be over too. I am so fed up of this world that if it weren't for my poor little children, I swear I would have eaten poison by now.

Aftab Begum: Have you lost your senses? You are hardly of an age that you should talk of dying! You are in the spring of your life. Masha Allah, your children are growing up. Talking of poison, indeed! Look at me...

Muhammadi Begum: Why? My feelings have nothing to do with age; it isn't as if only the old get fed up with life. The greed for life that I have seen in the old, I have never seen in the young. All around me I see people dying. I don't know why Death is so elusive! Children forget easily and after some time everything becomes...

Aftab Begum: Come to your senses, my dear girl! You shouldn't be talking about death at your age. You are young, at least ten or twelve years younger than me. There was talk of my marriage the year you were born. It was the year the Queen had died. I can remember clearly how pleased your mother was; she kept saying this baby is like a son for me. You were born at least thirty years after your parents were wed. There was such feasting and dancing and how the domnis sang! What is more, when it was time for your marriage, there were again such elaborate arrangements and celebrations that all of Delhi was agog! Who can be as fortunate as you? You should think of me... You have a home, a husband, children, everything.

Muhammadi Begum: Yes, that's right. Husband, home, children... I have everything. Young? Who can call me young? I look like a seventy year old hag. I am ill every day. I send for a doctor or hakim every day and give birth to a child every year. Yes, who can be more fortunate than me? (*As her eyes well up with tears, she wipes them with a handkerchief, spits into the ugaldaan near her, and then resumes talking.*) About two months ago, before the last pregnancy, I was advised to send for a lady doctor. Even Dr Ghayas said that possibly I was suffering from a fever due to some internal complication and it would be best if a lady doctor examined me. The lady doctor came. She asked me my age. I said: 32 years. She smiled disbelievingly at me. I said: 'Miss saheb, why do you smile? Do you know that I was married at seventeen years of age and since then I have borne a child every year except that one year when my husband had gone abroad and once when he and I had had a fight. And these teeth... Dr Ghayas pulled out my teeth because I had pyorrhoea or whatever it is called. The thing is that when my husband returned from abroad, he said my breath stank.' The lady doctor laughed when I told her this.

Aftab Begum: You do say the oddest of things; what else could she do?

Muhammadi Begum: Anyhow, that poor woman examined my chest, and then my abdomen. When she examined my womb from inside, the poor thing was startled. She said, 'Begum Saheb, you seem to have a two-month pregnancy.' And I? I was stunned... There I go again, I said to myself. (*The voice of children, crying and shouting, could be heard from the other room. Begum Saheba sat up from her reclining position against the gaotakhiya and shouted.*) Hey, you wretches, you don't give me a moment's respite to talk to someone or to rest. There are so many of these bitches roaming around and yet these children of mine are creating such a din. May God take me away from this mess!

(*The door opens and two ayahs come in, wearing clean white clothes, pajamas with matching mulmul dupattas and kurtas. Behind them some children can be seen standing in the doorway. The children are frail and sickly looking. Through the door, you can see the open space of the courtyard beyond.*)

First Maid: Begum saheb, Munne Miyan refuses to listen to us. Every time he enters the room, he teases the little ones and does not let them play. Now he has run off with Nanhi Bi's doll and Chhote Miyan's ball and gone straight to the men's quarter. Several times...

Muhammadi Begum (*getting angry*): He is a butcher, nothing but a butcher! He does not let anyone live in peace. After all, he is his father's son!

(*She pulls the children onto her lap, kisses them, opens the small chest kept nearby and gives them both something to eat. Then she tells the ayahs to leave.*)

Go, for heaven's sake, scoot! Screaming and shouting all day long... that's all you do! Wait! Wait! (*As the ayahs go away and leave the door ajar.*) Hey, shut the door! How many times have I said this since the morning? Every time they come here, they leave the door open.

Aftab Begum: Whenever I come to your home, I find a doctor waiting here, yet look at your children... they are pale and sickly, as though they are victims of starvation.

Muhammadi Begum: Well, it is no wonder; after all, the poor mites have never had a drop of their mother's milk. Ayahs were kept for each one of them... pock-marked, one-eyed, fat, thin, whoever was found was kept. My husband's command is that since, by the grace of God, we have enough money, why should I have to take the trouble of feeding my babies. Whereas the truth is, it's all about his pleasure; if the child stays with me, it will ruin his pleasure in sex. Day or night... nothing matters to him... he wants his wife all the time! And not just his wife... he is not exactly shy of straying.

Aftab Begum: You blame your husband for everything! If he keeps an ayah, he is at fault; if he had not kept one, then too you would have blamed him. Have some fear of God, my dear!

Muhammadi Begum: Ai hai, Apa, you were not here when Naseer died. That poor four-month old baby experienced such pain... I wouldn't wish it on my worst enemy! Even outsiders couldn't bear to see his suffering. He had this ayah, who appeared to be healthy enough and quite fat too, but was suffering from venereal disease. Who could have guessed from her appearance? My baby's body erupted in huge boils and when they burst, we could see his tender, raw flesh beneath the blisters. Every inch of his body was filled with infected sores. Dr Ghayas used to draw up pus by the basin full from that tiny body. I used to watch from behind the curtain, not knowing whether to pray for his recovery or hope for his release. After two months of rotting away, bit by bit, the child finally departed. After that, three more babies were born. Each time, I insisted that I would nurse my babies. But who listens to me? He threatens me that if I suckle my baby, he will marry another woman and bring her home. 'I want a woman all the time,' he says, 'I don't have the patience to wait while you nurse your child.' And then you say...

Aftab Begum: Ai hai, so that's it! How could I have known? God save us from such men; they are worse than animals. We didn't have such things in our time; now every man one hears ofhas the same problem. Take the case of your brother-in-law... of course he is old now but in his youth, he never forced himself on me. (*Smiles*) By God, how I used to make him beg for hours!

Muhammadi Begum (*sighing deeply*): Each to her own fate! By the way, I had not finished telling you about the lady doctor and look how far we have moved away! When she told me I had a two-month old pregnancy, she looked at me with deep surprise and said. 'You were telling me, Begum saheba, that you have been bed-ridden for four months and that you get a fever in the evenings and Dr Ghayas also told me that you run a fever by the end of the day every day. Are you trying to tell me that even then your...?' I told her, 'Ai Miss saheb, you are much better off. You earn your own money, eat what you want, sleep well at night. Here, whether one is going through heaven or hell, he is only concerned with his pleasure. Whether the wife is all right or is dying, men are only concerned with sex.' The poor woman fell silent. Then she said, 'You are so ill.' And why just her... all the other doctors have told me how can my children be healthy if I am so sick all the time, and if my children are

born so frequently one after the other? What is one to do? It
would have been better if one had been a Christian!'

Aftab Begum: Heaven forbid! Don't talk such blasphemous
nonsense. May God remove the kafirs! I have only one son
and he has gone off and married a Christian woman. How I
had dreamt of his marriage to my brother's daughter. And
my brother has had her engaged to someone else. How I
burn at the thought that the girl I had asked for at her birth,
will go off to someone else's home! If only he hadn't been
born! He is dead as far as I am concerned.

Muhammadi Begum: How can you curse your own son? He
is the strength of your old age. He will be all right one day.

Aftab Begum: Ai, he will never be all right. It has been two
years and I am dying to see his face. He lives in this very
city but he never even comes to peep in. I have heard that
he earns a hundred and fifty rupees. I can only praise the
Lord that as yet there is no child. My only wish is that even
if there is no one to light a candle at my grave, let that
Christian bitch never conceive! Hai, Biwi, who does one
share one's sorrows with; everyone has their own troubles...
Muhammadi Begum, have you heard? ... Mirza Maqbool Ali
Shah has got married again. Two of his wives are dead, even
his grand-daughters have become mothers ... and this new
wife of his... she has such an innocent face. She must be
young, very young, no more than twenty years of age. The
poor wretch ... her life is ruined. She has six unmarried
sisters sitting at home. No wonder her poor parents...

(*Suddenly, the eldest son, who is about twelve years old, shows up. The
bottoms of his pajamas are filthy with mud. He is holding aloft a toy
train in one hand and a pair of scissors in the other. Running behind
him is a girl, healthy but dressed in grimy clothes; she is wearing tight
pajamas and her dupatta is trailing on the ground.*)

Girl: Look at him, Amma! He is refusing to listen to me; he
has chopped off my pajama. (*And so saying, she raises her
kurta*) I wasn't even talking to him; I was sitting quietly and
sewing a button on Abba jaan's achkan. And, see, he has
torn my dupatta too. (*And sliding against the wall, she begins to
cry while the boy mimics her crying.*)

Boy: Ow, ow, ow! Won't you tell what you were doing? Were
you sitting and sewing, or were you reading dirty books?
Was it 'The Brave-heart Lover' or 'The Young Rake'? I'm
not sure which as I couldn't see which one it was.

Girl (*turning around*): For heaven's sake, don't lie so! I swear,
Amma, I was reading Maulana Ashraf Ali Saheb's *Bahishti
Zewar*. He was after me to show him the book and when I
didn't, he cut my pajama. But you never say anything to
him.

Muhammadi Begum (*clapping her hands*):Well done! Bravo,
dear daughter! Whether your mother lives or dies, would
you ever think of lending a helping hand? Oh no, you are
far too busy fighting with your younger brothers and sisters.
(*Turning towards her son*) And this wretched fellow goes around
troubling people all day long! Go away, run along from here!

Aftab Begum: Here, Miyan, give those scissors to me. And
why do you trouble your Apa like that? How many more
days is she going to be here with you? She will get married
in another year or two and go away to her in-laws' home.
And then you will miss the sight of her face.

(*The girl, Sabira, instantly ducks her head shyly as soon as she hears
this sentence and sidles out of the room. The boy sits astride a gaotakhiya,
as though on a horse, and after a moment's pause, begins bucking up
and down.*)

Boy: Then why was she not showing me her book?

Muhammadi Begum: Ai Hai, Bade Mirza, for heaven's sake,
have some pity and stop shaking me about like this! You

have rattled me to the bone, you wretched boy. My heart is beating so fast. Go outside, go to your father. And Maulvi Saheb must be coming to teach you; have you revised your lesson?

(*Hearing the word 'lesson', Bade Mirza thought it best to leave the room quietly.*)

Aftab Begum: If you have a lot of children, Masha Allah, while the house seems nicely filled up the constant din drives you mad. When I am alone at home, I spend the whole day sitting as still as a scarecrow. My husband comes home, sits for a while, says his prayers, and then goes off to the men's quarter. May God save one from such terrible loneliness! I had had such dreams...

(*The door opens and a maid enters, carrying a covered dish.*)

Maid: Salaam, Begum Saheb! Badi Begum Saheb, I was about to go to your house with your share... How are you, Begum Saheb? How are your children?

Muhammadi Begum: Well, I am as all right as I can be expected to be. Tell me, how is my sister-in-law? Are the children well? May her grandson be blessed! Has she sent panjiri?... Rahiman, empty the dish. (*Opening the small chest kept near her*) Apa, make a paan for me.

Aftab Begum: Rahiman, take my share here, too.

(*As Aftab Begum busies herself in making paan, Muhammadi Begum gives two annas to the maid.*)

Muhammadi Begum: Convey my salaams to everyone and give my best wishes too. Some day, when I am feeling better, I will come by. Tell them I am dying to meet everyone and especially to see the newborn, and ask my sister-in-law if she has sworn never to come and see me?

(*Aftab hands her the paan and, taking out two annas tucked away in her waist-band, gives them to the maid.*)

Maid: Begum Saheb, my mistress too remembers you a lot but she just doesn't get the time to stir out. In any case, these days, the house is filled with guests

Aftab Begum: Give my best wishes to Sultan Dulhan; may her grandson be blessed. Tell her that I will come to meet her on Friday.

(*The maid picks up the two dishes, offers her salaam to the two ladies, and leaves.*)

Muhammadi Begum: Apa, this sister-in-law of mine, Sultan Begum, is quite something! Her husband has never earned more than forty rupees yet she has such skills, Masha Allah, that she has managed to do everything – had her sons married and then her daughters too. Now, with the grace of God, her son has got a good job; he earns a hundred and twenty-five rupees and there is scope for advancement.

Aftab Begum: Yes, and the daughter-in-law is good, too. (*Sighing deeply*) Each one has her own destiny. Look at me... Anyhow, let that be... Tell me, have you heard anything about Razia? Your Mamu married her in such haste that he didn't even invite anyone for the wedding!

Muhammadi Begum: So what if he didn't invite anyone? He distributed enough food to everyone's house – almost three times what anyone might ordinarily send. And that poor girl was married in such haste simply to avert a scandal. And here, too, my husband can take all the credit.

Aftab Begum: Ai hai, I had no idea! So, tell me what happened?

Muhammadi Begum: You mean, you don't know? Everyone knows by now... That poor girl, she is barely a child. She must be two or two-and-a-half years older than my Sabira. She was born after I got married, when Chhote Mamu

returned from Calcutta. He had come back after being away
for years. We were all gathered there and my grandmother
was so happy, even though she was suffering from paralysis...
A few months ago, I had brought Razia home with me when
Chhoti Mumani had gone to stay with her parents. Razia
loves her father's side of the family and doesn't much care
for the mother's. After all, I am like an elder sister for her;
there is no harm if she comes to stay here. I would never
have dreamt in my wildest dreams that anything was amiss.
When her mother returned, Razia went back to her own
house. One day, I received a note from Razia begging me to
come and see her immediately. How can I describe what
happened when I reached there? You know what my Chhoti
Mumani is like and how she talks in her hypocritical manner!
She greeted me effusively and was volubly hospitable. But
Razia handed me a note telling me that my husband, whom
she calls Dulha Bhai, visits their home daily, how her mother
fusses over him and the two talk in whispers. What more
can an unmarried girl say? As it is, she showed exemplary
courage. She also showed me the letter my husband had
written to her; it was more romantic than anything you might
find in a novel. I read it and went up in flames. I told Razia
not to tell anyone anything, I came home, smouldering with
anger, and spoke to him. Ai, Apa, I swear, he stared straight
into my eyes and asked me what was wrong in it. He said he
wanted to marry Razia, even if it meant divorcing me. I said
to him, 'Miyan, are you in your right mind or have you taken
complete leave of your senses? She is a girl from a sharif
household. If you so much as take her name, her father,
uncles and brothers will chop you into little pieces. It's best
that you don't nurture any false hopes.'

Aftab Begum: So, your aunt must have fixed everything on
the sly; that's why he was showing such brazenness.

Muhammadi Begum: Yes, of course! Mumani jaan has always

hated me and my late lamented mother. Even when my mother was ill and dying, Mumani jaan used to swear that she would not rest in peace till she had destroyed Muhammadi's home. And when Razia's engagement was fixed in her Chacha's home, she swore that she would not give her daughter to the 'enemy'.

Aftab Begum (*laughing*): But why choose your husband? He is married with children, though, yes, he has money. Not that your uncle is any less wealthy. I say, I have never heard of such things among sharif families. Among the wretched Punjabis one has heard of the practice of two sisters marrying off their daughters to the same man but we don't do that.[7] But, then, in this modern age anything goes. So, what happened then?

Muhammadi Begum: When I got angry and started ticking him off, he began to plead and beg. He said he was in love with the girl. 'Hai, for the love of God, help me. It is your duty to help me,' he said. Then, sitting down and opening the Holy Quran, he read out verses telling me that if I did not help him, terrible things would happen to me after death. Tell me, can the fires of hell be any worse than this constant burning? Anyhow, the long and short of it all is that he would constantly tell me that he would go mad. He would shut himself in his room and lie in bed and moan, 'Hai Razia! Hai Razia!' And I... I would have to listen to it. I swear Apa, I am so fed up of my life that all this money means nothing but trouble. If only I had happiness; I wouldn't mind it if I had to live on dry roti... Make a paan for me, Apa. All this talking is making my throat dry.

(*She pours some water from the surahi and drinks it. Aftab eats a paan herself and gives one to Muhammadi.*)

And so things continued... he used romantic words for that poor virginal girl and I had to listen to everything and choke on every word. And my aunt kept up her fawning ways. Everytime my husband went to her home, she would simper, 'Look, Razia, your Dulha Bhai is here. Give him some paan, get him some elaichi...'

Aftab Begum: Do you mean to say it was all your aunt's doing?

Muhammadi Begum: What else? That poor girl used to cry for hours. If I met her somewhere, she would open up her heart to me. For a about a month, I stayed quiet. Then one day both my uncles came to visit me. I said, 'Is it true Mamu jaan that Razia's engagement has been broken off?' Both of them were taken aback. I, who had been sitting silently for so long with everything clamped inside me, suddenly broke down. My feelings welled up and I told them everything. The two of them must have had a consultation for on the third day Razia was married off.

Aftab Begum: It's a good thing she was!

Muhammadi Begum: But, Bua, my husband did not come home for the next six months; he stayed in Chawri[8] the whole time. But I was happy. As God is my witness, on the days that he goes here or there, I get a full night's sleep. These days his daily threat is: 'You are ill every day; how long am I expected to be patient? I am going to get married a second time.' But then he also insists: 'You get my second marriage fixed. The Shariah allows a man to marry four times; so, why shouldn't I marry?' I tell him, 'By all means, say Bismillah and start! A year from now, Sabira will be getting married. Let the father and daughter get married at the same time. You can hold your grandson in one arm and your son from your new wife in the other.'... he starts fighting with me when I say such things and says, 'What would women know? God has not given them sexual desire.' And I say, 'All the lust of all the men in this world is to be found in you, so what else...'

Aftab Begum (*sounding angry*)**:** Muhammadi Begum, it is the same story everywhere these days. Men have played their cards so well that no matter what, they win hands down each time. Now, can there be any thing crueller than to say that he will get married again and that his second marriage must be arranged by the poor wretched first wife...

Muhammadi Begum: Is it any wonder that after listening to such things, I pray for death? There is my own declining health and on top of that, the constant squabbling among my brood of children. Though my elder children are, Masha Allah, healthy enough; it is these younger ones who are ill every day. No wonder I have lost any pleasure in life. I know he will marry again; this daily threat has become intolerable. May God take me before I have to see the face of my husband's new wife! Do you know the things I have done out of fear of my husband getting a new wife? Do you know I have even had two operations?

Aftab Begum: Yes, I had heard that you have had something done so you don't have any more children.

Muhammadi Begum: Who told you that? The truth is that my womb and all the lower parts had slipped so far down that I had to get them fixed, so that my husband would get the same pleasure he might from a new wife. Ai Bua, how long can a woman who bears a child every year expect to have her body remain in good condition? It slipped again. Again he went after me, nagged and threatened me into going under the butcher's knife. But he is still not happy.

(*The sound of the azan can be heard wafting in from the mosque*)

Aftab Begum: Ai hai, Bua, it is the time for the *zuhr* prayer. I have been so engrossed in talking that I forgot everything. (*Tying up the strings of the kasna in which she has been chopping betel nuts*) I will offer my prayer here and then leave; your poor brother would be waiting for me.

Muhammadi Begum: Ai, Apa, I am so glad you came; I could talk to you to my heart's content. You should come more often. I am ill; I can hardly go about... Ai, Rahiman! Rahiman! Gulshabbo!

(Rahiman enters)

Go and help Badi Begum with her *wuzoo* and then spread the jaanamaz on the chowki for her.

(Curtain falls)

Woman
(a one-act play)

Characters

Maulvi Atiqullah

Fatima: Atiqullah's wife

Aziz: A young cousin, the son of Fatima's maternal uncle

Qadeer: Aziz's younger brother

Mumani: The mother of Aziz and Qadeer

The woman tenant

A woman with a child

A maidservant

Badi Bi: A woman servant employed by Atiqullah

Another woman

A boy, seven or eight years old

Time: Between the *zuhr* and *asr* prayer, late afternoon-early evening

Place: *A large courtyard in Fatima's house with two takhts placed on either side; both are covered with a white sheet, bolsters are placed on the sheet. A bed is placed in the middle; its bedding has been rolled and kept at the headstand and is used by Atiqullah as a pillow. A huqqah is kept on one side of the bed and an ugaldan on the other. Fatima is* *sitting on the takht facing the bed; she is stitching something. A paandaan, thaali, kasna and bughchiare lying close at hand. The floor is not plastered. A few low stools are scattered here and there. Several niches are set in the wall of the courtyard; porcelain and copper dishes are placed decoratively in these niches. On the left, there is a door that allows entry from outside into the courtyard; a jute curtain hangs over it. At the back, on the right side, is the door to the staircase. Two doors are visible at the back of the stage; they open into the rooms. One door is ajar; the other is shut.*

Atiqullah (*puffing away at his huqqah*): I cannot understand how my getting married a second time can possibly affect you. The house and the everyday expenses for running the household will remain in your control. I have said this so many times: I will look after both of you equally. I have to, perforce, marry again because your babies don't live.

Fatima (*raising her head*): If the babies don't live, is it because I wring their necks and kill them? If our babies are not willed by Allah Miyan to live, what can I do? Who can have their way against the will of God? What will you do if the other woman's children also die?

Atiq: A man must, after all, do the best he can. You are 40 years old and you have still not produced a single live baby. A child is the support of one's old age. And the Shariat too has permitted that if a woman is barren or her babies do not live, then a man can marry a second time.

Fatima: This is the first I have heard about the Shariat saying anything about children who don't live! You can produce any Shariat you like. May God help me, but I am not barren. I have carried 10 or 12 children – full-term and mid-term – in all. If none of them lived, is it my fault that I must be punished? You go around giving charms and amulets to the whole world; why don't you give yourself the benefit of your wisdom?

Atiq: But that is exactly what I am trying to tell you... Last Thursday, an old man appeared in my dream and told me: You will never have living children from this woman. Marry again so that your heart's desire may come true. If God doesn't will it...

Fatima: You pretend to be this great Maulvi, the whole world respects you and gets you to deliver fatwas. But I swear, these imaginary dreams of yours burn my heart to cinders. Your lies have no effect on me anymore. A moment ago you were saying that some disciple of yours is after you to marry his daughter. And now some old seer comes in your dream to say the same thing on a Thursday! Why don't you tell the truth? That girl was sick. You had gone to rid her of the jinn. The jinn is gone; now you want to take its place. (*Getting angry*) Get married if you must; why ask me? Do you ask me for everything that you do? Why must you lie?

Atiq (*throwing the nozzle of the huqqah away*): What a strange woman! She is calling her husband a liar? No wonder your children die!

Fatima: Now that the second one ...

(*A woman wearing a tight pajama enters. She is wearing a dirty burqa and is holding a small child in her arms. The child is as grubby as the mother and is wearing a necklace of amulets around its neck. Atiq and Fatima fall silent as they catch sight of the woman. Fatima goes back to her sewing, Atiqullah resumes puffing on his huqqah. The woman steps forward and greets Atiq and then Fatima by offering her salaam. Then she sits down on one of the low stools between the bed and the takht.*)

Atiq: So, is your child well?

Woman: Thanks to your blessings, yes, huzoor. But the young master is still not well. His fever is raging. He is fretful and restless. Can you please change his amulet? And, Maulvi Saheb, my mistress has said that she would be very grateful if you could stop by her place in the evening and look at the child.

Atiq(*frowning*): Look here, I don't like going to people's houses every now and then, especially to the homes of those who lack faith. (*Pulling on his huqqah*) Her husband pretends to be an English lord. Tell your mistress that if she gives the child English medicine, then I can do no more.

Woman: Why, huzoor, how can you say you can't do anything? You can do everything! My mistress kept shouting, but her husband went and brought some wretch of a doctor. He prescribed castor oil, wrote out a prescription and diagnosed it as a case of indigestion.

Atiq (*laughing sarcastically*): Indigestion! Why, that is so funny! There is a shadow over the boy! (*Angrily*) If she wanted me to treat the boy, why did she allow English medicine to be given? I shall not go to see the child now. If they want they can bring the child here.

Woman (*sliding the stool forward*): Maulvi Saheb, the medicine has not yet been given, though the master had had the child drink the oil rightaway. My mistress has asked me to tell you not to be angry. What could the poor lady do; she was helpless in front of her husband. And, huzoor, my mistress has said that the poor child is not fit enough to get off his bed or else she would never have dreamt of troubling you. She would herself have brought the child here and laid him at your feet. No doubt it will be a terrible hardship for you, huzoor, but I will come to fetch you whenever you are free to come.

Atiq: Unnhh. I too am concerned about that poor little mite. Otherwise, I don't go to people's houses, nor do I treat those who disobey my orders. Why trouble me if they want to administer the medicines of those kafirs?

Woman: Huzoor, what shall I do now? We women can't pit ourselves against our men. My mistress has complete faith in you, and rightly so. Look (*pointing towards her own child*), my child's teeth are coming out only thanks to your amulet.

No fever, no itchy eyes! Ask anyone... everyone praises your miracles.

Atiq: I don't deserve any praise; it is God's word. Everything is thanks to Him.

Woman: But, Maulvi Saheb, everyone cannot understand the word of God. (*Nudging her stool closer to the bed*) After all, a Maulvi Saheb lives in the alley with the neem tree... let me not start about him!

(*The sound of someone rapping the bolt loudly on the door outside can be heard.*)

Atiq: Who is there?

(*The noise from the loud clanking of the bolt continues.*)

Atiq (*to the woman*): Go and see who is outside.

(*The woman puts down the baby and goes out.*)

Fatima (*in a bitter tone*): The child should be treated by a doctor; he has indigestion. He has already been given a laxative. It will bring the fever down; and the Maulvi Saheb will be praised for it. It is these frauds who draw people towards you...

(*The woman returns with a letter. Fatima falls silent as Atiq begins to read.*)

Atiq (*addressing Fatima*): Here, it is addressed to you; a letter from your aunt. She will come to visit you, yet again, this evening. (*Addressing the woman*) All right, my girl, you can go now. You can come to take me after sunset.

(*The woman offers salaam, picks up her baby and leaves.*)

Atiq: This aunt of yours visited you barely four days ago. Does she have nothing to do in her own home? This is a new trend... women don't seem to want to stay put for two days in their houses.

Fatima: How does it bother you if she drops in for a while now and then?

Atiq: No doubt her sons will come with her. Actually, you should observe parda from them.

Fatima: Why? Both of them are younger than me. Moreover, they have come to live in Delhi after years. How I had been longing to see their faces! And you are saying I should observe parda from them!

Atiq: I don't like the ways of your uncle's household. If a person stays away from home, it does not mean that he should forsake his time-honoured ways and become a Christian! And the boys... they go around looking like Christians. And that aunt of yours has learnt to tie a sari in her old age.

Fatima: Well, certainly not in her old age! She has always worn a sari. She got married to my uncle and they went to live abroad. May God grant paradise to my uncle, as long as he lived he was inseparable from his wife! Many of their acquaintances were Hindu. (*Flaring up suddenly*) And what is wrong with wearing a sari?

Atiq: What isn't wrong with it? Leaving your own Islamic dress for one and mixing with kafirs for another... is it decent behaviour? Anyway, forget the mother. Look at the sons who go swaggering about in their English clothes! What is one to make of that? (*Pauses*) First of all, those men are na-mehram for you and you must observe parda from them. And, secondly, *I* don't want you to appear before Aziz and Qadeer.

Fatima: You become obstinate about any one thing. What about my elder uncle? I don't observe parda before his elder son. But that is all right because he is your friend and admirer; therefore he is mehram for me! You call him to our house all the time; he drops in on his own, too. And he is not na-mehram. And Aziz and Qadeer, with whom I have exactly the same blood relation, they are na-mehram! Tell me how?

Atiq: I don't have to tell you everything. It is the duty of a wife to obey her husband's command without doubt or delay. Whereas you, you question and interrogate everything I say. If you really want to know my answer, then listen... These days, there is no accounting for the ways of young men. They have no faith, no religion no fear of God or His Prophet in their hearts. They drink and eat the meat of forbidden animals. (*In his excitement he sits up in the bed.*) Can there be anyone more debauched than these young men? They cast lascivious eyes at the virtuous women of other men. They are kafirs!

Fatima (*angrily*): God forbid that they should be kafir! Why should they be kafir? Is it a pious act to call someone a kafir? And must you start digging up old corpses again? Casting lascivious eyes, indeed! As though your sister is pure! Poor Qadeer only expressed a desire to marry her; that can't be termed as casting lascivious glances.

Atiq: No, no, it is casting saintly looks! Coming into other people's homes and looking at girls, is that good behaviour?

Fatima: Who looked where? Your sister used to show up, bare headed and bare faced! And it isn't as though she was a babe in the arms! She was a few years older than Qadeer; he was, after all, a boy. Why go after Qadeer; why not look at yourself? Look at you, you are crazy over Kaneez Fatima and you are blaming me for being childless. (*Angrily*) No one ever sees their own flaws.

Atiq: Astakhfurullah! Kaneez's parents are begging me to marry her because they think I am noble and exalted.

Fatima: Yes, yes, God knows how many people will rue their fate because of your nobility and exaltedness. My own father sacrificed me over it... (*The maid enters. Fatima turns around and begins talking to her without a pause.*) Look here, Badi Bi, you forgot to sweep the kitchen before you left; the place is buzzing with flies. And now you have shown up so late!

Maid (*comes close and sits down on the stool*): I got a bit late. I had gone to meet my friend; her daughter is visiting from her in-laws'. Time passed so quickly when we sat down to talk that I didn't realise it! (*After a pause*) Biwi, give me a piece of paan... Will you give some money to buy groceries, or will the food be sent from somewhere?

Fatima (*handing her the paan, and speaking sarcastically*): Don't worry about food! May God keep our Maulvi Saheb alive, we get to eat free pulau and qorma every day! One of his devotees is getting married today; they will send the food. For now, pick through the fennel I had put in the sun to dry. Clean and pound it; I will make chutki out of it tomorrow.

(*The maid gets up to leave.*)

Fatima: And, listen, Badi Bi, clean the dishes properly and sweep the kitchen thoroughly. Hurry up! My Mumani is expected.

Atiq (*burps*): Badi Bi, get me some water first.

Fatima (*cutting him short*): Go, go and do your work. He will get his water. (*Fatima gets up, pours water in a bowl, dumps it forcefully beside Atiqullah and begins to walk away.*)

Atiq (*holding the bowl of water in one hand*): This Qadeer who has been practising law for the last two years... does he earn anything from it?

Fatima: Of course, he earns! He doesn't go around spreading his hand in front of everyone.

Atiq (*sliding down on the takht once again*): Why doesn't he get married if he is earning?

Fatima: He will get married, what is the hurry? He is still young; he says he will get married to a girl of his choice. I am ever grateful to God that he didn't marry your sister; the poor boy would have ruined his life. How you must be regretting the loss!'

Atiq: (*sitting up straight*): How could that kafir have even dared to win my sister? I would never have permitted their match in my lifetime.

Fatima: All right, so let him be a kafir, a low caste, full of every imaginable vice. That sister of yours who has been married into a high-caste Saiyyed family, is she happy?

Atiq: They are pure blooded. Their family...

Fatima: Ai hai! If Qadeer's blood is so inferior, why did you marry into his family?

Atiq: I? I didn't do anything. It was your father who was so enamoured of me that he begged me to marry you.

Fatima: Well, all right, my father begged you and your father and wrecked my life. But this new marriage that you are embarking on ... is she also a Saiyyedani? You are, by God's grace, forty years old; you are not exactly a lad. Spare a thought for your years.

Atiq: What's the point of all this nonsense?

(*Fatima picks up her sewing from the bughchi and begins to sew.*)

Atiq (*after a short silence*): I am thinking of getting rid of the tenants on the first floor.

Fatima: (*angrily*): Why? It is my house. First of all, we get a rent for it. Secondly, the tenant's wife is a good woman. She is there for me in good times and bad. I will never allow this tenant to be thrown out.

Atiq: What has happened to you these days? You argue and dispute everything.

(*Suddenly, a seven or eight year old boy enters, carrying a tray covered by a cloth on his head. He speaks hurriedly.*)

Boy: Salaam, Mullani ji. Biwi has sent this portion of sweets. Empty the dish and return it.

Fatima: Where have you brought it from? And what is the occasion?

Boy: I have brought it from the Lane of the Pandits. Empty the dish and return it.

Fatima: I'll do it; give me a moment. What are the sweets for?

Boy: A lot of ladies had come.

Fatima: But, child, a lot of people live in the Lane of the Pandits; tell me whose house?

Boy: They are from the house with the tamarind tree.

Atiq: Why ask him all these questions? How does it matter where they have come from? We are only interested in the sweets... they must be from the home of some disciple... What a pretty dish this is! (*To the boy*) Go tell your mistress that the sweets are for the Mullaniji, and Maulvi Saheb has kept the dish.

Fatima: Keep the tray as well; why leave that? After all, it is more expensive.

Boy (*Scared*): My mistress had asked me to bring the dish back. If I don't, she will beat me.

Atiq: Go, go and tell her what I have said; she won't beat you then.

(*The boy stands quietly; he doesn't leave.*)

Atiq (*Loudly*): Arre, why don't you go?

(*The boy leaves, moving slowly, turning back every few steps to look at the dish.*)

Atiq: Pass me the sweets; let me see what sort they are.

Fatima (*Bends and passes him the dish. Atiq picks up one and pops it in his mouth*): Look here, you were unwell a minute ago, now you are eating these rich, heavy sweets, in the evening you will again eat rich banquet foods at the wedding. Will you fall ill, or not? Anyhow, why should I bother? (*Picking up the dish*): Are you done, or will you have more?

Atiq (*Picking up one more piece*): That's it, I don't want any more.

(*Fatima takes the sweets and goes inside. Atiq finishes the sweet in his mouth and begins to pick the crumbs fallen on the bed, putting them in his mouth and burping all the while. A woman enters; wrapped in a burqa, she looks around. She offers her salaam and stands.*)

Woman: Where is the Mullaniji?

Atiq (*Looking all around him*): She has gone in; why?

Woman: Maulvi Saheb, I have come from the house of Mirza Haider Baig. I want to speak to you; can you come to the baithak outside?

Atiq (*Yawning*): No, no, you can speak here; she has gone in.

(*The woman sits down on the low stool.*)

Woman: The girl's side are saying that you sent the proposal and then went quiet. They have received another offer. But they have decided to wait till they hear a 'yes' or 'no' from your side before they consider the other one.

Atiq (*Sitting up in a hurry*): No, no, tell them to refuse the other offer immediately. I was in two minds whether I should marry again or not, but now there is no question of indecision. A voice in my dream has instructed me to get married a second time; how can I now step back? Tell Haider Baig that soon all will be well.

(*Fatima comes out and stands, silently listening.*)

Woman: May God keep you happy! My master says those women are fortunate who are lucky enough to get a husband like you. He will be very happy to hear this; he is your devout follower. He says he has never seen a man as pious and God-loving as you. But my mistress says that after everything is said and done, her daughter will still be a second wife.

Atiq: Arre, tell her not to think of such things. My wife herself is after me; she tells me to get married again so that I can have living children. I would never have thought of doing such a thing without her consent. Moreover, she isn't the quarrelsome kind. If her children do not survive, what can we do; she and I are both helpless. Moreover, Allah has commanded men to marry four times.There is no injustice for anyone in this.

Woman: That is exactly what my master says: if a man can treat them both equally then it is a pious act to marry twice. Maulvi Saheb, may God keep you happy, but where will she live?

Atiq: I will get rid of the tenant upstairs and have the rooms repaired and made fit for her.

Fatima (*Stepping forward angrily*): Get rid of the tenant indeed! Let me see how you will remove the tenant. This house was given to me by my father. Forget you, even your jinnat cannot remove the tenant from this house. And you...

Atiq (*Making an effort to curb his anger and speaking softly*): What is the need for this nonsense? You can say whatever you have to to me, later.

Fatima: Why? Am I scared of anyone?

(*Atiq makes a sign to the woman; she leaves hurriedly.*)

Atiq (*Pulling himself up*): Look here, what is the meaning of this? (*In a terribly strict voice*): What do you mean by jumping like this into the middle of a conversation? Have you completely lost your senses?

Fatima (*In a loud voice*): Me? What have I done? Instead of being ashamed of yourself for lying, you are shouting at me. What do you think of yourself? Do you think you can sit here in my house and talk like this and expect me to sit quietly and accept everything?

Atiq (*His anger mounting*): And you? What are you? The highest and mightiest of ladies have had to accept a second wife. And they didn't say a word; instead, they spent their entire lives in devotion to their husband. (*Shouting*): You are a sinful and terrible woman. You are preparing a place for yourself in hell by enraging me.

Fatima (*In a voice quivering with rage*): And what pious acts are you doing? Do you think you will go to heaven for this? Forget one hell, I am willing to endure a thousand hells. You listen to me carefully: that wife of yours cannot enter this house.

Atiq (*Enraged, he stands up*): Is there no end to your nonsense? If you have no fear of God and His Prophet and your husband who is your earthly God, then you're the basest, vilest and most shameless of all creatures. I am not going to stop my remarriage because of your nonsense. I will marry again no matter what! And she will stay in this very house. Your status will be less than a dog's because that is what you deserve.

(*With this magisterial pronouncement, Atiq turns to go out.*)

Fatima (*Steps forward and screams*): Wait and listen to this: I will grind all your 'Maulviyat' and your good name into dust and I will not let that beloved of yours set foot in this house. I am not the daughter of some impoverished Saiyyed that I will be intimidated by you.

Atiq (*Turning around*): You illiterate, hell-bound woman, if you cannot understand my words, can you understand this? (*He lands a resounding slap on Fatima's face and turns to go out.*)

Fatima (*Incensed beyond all control, Fatima gnashes her teeth and grabs the Maulvi by his kurta*): If you have to hit me, hit me properly. I swear by God and His Prophet that if I don't turn your honour and your very existence into dust, I am not the daughter of Hameed Baig, but born of some low-caste sweeper.

(*Atiq frees his kurta from her grasp and, shaking with anger, leaves the house.*)

Fatima (*Helplessly*): Where are you going? Some big-shot Maulvi you are! Liar! Cheat!

(*Fatima hides her face in her dupatta and begins to sob. The sound of footsteps coming down the stairs can be heard. A woman first thrusts her head in to peer and then comes forward.*)

Tenant: What happened, Mullani ji? Why are you crying? Is everything all right?

(*The tenant comes and stands near her. Then she holds her by the hand and makes her sit down on the takht.*)

Tenant: After all, say something... what is wrong? I could hear the Maulvi Saheb speaking loudly and getting very angry. I could hear his voice all the way up. Tell me, what happened?

Fatima(*Sobbing*): Second marriage... he is getting married again... And he hit me. (*Getting angry*) O God, punish such wicked people!

Tenant: Hit you? Maulvi Saheb did? No, no, I can't believe it! Honestly, tell me the truth, I beg you!

Fatima (*Wiping her face with the end of her dupatta*): Anyhow, he will soon meet his match. He shouldn't think that I am fatherless and brotherless. He can't do as he pleases...

Tenant: No wonder he was telling us to vacate our rooms. I was wondering why... But what is the matter?

Fatima (*Wiping her face and sobbing*): He asked you to vacate the rooms? When did he say that?

Tenant: He told my husband last night.

Fatima: She hasn't even set foot here and already he has begun to hit me. God knows what will happen to me once she comes. Tell your husband not to move out.

Tenant: Arre, heaven forbid, will he listen to you, or Maulvi Saheb?

(*The maid too comes and stands near them; she is looking at Fatima with pitying eyes.*)

Maid: Maulvi Saheb was in such a towering rage today.

Tenant: See, you can see the imprint of all five fingers on her cheek.

Maid: Hai, such a great Maulvi and he lifts his hand against a woman!

(*Fatima wipes more tears.*)

Tenant: He has never beaten you before; it's because of this new marriage that he is planning. By God, it makes no difference whether a man is a Maulvi or not, it does not take long for a man to change colours. I don't care if anyone likes my words or not. I for one don't like this Maulvi's doings one little bit!

Fatima (*Spreading her hands*): Ai Allah! What sort of justice is this? You show such benevolence one moment, and then such cruelty? Why did You make us women so helpless? (*After a pause*): No matter what happens, I swear I will avenge myself for that slap and for that second marriage he is planning. Look at him, now he is blaming me for my children not surviving.

Tenant: Can there ever be a woman who would not rue the loss of her own children? To have to bear the loss of her children and on top of that get beaten by one's husband, what sort of justice is that? ... My husband set out in the morning to search for another house.

Maid: She lost three almost grown up children; the rest were all stillborn.

Tenant: Maulvi Saheb gives amulets to everyone, treats illnesses, captures evil spirits; why does he not treat his own wife?

Fatima: Treat the sick, my foot! It's all eyewash; nothing but a way of extracting money by fraud. And his greed is such that along with the sweets that someone sends him, he even keeps the dish!

Tenant: Well, I am telling you for the first time today. When I tell my husband the same thing, he begins to fight with me. He has tried his best, my husband says. If God doesn't will it, what can he do?

Maid: Ai, Biwi, do stop; how long will you cry? (*And wiping her own tears*): Your destiny is flawed. Your husband is getting another wife and has also started beating you. He wasn't like this earlier. Of course, he always raved and ranted and shouted, but I've never seen him raise his hand against you before.

(*From outside, the voice of the palanquin-bearers can be heard.*)

Palanquin-bearers: Come and get your passenger... Come and get your passenger...

(*The maid wipes her tears and stands up and goes out slowly.*)

Maid: Why are you making such a din? I am coming.
Tenant: Who could it be?
Fatima: Must be my aunt.

(*The aunt enters, dressed in a crisp, starched sari. The tenant offers her salam. The aunt answers with a nod of her head and sits down beside Fatima. Fatima remains seated, quiet as before.*)

Aunt: Why, Beti, what's wrong? Are you not well? (*Inching closer*): Why are you crying?

(*Fatima stands up and bends to cling to her aunt. She is now crying, great wracking sobs.*)

Aunt: (*To the tenant*): What happened? Is all well?
Tenant: Maulvi Saheb hit her.
Aunt: Hai! What? Hit her? Why?... Fatima, Ai Beti, stop it.

Tell me what happened. (*Helps her sit straight and sits down on the takht beside her.*)

(*A man's voice can be heard outside.*)

Man's voice: Badi Bi, Badi Bi, can I come inside?
Aunt: Who is it? Aziz? Come in.
Tenant: Oh, wait a second; let me leave first.

(*Aziz enters, but upon seeing a strange woman present in their midst, he stops.*)

Aunt: Wait a second; let the parda lady leave.
(*The tenant makes a hasty exit.*)
Aunt: You can come in now.

(*A young man enters; he is dressed in a shervani and pajama. He remains standing.*)

Fatima (*wiping her tears*): Sit down, miyan; there is a bed in front of you.
Aziz: What happened, Apa jaan?
Fatima: What can I tell you, brother? A woman without a father or brother can only expect such dishonour and such a fate.
Aziz: Leave your complaints for a while; first tell me what is troubling you.

(*The aunt points towards Fatima's cheek.*)

Aziz (*Bending to peer at Fatima's face*): Why is your face red?
Fatima: Why is it red? Everyone – from God Almighty to fate to my husband – is slapping me in the face. What else can it be?
Aziz: For, heaven's sake, tell me what happened?
Fatima:Happened? He is planning to marry a second time. He says my children don't survive. So he will marry again.
Aunt: Second marriage?

Fatima: Yes, yes, he is planning a second marriage! And when I said I won't let his second wife enter my house, he shouted and screamed and slapped me hard on my face.

Aunt: What a nerve! It is your house, given to you by your father. He has no right to bring anyone else to this house. If he is so fond of getting married again, he should take another house for her.

Aziz: But does he even have the right to marry again when his first wife is around?

Aunt: Let's not talk of right, miyan; he is a man. Who can stop him? The Most Merciful, the Most Benevolent God Almighty, the Holy Quran, Shariat, community – everything allows him. Forget a second marriage; he can marry three more times. It is the women who must suffer.

Fatima: And on top of it all, he says he will treat us both equally, care in exactly the same way. She hasn't even come here as yet and already...

Aziz: Does he also say that he will love you both equally? There is a big difference between love and care.

Aunt: Who can love equally? The first wife always slips from the man's heart. Not even the greatest of men can claim to love equally; this poor man is, after all, only a Maulvi.

Fatima: He thinks no one is his equal in the whole wide world. He tells me the most pious of women have had to put up with co-wives without so much as a murmur of protest.

Aziz (*Laughs*): He is not wrong; after all, only women can get co-wives; cows or buffaloes can't!

Fatima: Miyan, if you were a woman...

Aunt: Exactly! What would he know? A man thinks as long as he has given a woman food and clothing, he has done enough. The more conscientious husband would think he is beingfair if he spends one night with one wife and the other with the second. As though wives are mere toys for their husband, he can play with either one he fancies. And who is to blame? What if the two women were to unite? What would the man do then?

Aziz: The man would leave both and marry a third!

Aunt: I don't just mean the two wives; I mean women generally. The real thing is that we women are basically unfortunate. When Allah Himself has given a higher status to men, then...

Fatima: Oh, come on! Men have written these books according to their own wishes. Those who create religions, write shariahs and laws – they are all men after all! They write everything to suit men; what would they know about a woman's heart? Had they been women, they would have known!

Aunt: God forbid, Beti, repent, repent! Don't spew such sacrilege in your anger. Those people were dear to God. Who are we before them? How can we question their wisdom or examine and test their actions? They were sinless and pure beings. They cannot be compared with these other men...

Aziz: But this is most unfair, Amma jaan! You are upbraiding Maulvi Saheb for obeying his rights, whereas I am praising him...

Aunt: The less said about you the better...

(*A knock can be heard on the door outside and a man's voice calls out.*)

Voice: Can I come in?

Aziz: Look, Apa jaan, Qadeer bhai too has come.

(*Aziz gets up to draw the curtain aside.*)

Aziz: Come in, Qadeer bhai, the coast is absolutely clear.

(*Qadeer enters, dressed in a suit.*)

Qadeer: Adabarz, Apa jaan. What's the matter? Why is everyone so quiet? Were you criticising me? No wonder my ears were burning!

Aziz: No, we weren't criticising you; we were praising Maulvi Saheb, at least I was.

Qadeer: How interesting! Well, is he once again making his predictions?

Fatima: No predictions now; this time, he has had a dream.

Qadeer: Thank God, he stopped short of meraj!

Aunt: The two of you can think of nothing but fun and jokes all the time. Can't you for once think of the trouble of other people around you?

Qadeer: Trouble? Who's in trouble?

Aunt: Your sister is going to get a co-wife. And you are making wisecracks at such a time!

Qadeer: By God, I had no idea! This is terrible! This must be a new development because when I was here last week, there was no mention of such a thing.

Fatima: I myself came to know only three days ago.

Qadeer: So, when is the Maulvi Saheb setting out with his wedding party? Will he go to the bride's house riding on a horse? Forgive me, Apa jaan, but I find this hilarious. (*He laughs uproariously*): Who is the lucky girl who is going to get this coveted place?

Fatima: She is the daughter of one of his disciples.

Qadeer: Really! Tell me everything.

Aunt: What is there to tell? First you laugh to your heart's content. He will marry again and bring his new wife to live in this house. And when your sister refused and said this is her house and she wouldn't let the second wife stay here, he hit her.

Qadeer: Did he hit you? Tell me the truth, Apa Jaan. How dare he lift a hand against you? And what is more surprising is that an honourable woman like you allowed him to hit you.

Fatima: What could I do, miyan? He hit me so hard. Should I have hit him back?

Qadeer: Why not? There is no doubt that Maulvi Saheb would have won in a wrestling bout, but you should have given him a couple of tight ones, too.

Aunt: There you go again... making light of everything.

Qadeer: Really, Amma jaan, you are the limit! Would I joke about something like this? I am being dead serious. You are the one who is taking it lightly. Ordinarily, no one can stay sober after listening to the manly exploits of our Maulvi Saheb. But this is making me very angry. How can you just sit there looking so helpless?

Fatima: Bhai, I am a woman without an heir or issue; what can I do to stop him?

Qadeer: Heir or issue? You are not a child that you should need support. As long as a human being does not have confidence in himself and does not become his own heir, no one in the whole wide world can help him.

Aunt: My dear, that is all very well but what can a childless woman from a cloistered world do without a man?

Fatima: Yes, Mumani jaan, you tell me in all fairness...

Qadeer: There is no reason to take offence. The sympathy I have for you is a given; talking about it will only fritter it away. But tell me, Apa jaan, what would you have me do? Do you want me too to sit with you and cry, the way my mother and Aziz seem to be doing?

Aziz: Don't take my name. Here I was fighting a valiant fight for poor Maulvi Saheb. After all, why can't the poor man marry again? I myself plan to keep four wives.

Aunt: Ai hai, I don't care for your wisecracks one bit! You find and keep one, then talk about four.

Qadeer: Apa jaan, first tell me exactly what it is that you want. And what can we do to help you?

Fatima: I don't want her to step foot in my house. He can keep her wherever he wants. (*Spreading the hem of her dress wide in supplication*): May God Almighty will her children to be born only to die like mine! Let others also know the pain of this false allegation.

Qadeer: Nothing will come of this cursing. Talk sense. Tell me, all you want is that she should not come to live here, isn't it? What if he does not agree? What will you then do?

Aunt: What can the poor thing do? What else but weep and wail and accept her lot?

Fatima: I won't weep and wail and sit quietly. I will shout from the rooftops and tell the whole neighbourhood about the cruelty he is heaping on a poor defenceless woman.

Qadeer: And what good would that do? She will, in any case, start living in your house. Your shouts will go no further than forty yards at the most.

Fatima (*With great passion*): Are there no courts left in this world? Is there no law that can help me stop her from entering my house?

Qadeer: Yes, there are laws. Because this is your own house, you can stop her from entering it. But will you have the courage to approach a court of law?

Fatima: If he brings her here then, by God, I will do everything I say I will!

Aunt (*Sounding scared*): Beti, don't take God's name in vain. You are angry now; you will regret your words when you have cooled down. Moreover, people from good families don't go knocking at the doors of courts and tribunals.

Qadeer: If they don't, it is time they did now! Amma jaan, why do you sap her of her strength and weaken her spirit?

Aunt: I, weaken her spirit? And how have you become her family elder? Don't forget Fatima's mother is still alive; she will be furious if she hears of this court business. The truth is that I too am dead against these legal shenanigans.

Aziz: Amma jaan, no one goes to the court unless they are pushed into doing so. If you were to stop getting the rent for your shop, would you not take legal steps?

Aunt: Look here, boys, have you lost your brains? Are you really planning to send your sister to a courthouse?

Qadeer: We won't push her but, yes, if Apa jaan asks us for our help we will do everything we can. Unlike you, we won't tell her to weep and wail and accept her lot. Anyhow, let's leave this argument aside. Tell me, how and why did he think of this new marriage?

Fatima: He says it isn't God's will that my children should live. Some saint appeared in his dream and told him that he must marry again; only then will your children live, the saint said.

Qadeer: Being a Maulvi is a jolly easy job! The children don't live because of his fault, and he is saying it is God's command!

Fatima: Three died in childhood, one due to smallpox. And I, I was left empty-handed.

Qadeer: It's all because of him; I bet he didn't let you get them inoculated.

Fatima: No, my poor mites did not get their inoculation shots; English medicines are anathema in this house. But the ones after them were either stillborn or died shortly after birth. Surely, this is my destiny. It is my misdeeds that stare me in the face.

Qadeer: Don't blame your destiny. And it is not your 'misdeeds', nor have you had the chance to commit any sins. The cause of the death of all your babies is no one else but Maulvi Saheb himself. In fact, I had come here to tell you precisely this. You remember that day when Dr Iqbal had come to take a sample of your blood... the result has come. I must tell you in private.

Fatima: Why in private? We don't have to hide anything from Mumani jaan or Aziz.

Qadeer: As you wish ... All I wanted to tell you was that my friend, Dr Iqbal, has told me that if you get proper medical attention, you can give birth to a healthy child – provided, of course, that Maulvi Saheb agrees to take the treatment.

Fatima: He will never agree to take English medication. Though I would have managed it somehow on the sly but now that he is getting married again, why would he even listen to me? Anyway, what is wrong with him?

Qadeer: You can say it is a heat of sorts.*

Fatima: What did you say? How can I get this foul disease? Surely, there must be a mistake somewhere. No one in my entire family, going back to several generations, has had such a disease.

Qadeer: You don't have it; Maulvi Saheb has it.

Aunt: God forbid, be careful what you say! He is a Maulvi after all; he can heap as many cruelties as he wants but he won't do this kind of dirty business.

Aziz: How would you know: do you run after every Maulvi to check what he is up to?

Fatima: I, too, am finding this hard to believe.

Qadeer: You may or may not believe it. I cannot say anything about Maulvi Saheb. His blood has not been examined, but you certainly have the disease.

Fatima: But how did I get it?

Qadeer: I think you would have got it from Maulvi Saheb.

Fatima (*With sudden passion*): If you are right and if he is indeed responsible for killing my babies, I will teach him a lesson that he – and that dewy new bride of his – will remember all their life, even if I end up begging on the streets! Mumani jaan, I want to give you my jewellery box and papers relating to the house and other properties for safekeeping; God knows when I might need them.

Aunt: But, my dear, that is a huge responsibility! Why don't you give them to your mother?

---

* Sexually transmitted diseases were referred to as *garmi*, or a sickness caused by excess 'heat' in the body.

Fatima: You know what my mother is like... she will never listen to me; she will only believe my husband's version. She always does exactly as he says. No one can love a daughter as well or as dearly as she loves her son-in-law. If he tells me to will all my property to the other woman, my mother will say I must do so. If she has her way, I could die but still not do enough for him.

Qadeer: Apa jaan, if you trust me, I am willing to keep your jewellery and papers. My mother is no better than yours. She will also say: You can die but never do enough for your husband.

Fatima: May God keep you happy! I will bring them.

(She goes in.)

Aunt: What is wrong with you, Qadeer? Why are you getting into the private matters of other people? As it is, Maulvi Saheb hates your guts. And you are not a child any more...

Aziz: But, Amma jaan, when she is asking us for our help, it is against humanity to refuse her at such a time.

Aunt: This is a fine time to talk of humanity! Her mother is alive, her mother's brother is alive. She has an uncle from her father's side and other cousins too. Why must you get involved?

Qadeer: Her mother, uncles and cousins will end up pushing her back into the hell she lives in. When she says she does not want Maulvi Saheb's second wife to live in her house — and it is certain that he will want to bring his second wife to this house – why should we not help her?

Aunt: Tomorrow, if Atiqullah were to charge us with abducting his wife... what would we do then?

Qadeer: His wife is not a child. There is no need to do anything on the sly. Why would we abduct her? Though, yes, if she comes to us, we should not shut our door on her.

Aunt: The two of you will never listen to me. I should blame the 'New Light'* for this... Hush, she is coming out.

(*Fatima comes out of her room holding a small box in her hands.*)

Fatima: Here, it has all my money, jewellery... a few things are at my mother's.

Qadeer (*Taking the box from her*): It weighs a ton! Is it filled with bricks of gold?

Fatima: Hardly! You take it with you now. He must be about to return... Aziz, will you come by tomorrow morning... I have some more papers that I want to give you.

Aunt: Beti, I don't have the courage to walk away with this.

Qadeer: Don't worry, Amma jaan, I will keep it in your doli; you can leave with it.

(*He goes out holding the box.*)

Aunt: You boys are the limit...

Aziz: Just think, Amma jaan, if he were to return, we will lose the contents of this box forever. Her jewels will be worn by another woman. You were just telling me that I am no use in times of trouble...

(*Qadeer returns; the aunt gets to her feet.*)

Aunt: No one listens to one's elders anymore. May God keep you happy! May God change Atiq's intentions! And may I return what you have given to me for safekeeping; you are placing a huge burden on me.

(*Maulvi Atiqullah can be heard clearing his throat; everyone falls silent as he enters.*)

Atiq: Assalamwaaleikum!

Aziz and Qadeer: Adabarz!

---

* The 'New Light' was the new wave spreading awareness about *Nai Taleem* or new western-style education, pioneered by Sir Syed Ahmad Khan at Aligarh.

Atiq: A re you going away upon seeing me?

Aunt: No, we were about to go in any case. I was just saying my farewells when you entered.

(*The aunt looks at her sons and makes a face; her look says: May God help you!*)

Qadeer: I had come with a message from A pajaan's doctor. I shall seek your leave now. A dabarz, A pajaan. (*To Atiq*) A dabarz.

Aziz: A dabarz.

Aunt (*Hugging Fatima, she whispers*): T hink very carefully, B eti, before you do anything.

(*Everyone, except Atiq, turns to go. Fatima walks them till the door where everyone takes leave of her. Fatima comes back and begins to walk in the other direction without looking at Atiqullah.*)

Atiq: W hat doctor was Q adeer referring to? I don't know anything about this. A re you sick? A nd how dare you see a doctor without my permission?

Fatima (*Standing stock still*): I have the disease you have given me... you have caused my innocent babies to die. You murderer! I will get myself treated by whoever I want. N o one can stop me now. I have suffered enough at your hands by listening to your commands.

Atiq: W hat is the meaning of this nonsense? D on't think you can speak to me on the strength of your cousins. A nd I will see how these people enter my house again...

Fatima: Your house? H as anyone in your entire family ever owned a house? N o better than beggars... the lot of you! A s long as I am alive, my family will not leave me. You can go; they won't go. S ome nerve you have...

Atiq (*Angrily*): I swear by my A lmighty G od, I will teach you such a lesson for your insolence! You deserve the most severe punishment. You ill-fated woman, you have still not learnt to repent for your misdeeds. I will teach you a lesson that even you will remember...

(*Atiq gets up from the takht and begins to walk towards her in a towering rage. His right hand is raised high to slap her as he approaches her.*)

Fatima (*Making an effort to control her temper*): Careful! I tell you Sit down ... if you care one jot about your honour. If you raise your hand one more time, I promise you I will not be responsible for my actions.

(*Fatima takes a couple of steps in his direction. For a second, Atiq stands still. Then his right hand begins to lower itself. He takes a couple of steps backwards and walks towards the takht where he sits down.*)

Fatima (*After Atiq has sat down on the takht*): Some man he thinks he is... thinking of getting married a second time!

(*Saying this, she walks away. The curtain falls.*)

Published Stories & Plays

Aurat aur Digar Afsane, 1937

- *Aurat*
- *Sauda*
- *Mera ek Safar*
- *Sadak*
- *Punn*
- *Gharibon ka Bhagwan*
- *Istekhara*

Shola-e-Jawwala (ed) Hamida Saiduzzafar, 1974

- *Iftari*
- *Mujrim Kaun*
- *Chhidda ki Ma*
- *Faisla*
- *Sifar*
- *Asif Jahan ki Bahu*
- *Woh*
- *Saas aur Bahu*
- *Andhe ki Lathi*
- *Woh Jal Gayi*
- *Bezubaan*

- *Mard aur Aurat*
- *Salma*

Rashid Jahan ki Kahaniyan (ed) Shakil Siddiqui, 2006

- *Dilli ki Sair*
- *Iftari*
- *Asif Jahan ki Bahu*
- *Saas aur Bahu*
- *Chhidda ki Ma*
- *Woh*
- *Mera ek Safar*
- *Bezubaan*
- *Woh Jal Gayi*
- *Qanoon aur Insaf*
- *Sauda*
- *Ghalat Sohbat*
- *Chor*
- *Mard aur Aurat*
- *Salma*

Nasr-e-Rashid Jahan (ed) Humaira Ashfaq, 2012

- *Iftari*
- *Asif Jahan ki Bahu*
- *Chor*
- *Sauda*
- *Chhidda ki Ma*
- *Woh*
- *Saas aur Bahu*
- *Mera ek Safar*
- *Bezubaan*
- *Mujrim Kaun?*
- *Sifar*
- *Sadak*

- *Punn*
- *Gharibon ka Bhagwan*
- *Istekhara*
- *Dilli ki Sair*
- *Gosha-e-Aafiyat*
- *Hindustani*
- *Parde ke Peechche* (a play)
- *Padosi*
- *Aurat* (a play)
- *Kantewala*
- *Munshi Premchand aur Tarraqui Pasand Adibon ke Pehli Conference*
- *Hamari Azadi*
- *Adab aur Awam*
- *Urdu Adabiyat Mein Inquilab ki Zaroorat*
- *Aurat Ghar se Bahar*
- *Chandar Singh Garhwali*

Bibliography

Interviews

Sarwat Rahman, Dehradun
Shaukat Siddiqui, Lucknow
Abid Sohail, Lucknow
Sharib Rudaulvi, Lucknow
A.A. Fatimi, Allahabad
Munibur Rahman, Aligarh
S.M. Mahdi, Aligarh
Aulad Ahmad Siddiqui, Aligarh
Shahryar, Aligarh
Zahida Zaidi, Aligarh
Zohra Segal, New Delhi
Bano and Naren Gupta, New Delhi
Birjees Kidwai, New Delhi
Salima Raza, New Delhi
Shahla Haider, New Delhi
Akhilesh Mittal, New Delhi
Arif Naqvi, New Delhi
Raza Imam, New Delhi
Zehra Nigah, New Delhi and Karachi.
Kamran Asdar, Karachi.

Published Books/Articles (English)

Ahmed, Talat. 2009. *Literature and Politics in the Age of Nationalism: The Progressive Episode in South Asia, 1932-56*. New Delhi: Routledge.

Ali, Ahmed. 1974. 'The Progressive Writers' Movement and Creative Writers in Urdu', in Carlo Coppola (ed.), *Marxist Influences and South Asian Literature*. South Asia Series, Occasional Paper No. 23, Vol. I. East Lansing: Michigan State University.

Barrier, Gerald Norman. 1974. *Banned: Controversial Literature and Political Control in British India, 1907-1947*. Columbia: University of Missouri Press.

Bartolovich, Crystal and Lazarus, Neil (eds.). 2002. *Marxism, Modernity and Post-Colonial Studies*. Cambridge: Cambridge University Press.

Burton, Antoinette M. 2003. *Dwelling in the Archive: Women Writing House, Home, and History in Late Colonial India*. Oxford: Oxford University Press.

Coppola, Carlo (ed.). 1974. *Marxist Influences and South Asian Literature*. East Lansing: Michigan State University.

Dimmitt, Marjorie A. (ed.). 1932. *When the Tom Tom Beats & Other Stories*. Lucknow: Methodist Publishing House.

Farooqi, M. 1969. *The Communist Party and the Problems of Muslim Minority*. New Delhi: The Communist Party Publications.

Flemming, Leslie (Introduction). 1985. *Another Lonely Voice: The Life and Works of Saadat Hasan Manto*. Short stories translated by Tahira Naqvi. Lahore: Vanguard.

Gopal, Priyamvada. 2002. 'Sex, Space and Modernity in the Work of Rashid Jahan Angarewali', in Crystal Bartlovich and Neil Lazarus (eds.), *Marxism, Modernity and Postcolonial Studies*. Cambridge: Cambridge University Press.

Gopal, Priyamvada. 2005. *Literary Radicalism in India: Gender, Nation and the Transition to Independence*. Routledge.

Gopal, Priyamvada. 2007. 'A Forgotten History – From Rashid Jahan to TaslimaNasreen, the CPI (M)'. www.Europe Solidaire Sans Frontiere.com. 6 December.

Haithcox, J. P. 1971. *Communism and Nationalism in India: M. N. Roy and Cominitern Policy, 1920-1939*. Princeton: Princeton University Press.

Hardy, Peter. 1972. *The Muslims of British India*. Cambridge: Cambridge University Press.

Kazim, Lubna (ed). 2005. *A Woman of Substance: The Memoirs of Begum Khurshid Jahan*. New Delhi: Zubaan.

Kumar, Girija. 1997. *The Book on Trial: Fundamentalism and Censorship in India*. New Delhi: Har-Anand.

Kumar, Nita. 1994. *Women as Subjects: South Asian Histories*. Calcutta: Stree.

Mahmud, Shabana. 1996. '*Angare* and the Founding of the Progressive Writers' Association', *Modern Asian Studies*. May, Vol. 30. No. 2, pp. 39-43.

Mahmuduzzafar, S. 1954. *Quest for Life*. Bombay: People's Publishing House.

Malik, Hafeez. 1967. 'The Marxist Literary Movement in India and Pakistan', *The Journal of Asian Studies*, August, Vol. 26. No. 4, pp. 649-664.

Masani, M. R. 1954. *The Communist Party of India: A Short History*. London: Derek Vershcoyle.

Minault, Gail. 1998. *Secluded Scholars: Women's Education and Muslim Social Reform in Colonial India*. New Delhi:Oxford University Press.

Minault, Gail. 2009. *Gender, Language and Learning: Essays in Indo-Muslim Cultural History*. Ranikhet: Permanent Black.

Overstreet, Gene D. and Marshall Windmiller. 1960. *Communism in India*. Bombay: The Perennial Press.

Poulos, Steven M. 'Rashid Jahan of *Angare*: Her Life and Work'. *Indian Literature*. New Delhi: Sahitya Akademi.

Petrie, David. 1927. *Communism in India, 1924-1927*. Calcutta: GOI Press.

Pradhan, Sudhi (ed.). 1979. *Marxist Cultural Movements in India: Chronicles and Documents (1936-47)*, Vols. I & II.Calcutta: Distributed by National Book Agency.

Rais, Qamar (ed.). 1978. *October Revolution and Impact on Indian Literature*. New Delhi: Sterling Publishers.

Rajimwale, Anil. 2007. 'P. C. Joshi and Indian Cultural Renaissance', *Mainstream*, New Delhi, June. Vol. XLV, No 25.

Russell, Ralph. 1995. *Hidden in the Lute: An Anthology of Two Centuries of Urdu Literature*. New Delhi: Viking.

Russell, Ralph. 1992. *The Pursuit of Urdu Literature: A Select History*. London: Zed Books Ltd.

Russell, Ralph. 1977. 'Leadership in the All-India Progressive Writers' Movement, 1935-1947' in B. N. Pandey (ed.). *Leadership in South Asia*. New Delhi: Vikas Publishing House.

Sadiq, Muhammad. 1983. *Twentieth Century Urdu Literature*. Karachi: Royal Book Company.

Sadiq, Muhammad. 1984. *A History of Urdu Literature* (revised and enlarged). New Delhi: Oxford University Press.

Saiduzzafar, Hamida. 1996. *Autobiography, 1921-1988*. New Delhi: Trianka.

Segal, Kiran. 2012. *Fatty: Zohra Segal*. New Delhi: Niyogi Books.

Segal, Zohra. 2010. *Close-Up: Memoirs of a Life on Stage and Screen*. New Delhi: Women Unlimited.

Shaw, Graham and Mary Lloyd (eds.). 1985. *Publications Proscribed by the Government of India: A Catalogue of the Collection in the India Office Library and Records and the Department of Oriental Manuscripts and Printed Books*, London: The British Library.

Suhrawardy, Shaista. 2006. *A Critical Survey of the Development of the Urdu Novel and Short Story.* Introduction by Asif Farrukhi. Karachi: Oxford University Press.

Surjeet, Harkishan Singh, et al (eds.). 2005. *History of the Communist Party of India (Marxist).* New Delhi: CPI (M) Publications in association with LeftWord Books.

Zaidi, Ali Jawad. 1993. *A History of Urdu Literature.* New Delhi: Sahitya Akademi.

Zeno. 1994. 'Professor Ahmed Ali and the Progressive Writers' Movement', *Annual of Urdu Studies.* Chicago: University of Wisconsin-Madison Vol. 9, pp 39-43.

Published Books/Articles (Urdu)

Abdullah, Shaikh Muhammad. 1969. *Mushahidaatwa Taasurraat.* Aligarh: Female Education Association.

Afraheem, Sagheer. 2009. *Urdu Afsana: Tarraqui Pasand Tehreek se Qabl.* Aligarh: Educational Book House.

Akhtar, Hameed. 2000. *Roodad-e Anjuman: Anjuman Tarraqui Pasand Mussanifin ki Roodad (1947-47).* Lahore: Bright Books.

Ahmad, Aziz. 1945. *Tarraqui Pasand Adab.* Delhi: Khwaja Press.

Alvi, Khalid. 1995. *Angarey ka Tareekhi Pasmanzar aur Tarraqui Pasand Tehrik.* Delhi: Educational Publishing House.

Ali, Ahmed. 1944. *Qaidkhana.* Delhi: Insha Press.

Ali, Ahmed. 1945. *Maut se Pehle.* Delhi: Dilli Printing Works.

Alvi, Khalid (ed.). 1995. *Angarey.* Delhi: Educational Publishing House.

Ashfaq, Humaira (ed). 2012. *Nasr-e-Rashid Jahan: Afsanon, Dramon aur Mazamin ka Intekhab.* Lahore: Sang-e-Meel.

Azhar, Naseeruddin. 2004. *Sajjad Zaheer: Hayaat-o-Jehat.* New Delhi: Mazhar Publications.

Azmi, Khalilur Rehman. 2002 (reprint). *Urdu Mein Tarraqui Pasand Adabi Tehrik* (reprint). Aligarh: Educational Book House.

Fatimi, Ali Ahmed. 2006. *Tarraqui Pasand Tehrik: Safar dar Safar.* Allahabad: Idara Naya Safar.

Husain, Syed Ehtesham. 1966. *Tanquidi Nazariyat,* Vol. 2. Lucknow: Idara Farogh-e-Urdu.

Husain, Syed Ehtesham. 1978. *Tanquidi Jaize.* Lucknow: Ahbab Publishers.

Jafri, Ali Sardar. 1957. *Tarraqui Pasand Adab.* Aligarh: Anjuman-i Tarraqui Urdu.

Jafri, Ali Sardar. 1964. *Lucknow ki Paanch Raatein aur Doosri Yaadein.* Lucknow: Nusrat Publishers.

248 *Bibliography*

Jafri, Ali Sardar. 1987. *Tarraqui Pasand Adab ki Nisf Sadi*. Nizam Lectures.
Jahan, Rashid. 1937. *Aurat aur Digar Afsane*. Lahore: Hashmi Book Depot.
Jahan, Rashid. 1974. (Published posthumously). *Shola-e-Jawwala*. Lucknow: India Publisher.
Jalibi, Jameel. 1982. *Tareekh-e-Adab-e-Urdu*. Vol. II. Delhi: Educational Publishing House.
Jamshedpuri, Aslam. 2002. *Tarraqui Pasand Urdu Afsana aur Chand Aham Afsananigar*. New Delhi: Modern Publishing House.
Khan, Idris Ahmad. 1996. *Daktar Rashid Jahan: Hayat aur Khidmat*
Mahdi, S. M. 2006. *Chand Tasweerein, Chand Khutoot*. New Delhi: NCPUL.
Rais, Qamar and Syed Ashoor Kazmi (eds.). 1987. *Tarraqui Pasand Adab: Pachas Sala Safar*. Delhi: Naya Safar Publications.
Sadri, Makhmoor. 2008. *Urdu Mein Tarraqui Pasand Tanqueed*. Delhi: Educational Publishing House.
Suroor, Ale Ahmad (ed.). 1968. *Tanquid ke Bunyadi Masahil*. Aligarh: Aligarh Muslim University Press.
Suroor, Ale Ahmad. 1976 (reprint). '*Tarraqui Pasand Tehrik Par Ek Nazar*', in *Tanquid Kya Hai?* New Delhi: Maktaba Jamia.
Zaheer, Sajjad (ed.) 1932. *Angarey*. Lucknow: Nizami Press.
Zaheer, Sajjad. 1985. *Roshnai*. New Delhi: Seema Publications.

Published Books/Articles (Hindi)

Ahmad, Z. A. 2008. *Mere Jivan ki Kuchch Yaadein*. Allahabad: Lokbharti.
Shakil, Siddiqui. 2011. *Rashid Jahan ki Kahaniyan*. New Delhi: Vani Prakashan.
Sharma, Rajendra (ed). 2012. *IPTA ki Yaadein*. New Delhi: SAHMAT.
Zaheer, Noor. 2005. *Mere Hisse ki Roshnai*. Shahadara: Medha Books.
Zaheer, Noor. 2006. *Sajjad Zaheer: Pratinidhi Rachnain*. Vols.I & II.Shahadara: Medha Books.
Zaheer, Noor. 2008. *Surkh Karvan ke Humsafar*. Shahadara: Medha Books.